The Divorce Recovery Sourcebook

Also by Dawn Bradley Berry:

The 50 Most Influential Women in American Law
The Domestic Violence Sourcebook
The Divorce Sourcebook
Equal Compensation for Women

The Divorce Recovery Sourcebook

DAWN BRADLEY BERRY

LOWELL HOUSE

LOS ANGELES

NTC/Contemporary Publishing Group

Library of Congress Cataloging-in-Publication Data

Berry, Dawn Bradley.
    The divorce recovery sourcebook / Dawn Bradley Berry.
      p.   cm.
    Includes bibliographical references (p.   ) and index.
    ISBN 0-7373-0002-7
    1. Divorced people—United States—Life skills guides.
    2. Divorced people—United States—Psychology. 3. Divorced
people—Services for—United States. 4. Divorce—United States.
I. Title. II. Title: Divorce recovery source book.
HQ834.B475   1998
646.7'008653—dc21   98-43488
                                            CIP

Published by Lowell House, a division of NTC/Contemporary
Publishing Group, Inc. 4255 West Touhy Avenue, Lincolnwood,
Illinois 60646-1975 U.S.A.

Design by Andrea Reider.

Printed and bound in the United States of America
International Standard Book Number: 0-7373-0002-7
10 9 8 7 6 5 4 3 2

Acknowledgments

I am extremely grateful to everyone who assisted me in bringing this book to life, especially to Jana Edmondson for excellent typing; to Willy Berry, Clarette Bradley, and innumerable friends for support and patience; to Kathryn Lang, Kathleen Robertson, Roberta Beyer, Lynn Peters, Lorraine Parker, Tim and Suzanne, Kathy Potter, David Riggert, Judy Lawrence, Frances Webb, Clayta Spear, and Becky Ralston.

Thanks also to everyone at Lowell House, especially Bud Sperry, Maria Magallanes, and Christina Ham.

Contents

Introduction

APPROXIMATELY HALF OF ALL AMERICAN MARRIAGES TODAY will eventually end by the choice of one or both partners. Millions of people will face a divorce and its aftermath at some point in their lives.

People expect to feel crazy and out of control during the divorce process, while they confront the task of dismantling a home and family, often pitted against a hostile adversary who was supposed to be a lifetime soul mate. Naturally, most expect that when the divorce itself is finally over, the pain and misery will end, and they will be able to pick up and get on with their lives. For many, however, the end of the divorce means that the most painful and difficult time of this transition is just beginning.

Divorce has been described as an amputation. The ghostly presence of the former spouse may haunt you long after his or her physical presence is gone, in the same way amputees often feel pain or other sensations in a phantom limb. The aftermath of divorce brings a multitude of new emotions and responsibilities that may seem overwhelming. A new home must be established or an old one restructured. Finances are often in turmoil. Children may be depressed, angry, and bewildered. You are probably feeling depressed, angry, and bewildered as well, at the very time you thought you would be finished with such emotions.

Even for those who couldn't wait to leave their partners, divorce represents a loss—the loss of an ideal, an image, the hopes and dreams that each partner had for the marriage when it was new. Many people are stunned to find themselves feeling bereft and miserable once the initial elation of freedom has subsided.

One of the most challenging duties life can present awaits divorced parents. People who no longer want to share their lives must now put aside their pain, grief, and hostility and build a new kind of peaceful or at least civil relationship for the good of their children. This may seem an insurmountable task, for which few guidelines exist, but one which absolutely must be accomplished. And it can be, as the many parents who have done so can confirm.

Do bear in mind as you pass through this tough time of transition that we are all human beings, prone to mistakes and foibles. None of us behaves perfectly all of the time, even when life is running smoothly. It is likely that you will make some bad choices, lose your temper, and mess up in ways that will surprise you. Don't beat yourself up over these things; take note of what you learn and move on. One day spent swilling booze and sobbing over lost love does not mean you are ready for rehab. One tactical error in financial planning is unlikely to doom you to a life of poverty. One nasty comment about your ex made in front of the kids won't scar them for life. Do the best you can, remember that you are human, and then let it be.

Remind yourself often that divorce is not a failure, it is a transition. Many of the difficulties of surviving divorce in our society arise out of our distorted view of marriage and the unrealistic expectations with which many people enter into it. Psychologists point out the absurdity of the common myth that when a couple marries, "the two shall become one." In a healthy marriage, two people remain individuals who interact on an equal basis, communicate with and respect one another, and grow as unique selves with mutual support. For many, it takes more than one try to achieve this type of equal and satisfying relationship.

In addition, lifelong marriage is simply not for everyone. Many behavioral scientists believe that human beings are not genetically programmed to mate for life, and that biological, demographic, and sociological forces are moving modern humans toward a period in which serial monogamy, a succession of positive and successful—but finite—relationships will be considered every bit as normal as one lifelong marriage.

Every family is unique, and every divorce different. Yet most people share certain common reactions, and pass through similar stages during the process of recovery and healing after a divorce. Understanding what to expect, what is and is not considered normal, and where to find assistance for various difficulties can help make the period after divorce easier to navigate and endure.

The information I chose to include in this book has been distilled from professionals experienced in fields ranging from psychology to finance to law; there is also practical advice from those who have been through the process of healing and rebuilding. I have endeavored to provide an overview of the options and services available to those coping with the challenges that frequently arise during the difficult period following divorce, and to explain how and where to find assistance. At the back of the book you'll find an extensive list of sources of help, including books, videotapes, church programs, community resources, hotlines, and Internet Web sites. One universal trait shared by virtually all successful people is their willingness to ask for help. Do not hesitate to take advantage of the many, many services and sources of support available to people seeking to rebuild their lives after divorce.

While emotionally devastating for many people, divorce always carries some potential benefits. When you're feeling low, stop to consider that divorce can be a catalyst for other changes you need to make in your lifestyle, job, and home environment. For many people, the relationship with their children is improved when the constant stress of an unhappy marriage is resolved. Divorce often leads to personal growth and freedom, a desire to get organized and to take a long look at what you do and don't want your future to include.

Millions of people have weathered the tempestuous time that follows divorce; and they have not only survived, but thrived and flourished. Most have gone on to build better lives, more satisfying relationships, and more stable homes. Ernest Hemingway wrote, "The world breaks everyone and afterward many are strong at the broken places." You will learn, with time, that he was right.

The
Divorce
Recovery
Sourcebook

CHAPTER

1

The Emotional Impact of Divorce

IN HER BOOK *CRAZY TIME: SURVIVING DIVORCE AND BUILDING a New Life,* counselor Abigail Trafford describes divorce as a "savage emotional journey," in which you ricochet between the failure of the past and the uncertainty of the future, all the while struggling to understand what went wrong and to apportion blame. According to those who have been through a divorce and its aftermath, this is an apt description.

Some experts believe that the emotional impact of divorce is greater than that of a spouse's death. Author and counselor John Gray has written that of all possible losses, a divorce can be the most difficult to grieve. Divorce is more complicated emotionally than the death of a spouse. Death is final, but divorce leaves people not only with feelings of loss, but often hurt, resentment, jealousy, and blame as well.

Author, educator, and counselor John Bradshaw also believes that divorce is actually more stressful than the death of a spouse. Those who are widowed must suffer through a wrenching sense of loss and grief, but do not have to face the ambivalence and sense of failure brought about by divorce.

Also, the pain of a divorce is often prolonged by the necessity of continued contact with a spouse when there are children from the marriage.

Those emerging from a divorce, however, can gain strength during its aftermath by reflecting on the ways in which they were tested and the challenges they survived. People who have endured a divorce emphasize the importance of understanding that life will never be the same. Divorce is both the death of an old relationship and old dreams, and the beginning of a new life full of exhilarating possibilities.

The legal and practical disentanglement of a marriage is only the beginning of the divorce. Yet once the papers are signed and filed, the possessions divided up, and the children assigned visitation schedules, it is supposed to be complete, with everything neatly falling into place. There are few guidelines to assist people in navigating this period of upheaval and strangeness. As common as divorce has become, the emotional and practical process of recovery is always a new and thoroughly confusing experience for one who has never been through it.

WHAT TO EXPECT ON AN EMOTIONAL LEVEL

While no two divorces are alike, most people experience similar reactions as they prepare to build new lives after the divorce itself is concluded. Psychologists note that a person facing a divorce always feels, at some point, like a failure. Not surprisingly, emotional turbulence and wild mood swings are normal during this time. Euphoria, rage, and depression are all to be expected. Nearly everyone feels some pain, confusion, grief, and sense of chaos. Emotional turmoil, while far from pleasant, is normal and necessary, and must be experienced in order to complete the psychological process of separation from the old life and former mate. How do you know what to expect, or how to cope with these wild and confusing emotions?

Starting over requires letting go of the past, a task which is both an art and a skill. It does no good to try to force painful feelings to go away. Virtually all professionals who work with those recovering from a divorce stress the importance of facing the loss and taking time to feel and work through the grief. John Gray notes that many people experience an emotional lag time, a period in which the mind wants to move on before the heart is ready. Ordinarily, such reactions are normal, even healthy. It is a rule of survival that human beings seek out pleasure and try to avoid pain. During the time of healing after divorce, however, this may cause problems. The natural tendency to resist unpleasant feelings can lead to depression and a whole host of other emotional ills that can, if not addressed, persist for years and, quite literally, ruin lives.

Career counselor Anne Walther, author of *Divorce Hangover*, has found that the problems her clients encounter in their professional and financial lives are often rooted in what Walther terms the "divorce hangover." She describes this state as a crippling condition characterized by persistent feelings of pain, anger, anxiety, or depression, which keeps one from living fully in the present and moving forward into the future. "Divorce hangover," writes Walther, "is a network of strong emotions that keep you connected to your ex-spouse and stuck in the past."

Walther and other professionals emphasize the importance of achieving closure after a divorce. The most important step in beginning the emotional healing that leads to such closure is deciding to do it; knowing that the time has come for you to free yourself from the past, come to terms with it, and make peace with it so you will be able to begin a rich, new life. By picking up a book on divorce recovery, you have taken that first step.

The Grieving Process

Mental health professionals emphasize that both parties go through a grieving process after a divorce. "The one who files for the divorce often feels an initial sense of freedom and elation, but will usually go through an emotional transition about six months later," explains licensed clinical mental health counselor Kathryn Lang. "If he or she has someone else waiting in the wings or begins dating right away, this can prevent grieving or delay it, which only makes it more difficult and painful in the long run. I believe that you don't go through this essential process unless you spend some time alone. You don't get a real feel for the pain you need to work through. Everyone needs to come to terms with aloneness, and learn to be a one before you can be a two. You need that time to learn who you are."

Lang's own marriage ended when she was the mother of two young daughters, and she now feels the experience gave her a greater appreciation of the pain and shock that both people suffer in a divorce. "I consider myself an extremely stable person. Not much shakes me. But divorce shakes everybody severely," she remarks. "When I first left the marriage after fifteen years, I was walking on air—I felt unchained after being trapped, as though I could finally do whatever I pleased. Then about six months later, the depression hit. I never questioned my decision, but I still had to go through the grief of this ending."

Facing and Feeling the Emotions

The time after a divorce has been called a time of emotional anarchy, and with good reason. In the aftermath of a divorce, conflicting feelings of pain, anger, and even guilt are normal. The key is to face them, feel them, express them in a nondestructive way, and then move on. Millions do, sometimes alone, and sometimes with the assistance of mental health professionals or organized interaction with others who have survived similar challenges.

Frightening sensations may accost you during the recovery process. Over and over, people describe the time after divorce as an emotional roller coaster, in which feelings take on a life of their own and people feel that they are not themselves. Often, there seems to be no way to make sense of wildly changing feelings. Many feel uncertain about their very identities. People are not sure who or what they are once such a powerful role in life has been eliminated.

People often feel as though the divorce is the end of the world, that they will die, that God disapproves, that family members will hate them, that their kids will become delinquent, that they will starve and lose all their possessions, that they will never move ahead and feel better, that everyone is looking at them, that married people are superior. Such confusion is normal, but it is important to remember that these things are not true, and to look around at other people who have survived and flourished after divorce.

John Gray explains in *Mars and Venus Starting Over* that grieving the loss of love is an automatic process, but we tend to interfere. He believes that in order to release attachment to a person or a past relationship, people need to experience and release four emotions that are essential for healing: anger, sadness, fear, and sorrow.

It is necessary to accept each of these emotions, and realize how they work together. For example, when anger is suppressed, sadness can turn into self-pity, leaving a person feeling victimized, guilty, and stuck in the misery of the past. When anger is allowed to take precedence over the other feelings, it can be difficult to feel compassionate toward others and to grieve for yourself. All these emotions must be experienced in a balanced perspective. Once an angry person is able to face and feel her sadness, she can let go of anger and forgive.

Sadness   After a divorce, it is important to remember that a sense of loss and loneliness is to be expected. Most people experience some form of mild depression, especially during the early stages following a divorce (as discussed in the next chapter). Generally, the depression eases as the individual passes through the initial phase of grieving and begins healing.

For some, however, the passage of time is not enough. While feelings of depression are common during the different stages of healing after a divorce, chronic depression that doesn't go away can indicate clinical depression, which can be life threatening and requires professional treatment. Sadness should not persist indefinitely or exclude the other emotions that normally come after a divorce.

Anger   When the depression begins to lift, anger often surfaces. This, too, should be no surprise, since divorce inevitably brings about major life disruption. Men may fare better in coping with it, because society is more accepting of male anger than female anger. Psychologists stress, however, that it is important for everyone to connect with and accept the anger that follows a divorce, since suppressed anger will surface eventually and often does so in destructive ways.

Anger reconnects us to our passion for love and life, and once released, leaves us able to feel a new desire to be free of attachment to the past. The key is to find a healthy way to express and work off the energy produced by anger, then let go and move on.

Fear and Anxiety   Overwhelming fear is one of the most common—and most paralyzing—emotions people experience after a divorce. Anxiety, like anger, tends to surface as depression lifts, particularly anxiety about what the future will bring. People often wonder if they are still desirable to members of the opposite sex, and are terribly fearful that they will never again experience love. It is important to understand that such intense emotions are almost universal, and that much good can come out of facing and working through these fears.

In his videotape, *John Bradshaw on Surviving Divorce,* counselor John Bradshaw refers to emotional pain as a healer and a teacher that moves people to take action to make necessary changes in their lives. He emphasizes that it is wise to be fearful and upset about ending a relationship that began so full of hopes and dreams. Yet persistent, paralyzing fear can inhibit a person's ability to grow and heal. Therapy can be very helpful in learning to face and move on from fear, and may be an essential step for those who become so mired in their anxieties that they cannot make the changes they need and want to make.

Sorrow and Denial   Deep sorrow is a normal reaction to the end of an important relationship and a major stage of life. Even those who are certain that the end of the marriage was a positive change often feel a great deal of misery and doubt. Many people, however, find it very difficult to admit to and face feelings of sorrow.

Denial is a common reaction to the anguish that persists after a divorce. Men, especially, may tend to suppress or try to minimize the pain of divorce, because males are trained in our society not to show, or even to allow themselves to feel, emotions that indicate vulnerability. But it is crucial to allow one's feelings to progress and to undergo the legitimate suffering that follows a painful, life-changing event such as divorce.

The Danger of Suppressing Emotions

People sometimes get "stuck" in one particular feeling and exclude the others. Suppressing negative emotions leads to numbness and the inability to fully experience the positive feelings that make life rich and full, however. John Gray points out that one of the great delights of children is that they experience all of their emotions at full capacity until the world teaches them that certain reactions should not be shown. Yet negative emotions need to be addressed, balanced, and expressed in a positive way. Unfortunately, social conditioning often teaches us that certain emotions are not acceptable. For example, society generally condones anger in males but frowns on male expression of sorrow, fear, or sadness. Women often face the opposite problem.

People who insist on suppressing the painful emotions they feel after a divorce often get mired in a sense of unending sorrow, paralyzing anger, or unshakable despair. This is the inevitable result of not completing the grieving process. Psychologists warn that while all the emotions that come up after divorce must be faced and worked through, it is important not to become tied to certain patterns that can prevent or inhibit the healing process. John Gray cautions that feeling and blaming are not the same, and says that when we blame the ex for our own unhappiness we prevent the release of our own painful feelings. He recommends using feelings of blame to get in touch with your anger, then moving on to work on releasing it. Gray states, "to forgive is to release another from being responsible for how we feel." He explains that blaming makes people feel like victims, whereas forgiveness, then looking at our own feelings independently, empower us to let go, heal, and move on toward new solutions and new love.

Divorced parents, especially, need to put an end to the tendency to communicate with the other parent from a victim point of view. When people are able to express feelings to one another without a blaming attitude, each is better able to see the other's point of view without immediately taking a defensive stance. Gray emphasizes that both sides need to feel heard and respected to work out solutions to parenting problems.

In addition to blame, Gray cautions people to avoid becoming mired in six other attitudes that may prevent healing. These include resentment, indifference, guilt, insecurity, hopelessness, and jealousy or envy. He states that each of these attitudes is a sign of pain being ignored, and that it is important to face the message arising out of such attitudes, to locate and heal the hidden pain, in order to move on. Each of these attitudes should be faced in the context of the four healing emotions. Men, especially, tend to blame their partners for their unhappiness, while women tend to blame themselves.

These emotions need to be faced, worked out, and then let go. Until this happens, the legal divorce may be years in the past, but the real divorce process, the "emotional divorce," cannot be completed.

The Importance of Forgiveness

In recovering from the pain of a divorce, two distinct types of forgiveness are essential: forgiving yourself and forgiving your partner. Both usually require a good deal of time and focused effort to achieve. In order to detach, you may need to first face and reflect on what went wrong in the marriage, to forgive both yourself and your partner, and let go. Unless the relationship was truly hellish, as in the case of a violent marriage, most people wonder at some point whether the divorce was the right thing to do. Ambivalent feelings, nostalgia for the good times, and uncertainty over whether you should have worked harder to stay together are very common. It is essential to accept and work through this ambivalence.

Forgiving Yourself   People are often overwhelmed by a sense of failure following a divorce. As John Bradshaw explains, however, many people in American society have never really learned how to function well in an intimate relationship.

For most, the only model for intimate relationships were their parents. Those who were raised in families that did not function well enter their own marriages without the skills needed to form a healthy relationship with another adult.

In recognition of this common shortcoming, many schools and church groups are now actively teaching young people how to achieve the give and take, to attain a healthy balance of power, and to cope with the day-to-day demands of a healthy intimate relationship. Most adults today, however, embark on marriage without any training or preparation. Bradshaw urges those divorcing to remind themselves that they are doing the best they can with what they had to work with, and to remember that most people have romanticized notions and unrealistic expectations of what marriage is all about.

Many people also feel a great deal of shame after a divorce, especially those who were brought up in a religion or a family where few, if any, people ever got divorced. This feeds into the sense of failure experienced by so many divorcing people. John Gray urges people to remember that forgiving yourself doesn't depend on being forgiven by others, and to remember that a relationship that is not right for you cannot be right for your partner. As the poet John Donne wrote, "Whatever dies was not mixed equally."

Realize that you are in the midst of a great upheaval, and that you are allowed some mistakes, some blue days, and a certain degree of distraction. "You have to realize that it's okay not to be 100 percent all of the time when you're going through this," says Becky Ralston, reflecting on the difficult time after her divorce several years ago. "Remind yourself that you're a good person, although you may not feel too great now—it's okay."

The process of forgiving yourself does not mean denying or avoiding the work that must be done to recover and learn from the past experience; on the contrary, coming to an understanding of what occurred can help you put things in a more accurate perspective. As one divorced woman explained, "The real learning process comes from an individual taking personal responsibility for what contributions he or she made to the failure of that relationship, and then not repeating it in the next one. Part of this process is identifying the individual patterns—usually hidden in the subconscious—that we developed throughout our lifetime. The one common denominator in every failed relationship of mine is *me*! I finally realized this, at the age of thirty-five, and went on a quest to discover how I was sabotaging my own life and why."

Don't be afraid to ponder why the marriage ended. Think about what you want to be different in future relationships. If your partner was abusive—physically or emotionally—make a firm vow never to accept such treatment again. If you found it impossible to be faithful to one partner, consider whether you're meant to be in a committed, monogamous relationship—some people are not, and that's all right, too. If finances were the problem, make sure you get your financial life together, and think about the kind of situation you will want if and when you marry again. Don't take this analysis too far, though; be sure you see others for the unique individuals they are, and don't subject potential dating partners to endless comparisons with your ex. Learn to trust your instincts about people as well as the rational side of your mind.

Divorce frees couples from destructive relationships, and many learn to become more self-sufficient and creative, more knowledgeable about themselves, and more loving and generous after finding the strengths and abilities they need to survive this life crisis. They enter subsequent relationships as different persons, generally better equipped to make a new relationship work. Many psychologists note that divorce often forces people to grow up. Most don't merely survive; they flourish.

Forgiving Your Partner and Finding a New Perspective
Many counselors emphasize that an essential component of
healing a broken heart and preparing to start over is to
remember the love that was there in the former relationship,
and to take time to recall the special moments shared with your
partner. You must realize, however, that you can't go forward
with grieving the loss of the relationship as long as you are
hoping to reunite with your ex. Unless getting back together is
a realistic possibility that both partners want to explore, it is
vital to let go of this fantasy. Many people find that they cannot
do so without some assistance such as counseling, group
therapy, or at least a course of self-help exercises.

A common problem for those who must continue to deal
with a former spouse is the tendency to feel pain, and be hurt
by him or her, whenever you are in their presence. It is important to let go of this type of dependence, and to acknowledge
that the relationship is over and the time has come to stop
feeling like a victim. When you realize that you do not depend
on your ex to be happy and fulfilled, he or she can no longer
hurt you.

John Gray refers to this as a "simple but profound concept." When you no longer can be hurt by your ex in the
present, you can release the old hurt of the past and move
on. Even those who were truly victimized by the ex, such as
those who were abused, can acknowledge that while they
were victims, they no longer are today. We are all free to
change our feelings and desires.

It is also important to be patient with yourself. It is perfectly natural for feelings about the marriage and your ex,
both positive and negative, to linger and resurface from time
to time, even if you're doing everything within your power to
move forward into your new life. "In an era of instant everything, we expect ourselves to quickly heal and be rid of the ex
forever," says Sid Buckman, an Arizona family therapist and

divorce recovery specialist. "Even when we have children from the marriage, we expect ourselves not to have feelings toward our coparenting partner. This is unrealistic, as it places us in the dilemma of telling ourselves not to feel when feelings are a natural part of our healing and becoming whole again." Buckman explains that it takes time to let go of feelings and memories and to change the behaviors learned as a part of the marriage, especially since emotions are not subject to our typical way of rationally responding to life. "It isn't necessary to rid yourself of all the feelings and memories from the past marriage. The best guide is your intuition, your sense of what is correct for you. Another guide is when your feelings impede your growth in life. If a year has passed and you have not let go of many aspects of your marriage and divorce, this may indicate that you have unresolved feelings. It may not be easy to cleanse yourself of these murky emotions, but it is necessary if you are to have healthy relationships in your future."

If months have passed and you can't stop obsessing about your ex, either from a loving or hostile frame of mind, this is a sign that you could benefit from some form of counseling or group therapy. Likewise, if you can't regain your sense of self, can't grasp a new image of yourself as a single person apart from the marriage, you may need assistance to help you move forward.

Finding this type of balance and healing is especially important for parents (as discussed in detail later in the book). When parents have not yet released their anger, hurt, and resentment toward their former spouses, the children are more likely to be exposed to hostility. Buckman has found that such behavior tends to lessen as parents take steps to heal themselves. Parents who work to build a new, businesslike coparenting relationship reap the benefits of forgiveness and release in the process. Some even become friends. The key is to let a new kind of relationship develop naturally, within the context of the primary goal of parenting together without conflict. Trying to maintain a friendship that doesn't come naturally for both can keep a person tied to the past.

The time when your ex remarries may be tough if you have not yet completely let go and put the past in perspective. If you find yourself very upset when this happens, now is the time to actively detach—with the help of therapy, if you need it—and focus your energy on the future. This is especially essential if you have children. Now is the time to fine-tune the businesslike relationship you must maintain with your ex, and to clean up lingering emotional ties.

Mixed Emotions

It is very common for people healing after divorce to feel several emotions at once. Most people are not accustomed to this, and it can be very confusing, especially when these feelings oppose one another—anger and tenderness, revulsion and desire, fear and a fierce desire to move forward with life.

Conflicting emotions, which author and counselor Abigail Trafford dubs "double feel," such as love and hate for the former spouse, are common, and should be acknowledged as normal. Psychologists urge those who experience these conflicting feelings to explore them rather than trying to control them, and above all, don't block them. Again, the essential component of divorce recovery is to let go and accept the divorce and the emotions that go with it.

Inevitably, people reeling after a divorce feel confused and disorganized; they often experience a sense of ambiguity. People often are not sure what they feel, and do not understand what is going on in their emotional lives. This can be a source of tremendous anxiety. Relationships that were formerly well established and comfortable often feel strange, especially with children. This is similar to the pain and confusion of adolescence, in which goals and expectations are being forged and are not yet defined.

For those who have difficulty identifying and expressing their emotions, counseling is a safe place to share feelings and thoughts that they are not comfortable expressing to friends and family, who may also be hurt, confused, or judgmental after a divorce. Giving words to your feelings is a very freeing and healing experience. Support groups can be most effective in helping members share difficult emotions that surface in a safe context where such expression is encouraged. Self-help books such as John Gray's *Mars and Venus Starting Over* can also provide exercises and tools that people can use to access their feelings on their own.

Mixed emotions and profound confusion are especially common among those who experienced a divorce at one extreme end of the spectrum (either an amicable parting or an escape from a hellish marriage), because the sense that the ending of the marriage was the right decision is always tempered with some sadness. When a person has invested a large portion of his or her life in a relationship, and the relationship does not last, there is always some regret that it could not have worked out forever, or, in the case of a miserable relationship, that it could not have turned around and become better. Even those who know beyond any doubt that the divorce was the right decision need to acknowledge and face their ambivalence.

The Emotional Divorce

As John Gray writes, "Good endings make good beginnings." Regardless of how a relationship actually ends, or who chooses to end it, the close of a marriage is a loss. Accepting the importance of grieving the loss rather than sabotaging the emotional process required for healing is what makes a good ending, and completes what has been called the "emotional divorce." Many psychologists emphasize that we cannot heal emotions that we are not able to feel—that the only way out is through.

Renowned counselor and educator John Bradshaw, himself the product of a divorced family, has written extensively on divorce survival and recovery. Bradshaw emphasizes that for many people, the divorce procedure is a waste of time, in a sense, because they refuse to do the work that is required to really experience and survive a divorce, to come out whole and healthy and to use it as an occasion for growth. He explains that many people he sees in his therapy work do not really divorce well or completely; that is, they refuse to face the pain that follows divorce and let go of the past, a step that is essential for recovery. Bradshaw comments that he has seen people who are eight years out of a divorce but still fighting with their ex-spouses.

The emotional divorce must be finished before the individuals involved can go on with new lives. Those who are not able to face, feel, and get past old resentments cannot complete the healing process. Bradshaw emphasizes that the word *resentment* refers to recycled sentiments.

A Shift in Perspective Will Happen, with Time and Work

As the journey through this period of emotional turmoil continues, perspectives do change, although it may sometimes seem that everything is taking far too long. Yet eventually, those who commit to the necessity of completing the grieving process are able to feel grateful for the love and good times experienced in the past relationship, and to forgive both their former spouses and themselves.

John Gray reminds us that there is something to celebrate at the end of any relationship, including gratitude for the lessons learned and our own ability to release and heal. Of course, no one should ever be grateful for mistreatment, but we can feel gratitude for the strength and wisdom gained from breaking free, letting go, and then healing. Many gifts may come from healing this type of loss. Ending a painful situation frees a person to move on to a richer and more successful future, one that is approached with greater wisdom.

During the process of divorce recovery, you may choose to embrace change as a friend rather than a foe. Focus on the fact that being single is okay, and that your faith, your freedom, and your future dreams can remain intact. Seek out sources of encouragement. Remember that to encourage means to give courage. Turn to friends who have been through it and offer support, as well as others who may not have experienced it themselves but who are upbeat and reassuring.

Therapists who work with those recovering from a divorce often emphasize that it is truly possible to view a cup as half full or half empty, and the way a person looks back on the divorce and forward to life ahead can make a vast difference in his or her future. Most people do, with time, find a realistic perspective, with a bittersweet nostalgia. Most also gain a new type of wisdom born of survival and growth as they discover a new identity as a unique individual, apart from the identity experienced as part of a couple.

ACTIVE STEPS TOWARD MOVING AHEAD

Many people wonder just how to go about putting all the theories they read in books like this one into real-life practice. Listed below are a number of practical steps you can take to aid the natural healing process. Many of these are drawn from Anne Walther's excellent book *Divorce Hangover;* others come from different sources. All can help you gain a sense of movement and progress in a process that often seems to take longer than it should. All of these topics are discussed in greater depth later in the book, with more recommendations and stories from those who have made the recovery process real and workable in their own lives.

Do be aware that not all of these steps may be right for you now, depending on where you are in the process, and that you should not push yourself to take a particular step before the time feels right. But if you put these ideas into effect when they feel natural, they can be tremendously empowering.

1. Move from an emotional to a rational state of mind in your behavior. Decide to think, then act, rather than feel and then react. This proactive, rather than reactive, approach can be applied to all areas of your life: interacting with others, spending money, choosing a new home or job.

2. Answer the questions that keep plaguing you. Do the necessary "Monday-morning quarterbacking" about your marriage and divorce—including a look at why the relationship ended, and especially, what were the specific benefits you gained from the ending. There is always a positive side, ranging from "I escaped a brutal tyrant and saved my life" to "With all the stress I finally lost that pesky fifteen pounds."

3. Take stock of the changes and losses you face. Then come up with a step-by-step plan to cope with them. Give that local divorce support group a try. Make appointments with career counselors, college advisors, and financial planners, and learn about the changes you need to make, then set them in motion.

4. Recognize that anger is a core emotion of divorce, and find a healthy way to release the clean, honest, natural anger before it morphs into something misdirected and pathological. Shriek or sob along with your favorite "cry-

ing in my beer" music; kick the daylights out of a football; split wood; or write an enraged letter, then tear it into a million pieces.

5. Uncover the "hangover" spots. Step back and take a look at what you're doing to mask anger that needs to be released, or other negative emotions you need to face and work through. Once you recognize what you're fighting, you can deal with and eradicate it. Some common things to watch for are persistent sensations of feeling victimized, desperate sexual behavior, constantly saying nasty things about your ex to anyone who will listen, being unpleasant to others, workaholism, and using a new relationship with someone you don't really care about as a shield against pain. If you're plagued with emotions or behaviors you can't seem to work through on your own, seek professional help now. Find out about counseling or therapy, support groups in your community, or other available mental health resources.

6. Decide to take control over your life. If you have been drifting along with the flow, now is the time to grab the rudder, hoist the sail, take charge of navigating a new course for yourself. Think about the changes you would like to make and the steps you would need to take to set those changes in motion. Do you want to finish your degree, make a career change, move to another part of the country? Consider your dreams and goals.

7. Move from victim to victor. Embracing blame, guilt, or a sensation of failure distracts you from building a new life. Decide now to take care of the lingering baggage of the past so that you will be free to move into the future. If you don't, you'll simply drag your unresolved burdens around with you, like Marley's ghost in Charles Dickens's *A Christmas Carol*. Remind yourself that living well truly is the best revenge.

8. Determine that the time has come to cross the abyss. It is both terrifying and exhilarating to face the fact that the life you led and the role you filled before no longer exist. Embrace the excitement of realizing that you are a new person. Unearth any false hopes and illusions you may be hanging onto, such as the belief that things haven't changed that much or will be the way they were before. Accept that you are in a new place, take a deep breath, and step onto the bridge to the future, however rickety it may seem.

9. As you step out onto that bridge, find your sense of balance. John Gray writes about the two hands of healing. On the one hand, we give ourselves permission to feel what we feel; while on the other hand, we adopt a non-victim attitude. For example, while we do feel the pain caused by the breakup of the relationship, we also recognize it is in the past. This approach is not difficult, but it requires a deliberate intention. Likewise, we need to find a balance between exploring our worries and fears and being grateful for our blessings.

10. Make some decisions. A solid series of rational choices imparts power, eliminates confusion, and brings a satisfying sense of progress. These need not be earth-shattering changes, and tiny steps toward a major goal usually work best. The key is to start. Set realistic goals and start moving toward them, inch by inch. Let your accomplishments along the way bolster your sense of self-worth. Take risks and make mistakes. Embrace those mistakes and learn from them.

11. Turn negative attitudes into positive ones. Positive attitudes create positive behaviors. Check the vocabulary that plays in your head. Words do make a difference. Replace words like "trauma" and "failure" and "devastating" with realistic, but encouraging affirmations that

reflect how you would rather view this stage in your life—words such as "challenge" and "transition" and "new direction." Managing this "mind chatter," as Anne Walther calls it, can make an immense difference. A journal can help you keep track of this editing process.

12. Create a new vision of yourself. Begin to shore up your self-esteem by taking better care of yourself and rewarding yourself. Plan meals you will enjoy, try a new form of physical activity that interests you, make time to do things you love to do. Remember that you are human, and forgive yourself your foibles. Treat yourself to a little "retail therapy"—get a few new pieces of clothing that make you feel great. Go through your wardrobe and get rid of clothing that no longer fits your body or your self-image. Sarah Ban Brethnach offers a wonderful tool for making this choice in her book, *Simple Abundance:* If something doesn't make you look beautiful or feel fabulous when you wear it, let it go. Brethnach offers similar advice for sorting out other possessions (which I find also applies to clothing): If it isn't beautiful, useful, or sentimental, get rid of it. Sell, donate, pitch, or recycle what you don't need.

13. On the same note, refurbish your environment. Carefully choose the things with which you surround yourself. Keep things that validate your sense of self-worth and the person you are today. Savor the fact that you are now free to decorate your home according to your own tastes and preferences (and those of your children, if you have them). Begin some small redecorating projects.

14. While you're refurbishing, review your circle of friends and companions. Spend time with those who are accepting and supporting, who inspire you to take chances and encourage you to move ahead. If there are people in your life who bring you down, people who seem to enjoy your

misfortune, people you've kept in your life only because you were lonely or felt obligated, let them go. If "friends" urge you to "get even" or to continue battling with your ex when you are ready to rebuild a civil relationship, give them firm orders to cut it out, and if they don't, cut *them* out of your life.

15. Connect with a source of spiritual strength. Whether your preferred form of spiritual guidance is found in a traditional church, solitary religious reflection, connection with a friendly universe, or whatever resonates for you, this can bring tremendous solace. Those whose world is in upheaval need to believe in something greater than themselves. The sense of a grace existing somewhere outside you can help restore your sense of trust.

16. Forgive yourself and forgive your spouse. Recognize those things that were positive in the relationship. Practice generosity and kindness in all your dealings with others. Reclaim your power and use it benevolently. This may take time and repeated effort, but the rewards are well worth all the teeth-grinding and tongue-biting. Dealing with your ex can be a marvelous training ground for learning to equalize power issues and establish workable business relationships with adversaries. If nothing else, remember the old saying, "Love your enemies—it drives them nuts!" Keep your sense of humor, including black humor, well honed.

Stages of Recovery After Divorce: What to Expect When

WHILE DIFFERENT MENTAL HEALTH PROFESSIONALS GIVE THEM different names, most agree that recovery from divorce progresses through several stages, similar to the process of grieving after the death of a loved one or diagnosis of a terminal illness. Even so, the grieving process is unique for each individual. People progress through the necessary stages of healing at different paces, with different emotions surfacing at different times, and the process should not be rushed. It takes time to grieve the loss of the good times even in a difficult marriage, the unfulfilled dreams, and the unmet expectations.

WHY ALL THESE STAGES OF GRIEVING?

The end of a marriage always produces some sense of loss and confusion. Often, the breakup is not caused by the wrongdoing or shortcoming of either partner. People grow and change as years progress. Couples generally begin a marriage with comfortable roles and shared ambitions, but it is human nature to evolve as individuals, and those who were headed in a similar direction often have grown in different or even opposite directions ten years later. Economics, psychological factors, and the dynamics of the relationship all change.

When a couple splits, it is often a deep shock to one or both, even when both agree the marriage should end. Divorce is almost always an emotionally complex transition. People experiencing a divorce share common characteristics and progress through similar stages of grief and recovery. During this time of limbo and chaos, confusion and craziness are to be expected. Understanding these stages and the feelings that they are likely to bring can help make them more bearable and ease the anxiety that many people experience when they feel unstable and out of control.

The two years immediately following a couple's breakup, which writer and counselor Abigail Trafford dubs "crazy time," may be the most critical period in the emotional divorce process. There is work that must be faced and performed during this period if the process of recovery is to be completed successfully. It is essential to work through and stay with this grieving process, asking for help when necessary. This may be especially difficult—but no less vital—for caretakers, who are used to nurturing others and find it very difficult to ask for help when they themselves need it.

Yet great strength can emerge from doing the difficult work at each stage, in order to complete the healing process. Attributed to various philosophers, the popular phrase "what doesn't kill you makes you stronger" has special application to the divorce and postdivorce experience. Once you have been through it, it can never happen in the same way again.

Sadly, some who divorce legally never divorce psychologically and become trapped in bitterness, violence, or disabling depression. Those who do not face their pain and do the work to recover from the grief that follows a divorce are at special risk for certain problems. John Bradshaw and other mental health professionals emphasize that "you can't heal what you can't feel." Some get stuck in one of the stages and fail to progress. Many refuse to let go of the ex-spouse, and continue to obsess over his or her whereabouts and activities. This type of obsession, especially when it manifests in stalking and similar behavior, is extremely damaging to everyone affected by it.

Most people, however, progress through the necessary phases of grieving and eventually emerge healthy. Experts who have studied and worked with divorced people emphasize that most adults and children adjust and eventually look back on the divorce as a devastating but necessary transition in their lives.

WHAT ARE THESE STAGES?

Different professionals characterize the intervals people pass through after divorce by different names, and break them down in different ways, but most acknowledge three basic stages of recovery. The first is shock, in which people retreat, withdraw, discover what they are feeling, then gradually begin to experiment with openness and exposing their new identities to others. Many at this stage attempt to cope on their own, sometimes using self-help tools.

The second stage is adjustment. People accept that this change in their lives is real, and adjust their thinking about life. It is then that they begin to put their lives back together, assembling the pieces one at a time as one would do with a jigsaw puzzle—generally starting with the easier pieces first.

The third stage is growth, in which people experience a desire to move forward and begin to plan for the transition away from grappling with the past and into a fresh future. The pace of life slows and becomes less chaotic, they develop a new focus and learn the value of letting go of old emotions. They begin to take steps to trust again, realize that the divorce recovery process will take time, discover a new and healthy lifestyle, and begin to establish new relationships with others.

Although other experts break the process down into additional stages, as discussed below, these steps outline the fundamental progression. All encompass the same essential passages through similar emotional territory.

Shock and Denial

When a person's individual world is in total upheaval, a period of shocked disbelief along with denial that these events are really happening is very common. It is a time of surprise, of pain, and often of high drama. Each day requires navigating a thicket of unpredictable emotions, an effort that is often exhausting.

During this time daily activities may become surreal. It seems odd to many people that the world goes on around them while they are experiencing such upsetting change. Of course, individuals are different, and each person's reaction and behavior depends a great deal on his or her personality and usual manner of coping and reacting to the world. Most people experience the sensations that are likely to occur during this period in their own unique ways. For example, those who are comfortable with routine may be stunned, outraged, and panic stricken when faced with the need to completely restructure their lives.

Those who asked for the divorce may feel tremendous relief, which can delay the onset of shock. Eventually, this feeling of pleasure begins to be eroded by feelings of doubt, regret, or guilt. In some cases, where a marriage was terribly destructive, involving violence, addiction, or criminal behavior, the breakup is such a cause for celebration that this sense of relief becomes the dominant sensation throughout the readjustment process. Yet no divorce, even those that occur for the very best of reasons, is likely to be completely painless, unless the marriage itself was very short and very shallow.

Isolation   During the initial phase of shock, people often withdraw socially from others, leaving friends and family baffled. This can be a healthy time of reflection in which to assess unfamiliar feelings and learn, through self-help materials, about what you are experiencing. Most people gradually emerge from this "loner" phase.

A period of "psychological hibernation" can be beneficial if it lasts only a short time, to prepare for the steps that must be taken next. This is especially true for those who were in an intense state of denial prior to the marriage ending and for whom the divorce came as a complete surprise.

It can be very useful to allow yourself a time of going into a personal wilderness, in order to sort things out and allow your protective instincts to take over. A period of withdrawal may be a vital step for those who were extremely traumatized by the divorce, or who experienced other traumatic events, such as the death of loved ones, during the divorce process. This state of shock and numbness, even denial, can be a useful coping mechanism as long as it doesn't persist indefinitely.

Reconnecting with Others   Eventually, discussing the feelings and issues that follow a divorce with others who have experienced them, either through a support group or one on one, can be a vital component of healing. John Bradshaw urges those recently divorced to talk to people who have been out of a marriage for two years. He states that people need more support during the first nine months after a divorce—equivalent to the crucial period of time in mourning the death of a loved one—than at any other time. He stresses that this form of dependency is very healthy, since people who are grieving or depressed cannot think clearly. Others can offer help, point out choices, and help the bereaved individual get his or her thinking back on track.

Confusion and Wildness Divorce inevitably brings a change in the circumstances of everyday living, and people often feel a sense of anomie during the first months afterwards. *Anomie* is a sociological term that means a situation without laws or norms to guide behavior.

Reactions to such confused feelings may manifest themselves in seemingly senseless or disturbing behavior. Many people feel unsure about how they are supposed to act or even how they want to act, and go a little berserk. This is a very common transitional phase, and is generally not a problem unless it persists or results in extremely dangerous behavior. A short burst of crazy behavior is not necessarily a bad thing, as long as it doesn't get too extreme.

Wild behavior may be an effective way to block intense misery, and thus can be a survival tool in the short run, but very damaging if it persists or goes too far. For example, a promiscuous phase after a divorce is not uncommon, as people try to reassure themselves that they are attractive to the opposite sex and won't have to live the remainder of their lives without sex or love. As discussed later in the book, this can be a positive, fun time that paves the way for reentry into a more significant relationship later, as long as people pay attention to safety concerns, treat partners fairly, and keep things in perspective. It is very important, however, to pay attention to both physical and emotional safety.

Sex, like alcohol or drugs, can also be used as a mood-altering substance, a way to block and distract painful feelings that need to be faced. John Bradshaw emphasizes that feelings that are buried are buried alive, and that suppressed emotions

will catch up and erupt eventually, often in the form of physical maladies.

Rest assured that most people experience feelings that
seem out of control or make no sense at some time during the
two years following a divorce. This does not mean that
vicious, violent, or self-destructive behaviors are acceptable,
but feeling that way and fantasizing about such actions, along
with some reasonably wild activity, is normal. It is very helpful for those who are experiencing this kind of confusion to
talk to others who have been through it, especially in the context of a facilitated support group. Others who have experienced the confusion after a divorce can provide guidance and
raise the "red flags" that show a person is getting too close to
violence, madness, or despair.

Depression   During this period of initial regrouping, some
people may become locked into what Abigail Trafford terms
an "emotional purgatory" between marriage and divorce. Mired
in deep shock, they refuse to face the fact that the marriage
has ended and simply quit functioning. As discussed above, a
brief phase of isolation can be beneficial, if it is used for the
type of reflection and self-examination that eventually leads
the person to emerge from denial and move on.

Like denial, depression may be a part of the necessary
mourning, sadness, and grief that follow divorce, and to
become numb for a period of time can be a mechanism for coping with an excruciating loss. While not everyone experiences
serious depression after a divorce, a very high percentage of
people, especially women, suffer from depression that is
severe enough to interfere with their day-to-day functioning.
Those who were defined by the spouse's identity, such as the
wife who for many years acted as hostess and behind-the-
scenes support for a powerful husband, are especially vulnerable to depression after divorce. It can strike anyone, however.

Many men find themselves depressed as they suffer from the loss of regular contact with their children. Even women who were quite independent may become overwhelmed when they have to deal with new responsibilities and take full charge of managing a home and a family. Feelings of sadness, rejection, and guilt may become overwhelming, and it is not unusual to experience more physical illness during this time. People often wonder if they will make it through the day. Low self-esteem and guilt, also components of divorce, fuel depression. Again, whether depression may be considered pathological or a normal part of the grieving and healing process depends on how long it lasts, how disabling it is, and whether it manifests in destructive behavior.

Most people do live through this process and recover, but those stuck in despair should seek counseling. If you ever seriously contemplate suicide, this is a sign that counseling is absolutely essential. Unlike anger, depression is inward directed, and is most likely to manifest in self-destructive behavior. If you find yourself feeling more and more depressed all of the time, this is a danger sign; it would be wise to consider some form of counseling. Mood swings are normal during this period of time, rather than long-term, continuing, relentless depression. Depression should gradually segue into sadness and mourning and eventually nostalgia, rather than persisting for months and months.

Adjustment

During the adjustment phase that follows the initial period of shock and denial, new feelings begin to emerge. You may feel unexpectedly intense anger, inexplicable guilt, or other surprising emotions. This is a normal response to the realization that this major life change is real, and that you must now adjust to a different way of thinking about life.

Rage   A period of rage, resentment, and blame is natural after divorce. As discussed in the last chapter, virtually everyone who goes through a divorce experiences at least some anger, and finding a healthy way to release it is an essential component of recovery. It is during this second stage that previously suppressed anger often kicks in.

Many people, even those who requested the divorce, feel a deep sense of betrayal once the process is completed, and this naturally leads to anger. Many find that this rage has an unexpected intensity, especially since it usually peaks after the breakup, rather than at the time of the divorce. In addition to a fury specifically directed at events or behaviors, people often feel anger that is more vague. The rage may focus on dreams that are perceived as stolen away, and other losses that have been stockpiled over the period of the years of the marriage. Anger may also result from the loss of a comfortable home and a settled value system, and from a present that feels like a state of anarchy. Others may direct anger at themselves, or at both themselves and their former spouses, as they look back on roles they accepted and assumed in the marriage with great resentment.

This rage must be confronted. There are innumerable ways to release anger that are nondestructive, even positive. Such options range from twenty minutes of solid screaming to vigorous exercise to hard physical work to classes in anger management. Therapy may also be very helpful, either individually or in groups of others who are experiencing similar feelings. The practical work required to build a new life and make needed changes in the home, work life, and day-to-day activities can also provide a healthy outlet. Great anger can be a source of energy and a remarkable impetus for change. The danger is the fine line between constructive and destructive anger.

As with denial, another key in assessing whether anger is normal is how long the rage persists. There is no benefit from becoming locked into an endless screaming match with an ex-spouse, a slow seething boil that saps your energy, or an obsessive need to blame someone else for the pain you are feeling now. If two or three years have passed and you are still consumed with anger, or if it is the only emotion you are feeling, this is a sign that something is amiss.

The opposite is also true. Those who go through the aftermath of a divorce never feeling any anger are likely suppressing rage that may later emerge or manifest in negative ways, both emotionally and physically. Some people have been so thoroughly trained never to show anger that it takes the passage of many years, sometimes combined with therapy, before they can even recognize that what they have felt as a general sense that something wasn't right is anger.

Ambivalence   Uncertainty, mixed feelings, and conflicting emotions are characteristic of the adjustment period. Nearly everyone experiences some ambivalence following a divorce, and this can be a cause of great anxiety. Yet it actually signals the presence of common sense, a sign that the person is working through painful and conflicting emotions triggered by the loss of an important relationship.

Common feelings of ambivalence include a desire to spend time or have sex with the ex-spouse. Some feel a strong desire to reunite with the ex, but even those who do not may not want a complete separation, either. Researchers report that three-quarters of divorcing spouses experience some lingering attachment to the spouse after the separation. This may be especially true of those who must still function as parents of children.

Ambivalence toward an ex can take many forms. Sometimes former partners still get together for sex, which can be very risky in that it fuels the continued ambivalence. Some people feel great resentment as they see a former spouse growing and changing into a more compassionate person, especially if they still feel miserable and angry. Yet at the same time, they may see this person as a better potential partner and feel the desire to explore the possibility of a reunion. Often, people do not realize how emotionally entwined they still remain until after a period of separation.

The psychological nature of completing a separation is a long and complex process. During this time, it is essential to trust your own gut instincts, and to move forward under your own steam rather than looking to your former partner for cues—for example, refusing to let go of the hope of a reunion until your ex behaves in an especially nasty manner. It is vital to disengage in order to gain your own freedom, and to realize that the natural ambivalence that follows divorce will eventually mellow into a healthy nostalgia in which you will be able to remember the good times of the former marriage without experiencing anxiety about the future. During the adjustment phase, people tend to reassemble and rebuild the pieces of life one at a time. Many become impatient, but this time of sorting out—both physically and emotionally—is important.

Recovery is not achieved without a great deal of emotional upheaval and time. Building a new life involves a struggle between the past and the future, in which you must redefine and reestablish yourself. Some have compared it to finding a new place in the tribe. The adjustment phase of recovery continues to involve different levels of feeling and behavior, including an intense desire to seek out pleasure, a sense of confusion, bitterness, and pain. As it comes to a close, you will experience what has been called a phoenix phase, in which you are able to rise up, let go, and face the future with confidence.

Acceptance and Growth

During the final phase of healing, the pace of life slows and people begin to achieve a sense of comfort and belonging in their new lives. The value of letting go of the past becomes clearer, and the ability to trust begins to be restored. A new identity, and a new focus, emerge.

As the time after divorce progresses, old emotional bonds should begin to sever as you build a new life and recover a new sense of yourself. This is a time of growing strength. Little by little, you will find yourself able to take risks and make solid choices, and to put aside old emotions, such as lingering resentment of your former spouse.

This phase of growth is also the time of building new relationships. You feel strong enough to risk your heart, refreshed and anxious to move ahead in all phases of life. This is a time to relax and enjoy moving forward again.

Time Heals All Wounds—But When? It is difficult to place a timetable on divorce recovery, because the duration of the healing process is different for nearly everyone, depending on individual circumstances. For example, those who have been emotionally detached from their spouses for a long period of time prior to the divorce may have completed most stages of healing before the physical separation even takes place. Others, especially those who were anxious to escape the marriage and exhilarated at leaving, may not begin the "crash" and subsequent recovery until many months after the divorce is final. General emotional health, whether help is sought, and other factors such as work and financial stability also contribute to the time it takes to heal.

Psychologists urge people not to impose preconceived notions on themselves about when they should be "over" the emotional aftermath of divorce. The mourning process cannot be rushed, and it does no good to order yourself to "get over it" by some magic date. Unless you feel mired in one stage of grieving and cannot move forward at all, it is best to keep working patiently and let healing progress naturally. Again, this is where comparing feelings and experiences with others who have been through a divorce can help immeasurably.

Sid Buckman, a family therapist who specializes in divorce recovery and publishes *Healing Your Life After Divorce: A Divorce Recovery Newsletter*, explains that it takes time to let go of the many feelings and memories that were built during the years of a marriage. He adds that it is necessary to release many such feelings, but not all, and the best guide to which must be released and which may be retained is your own intuition—what is right for you, what feelings are impeding your growth. Buckman recommends that most people allow at least a year to pass between the divorce and the next serious relationship. He believes that full healing requires from one and a half to four years. Most therapists believe it takes at least two years to fully recover from any divorce—longer for many, especially those leaving a marriage of long duration and deep intensity. Counselor Kathryn Lang believes that the period of time people need to fully heal after divorce varies, but it may take up to five years for some.

This is a time when the proverbial "two steps forward, one step back" dance is very common. Healing is a gradual endeavor, with many layers, setbacks, and moments of waffling. Nearly everyone feels discouraged and impatient at times. This, psychologists explain, is normal, as long as it doesn't lead to suppression of feelings.

One common mistake many people make after a divorce is expecting that the healing and changes they want or need to make will happen automatically. Some are surprised to find that they are still unhappy after leaving a spouse they saw as the sole source of the misery in their lives. As psychologist Mel Krantzler has written, "Freedom means taking personal responsibility for one's own behavior, which is the difficult but necessary demand that divorce imposes on every man or woman who separates from a spouse."

Those who have been there agree that the recovery period usually takes longer than they anticipated. "It takes a long time to get over it, even if you know that leaving the marriage was the best decision you could do for your life," says Laura Murphy, reflecting on the end of her three-year marriage. "You're messed up for a long time. You feel like you've failed on some fundamental level." Laura found that it took far longer than she expected before she felt emotionally healthy again. Yet, she adds, "The good news is that eventually you do recover from the divorce completely. Now, years later, sometimes I literally forget I was married before. But it took a long time to get here."

Unfortunately, there are no shortcuts through the process of grieving and healing. Everyone must proceed at his or her own pace, according to an individual script written along the way. Counselor Abigail Trafford notes that the Chinese word for crisis combines the characters for danger and opportunity. She states, "In our country, that's the definition of divorce."

What Factors Contribute to How Well and How Fast the Healing Will Progress?   Many factors contribute to the ease or difficulty of healing after a divorce. Those who have been divorced more than once often remark that it is not the length of the marriage, but the emotional investment one had in the relationship, that determines whether the parting, and its aftermath, will be more or less wrenching. "It has to do with the depth of the relationship," says one woman, reflecting on her second divorce. "My first divorce was no big deal. My second marriage had more emotional involvement, more passion, as well as just the accumulation of more physical things."

The duration of the marriage is a factor of some significance for most. As one divorced woman stated, "I've heard that for every two years you were married, you need a year after the divorce to recover, and I think that's pretty close. I was married ten years, and now I've been divorced for four. I feel like I'm just about over it—but I think it will be another year until I've really finished the recovery completely. I've made peace with my former husband, and we still have a friendly relationship. I'm in another very good relationship with a wonderful man now, but it still bothers me when, for example, my ex tells me about his problems with his girlfriend."

The emotional closeness of the couple during the marriage, before it deteriorated, seems to have much more impact that the actual time. "I work with a woman who was married fourteen years, but her divorce seemed to have little effect on her," the same woman remarked. "She and her husband led very separate lives, and spent little time together."

Whether you or your spouse made the choice to end the marriage is another significant factor in recovery. Even when the parting was amicable, a truly unanimous decision to divorce is rare. One person usually makes the final decision to split, and this can have a profound effect on how each partner copes. "The one who makes the decision to leave the marriage often feels an initial sense of freedom and elation, but will often go through an emotional transition about six months later," says counselor Kathryn Lang, who herself experienced this reaction when she left her first marriage. "When I left after fifteen years, I was walking on air. I felt as though I was finally unchained after being trapped. Then about six months later, the depression hit. It wasn't a matter of looking back or questioning my decision to end the marriage, but I still had to go through the grief of this ending." Many people in this position find that they miss small, everyday things they took for granted, such as dinner routines and regular contact with in-laws. Also, the person who leaves the home after a divorce is likely to feel a greater sense of displacement.

Of course, how the partner who decides to leave tells the other has a tremendous impact on how the person who is left will react. Those who are surprised by a partner's sudden departure from a marriage he or she thought was just fine are often, quite understandably, completely devastated. "My wife just walked out the door and left on our first anniversary," Tim recalls. "No explanation, no note, nothing. She just disappeared. I was devastated." Tim's shock was so severe it cost him his job and nearly his life. "At one point I attempted suicide," he says. "I lost a really good job, moved around a lot, drifted. It took me a good five years to really get back on my feet."

In contrast, psychologist Genevieve Clapp, author of *Divorce and New Beginnings,* has found in her studies that those who are the most upset at the time of the breakup often heal more quickly and completely—perhaps because people in great emotional pain may be more willing to seek help. Clapp states that on the average, it takes most people about two years after a divorce before they feel they have regained their equilibrium. More time is required before most people feel completely detached from the divorce and have a real sense of stability and satisfaction.

THE GENDER FACTOR

Contrary to popular stereotypes, men suffer the pain of divorce just as intensely as women, and tend to feel the same emotions, although they often react to them in different ways due to the way they are socialized. In his book *Mars and Venus Starting Over,* John Gray writes that although the healing process is the same for men and women, the different genders often have to confront different challenges; a strategy that is productive for a man healing from a divorce may not be productive for a woman, and vice versa. He stresses that each individual is unique, and there is some overlap among the best methods of healing for each.

Gray explains that while men and women experience equally agonizing feelings after the loss of a love, they tend to cope differently, and to have different instinctive reactions. Starting over after a devastating loss can be the most challenging experience of a lifetime for both men and women. Many feel desperately frustrated at their inability to change what has happened. And, as Gray succinctly states, "We're not taught how to heal a broken heart in school." Gray compares a broken heart to a broken bone, which, if treated appropriately, will grow back even stronger than it was before the break. He advises those faced with such a healing challenge to get the help they need, grieve the loss, forgive, and become whole within themselves before starting over again with a new relationship. He believes that the best time to get involved again is when you feel you don't have to do so.

In his years of work with people healing from a loss, Gray has found that until the healing process is complete, men have trouble making a commitment and women have problems being able to trust again. Gray believes that of all the losses we face in our lives, the loss of love is the most painful, because when we suffer disappointments and injustices, it is love that comforts the soul and makes the pain bearable.

Women often tend to deny their need for love, and remain withdrawn from intimate relationships for a long period of time. Men, who tend to be solution oriented, often tend to bury themselves in work or rush headlong into another relationship before they have done the necessary healing on their own. Both sexes try to use their minds to invalidate feelings of heartache. Yet feelings work on a different level, and while we can control our reactions to them, we cannot use intellect and rational thought to control emotions. As one woman remarked, "You know that you're intelligent and that you're attractive and lovable on an intellectual level. But on an emotional level you remain convinced that you are not." Group therapy proved tremendously helpful to her in recovering her self-esteem.

Women Eleanor Roosevelt once said, "A woman is like a tea bag. You never know how strong she is until she gets into hot water." Studies of middle-aged women, in particular, indicate that a majority report feeling better about themselves after a divorce was over. Sociologist Gail Sheehy reports in her book *New Passages* that divorce, while inevitably painful, functions as a springboard for many women in their fifties, who enjoy rediscovery of their true selves, and are able to resume their educational pursuits and discover a new range of possibilities in their lives. Few such women focus on finding a new husband. Many guard their hard-earned confidence and freedom fiercely.

Yet women may fall prey to cultural norms, even today, that say women should not venture out on their own, that they should always be part of a couple. Counselor Kathryn Lang finds that many of her patients, especially women, feel that they must put their lives on hold until another partner comes along. "I have to remind people that they can get out and do things, enjoy life on their own as divorced women. I ask them to consider what they want to do with their lives," she says. "During my own single years, I did plenty of things with my daughters. We traveled through Europe, drove across the United States, and took trips to New York City. Some of my friends were shocked and horrified. They were so unaccustomed with the idea of a woman traveling without a man. They would ask, 'Aren't you afraid?' I told them there was nothing to be afraid of."

Fortunately, more and more women seem to be following Lang's adventurous approach to life. Demographers note that while the ranks of divorced women between the ages of forty and fifty-four have grown more rapidly than any other age group since 1970, these women are showing a radical difference in their remarriage patterns as compared to their earlier counterparts. Older women today are accepting and enjoying fulfilling lives without husbands, which often include lusty relationships, sexual adventures, and passion, often with younger lovers. These women are increasingly choosing to remain single, enjoying their independence as well as their financial and sexual freedom.

Women who leave marriage at a time in life when their children are either grown and independent or no longer require constant, everyday care and who emerge with their sense of financial and sexual independence intact often relish the chance to romp and have scant desire to reenter the role of wife and caretaker. Some report feeling younger and revitalized, relishing the opportunity for a second adolescence.

The overall increase in women's economic success may also have contributed to the increase in the rate of divorce among women over age forty. Many refuse to cling to unhappy marriages solely for economic security in midlife and beyond. Gail Sheehy reports that one of the biggest demographic shifts over the last twenty years is the fact that among divorced couples between the ages of forty-five and fifty-four, it is the women who are choosing to stay single more often than the men.

Sheehy acknowledges that the women she studied were unencumbered professionals who were financially sound, but even those with a lower degree of financial security reported enjoying the freedom to rent videos and curl up in bed on a Friday night if they so chose. For both men and women, a committed marriage to a best friend is one of the best predictors of a high level of well-being. In a mediocre or a poor marriage, however, it is the wife who fares worse when the marriage endures.

Social networks become more important as people age. While many women emerging from marriage at midlife do not want another traditional marriage, they long for a partnership with someone who can be a best friend and lover. Some become workaholics to blunt the loneliness, as men have traditionally done. Others may become more possessive with their children, which is especially problematic when the children are adolescents yearning to establish their own lives and assert their independence. But Sheehy found that most women who divorce at midlife do very well, contrary to popular myths.

Men   "Men, to some degree, tend to have different fears than women after a divorce," says counselor Kathryn Lang. "Many are afraid of not being good single fathers, especially if they never took on an active parenting role during the marriage. Yet some become better fathers after the divorce as a result of this, because they are actually more available to their children."

From a health standpoint, remarriage seems to be more important for men than women who are single in midlife and beyond. Marriage tends to protect men from depression. Those in their fifties or older, in contrast to their female counterparts, often actively seek to remarry, and studies show that those who do have wives live as much as ten years longer than their single peers.

Middle-aged men who find themselves single after a long marriage are often uncertain how to relate to women in their age group who have made drastic changes over the past twenty years. Many such men often find the company of other males in similar circumstances to be greatly rewarding and beneficial. Even those who would never dream of joining a "men's group" often form loose groups that meet at a restaurant, bar, or gym for camaraderie and companionship, especially during the after-work hours when the void created by a lack of intimacy in their homes is often the most difficult to fill.

Men who had traditional marriages often feel both desperate to replace the lost intimacy and intimidated by the new type of women they meet, especially when their wives' growth led to the breakup. "Middle-aged dating is adolescence all over again," says Sheehy. Older divorced men, especially, long for romance, security, and above all, companionship. Remarriage often provides a great relief from loneliness.

For both men and women, however, completing the work required to achieve a successful emotional divorce is the first and most essential step that must be taken before a new life can be forged, no matter what choices and changes the next era of living may bring.

CHAPTER

3

Sources of Support

EVERYONE INVOLVED IN A DIVORCE NEEDS SOME FORM OF emotional bolstering. For some, blessed with a steadfast network of supportive friends and family members, plus the self-motivation to do the research and emotional work they need to do on their own, this may be enough. But for others, perhaps most people, professional support can be very beneficial. Many psychologists who work with patients recovering from a divorce caution that the support of friends and relatives, while valuable, may not be enough, because such people lack the objectivity that a detached professional can offer.

Divorce may also bring out old, unresolved emotional residue that lingers from past experience. The time after a divorce is often a period in which ancient issues that existed even before the marriage will resurface. While it is never easy to cope with the eruption of intense emotions, the postdivorce period can be an excellent time to face these issues, seek assistance in the form of counseling, group therapy, or other forms of help, and do the work to emerge as a healthier person. The problems that arise in the fallout that follows a divorce are often deeper than the divorce itself. This may be a prime opportunity to learn more about yourself, work through old emotional issues, and gain insights that can make all the facets of your life happier and more fulfilling and enable you to build stronger relationships in the future.

Fortunately, social institutions have begun to respond to the reality that there are a great many people out there who need postdivorce assistance. More and more sources of support for divorced people and their children are becoming available. While some express concern that professional psychological help is often unavailable to those with limited financial means, others report that self-help therapy groups, usually set up or guided by trained professionals, are taking up the slack in an increasing number of places.

If you do not have insurance that covers mental health treatment and worry that you cannot afford it, rest assured that help is available to nearly everyone today, through private therapists and counselors, community-based mental health organizations, public health sources, HMOs or professionals included in medical insurance plans, churches, community centers, and other sources. Virtually all communities have some form of public mental health services. Your physician may be able to make a referral. If not, call your county public hospital or county mental health service for information and assistance. Some private practitioners offer sliding fees based on family income; others, especially those affiliated with churches, offer counseling on a donation basis. Therapy groups are often low-cost, donation-based, or free. Other professionals will work out a payment plan, accept credit cards, or agree to flexible fees. If there is a medical school or college nearby, check with the psychiatry or psychology department. Often excellent counseling is provided free of charge by student trainees working under the supervision of expert teaching professionals. Some of the organizations listed in the Appendix also provide referrals.

BEGIN WITH YOUR PHYSICIAN

If you believe that you or your child may need professional assistance, begin by contacting your regular physician. Sometimes it is necessary for both medical and practical reasons (such as HMO referral policies) to begin with a trip to your usual doctor. He or she can assess the symptoms and refer you to appropriate mental health treatment.

Physicians and psychologists often work together to treat people suffering from depression or anxiety disorders. While a psychiatrist can prescribe medications, a psychologist must generally refer a patient to a physician if drug therapy is indicated. If your mental health professional suggests antidepressant or other drugs, keep an open mind and consider the option. Many people balk at drug therapy, either because they see medication as a sign of weakness or they are afraid of becoming dependent on the medication. Yet short-term use of antidepressant drugs, or occasional use of tranquilizers to ward off panic attacks, can be extremely valuable when administered and monitored by a physician. Drug therapy is almost always combined with counseling to address the underlying causes of the distress. Many people suffering from depression or severe anxiety have found such medication to be, quite literally, a lifesaver.

"I don't think I would have made it without my good friends, an excellent counselor, and Prozac," one woman commented, reflecting on the short-term course of treatment that saw her through the first tough months following a difficult divorce.

HOW DO YOU KNOW IF YOU NEED THERAPY?

It is sometimes hard to assess whether you or your child may be seriously depressed or suffering from another type of emotional illness that needs professional attention. Special concerns and signs to watch for in children are discussed in more detail in the next chapter, but the basic warning signals apply to both children and adults.

You may be unable to tell whether you need to seek counseling, or are simply weathering one of the more difficult periods of healing. Is it simply a natural phase of moodiness or could there be serious emotional trouble? Watch for persistent trouble sleeping or concentrating, loss of energy, withdrawal from others, changes in eating habits, or the inability to enjoy things that always brought pleasure. Family therapist Sid Buckman states that if any lingering feelings toward an ex-spouse are impeding your personal growth, or if either spouse is using the children as a weapon against the other, professional assistance is advisable.

Psychologists note some additional warning signs of severe depression that can lead to suicide, in either children or adults: a persistent, unrelenting sense of hopelessness; repeated high-risk, self-destructive behavior; deep depression that never lets up; or a persistent lack of caring about one's self and one's future. Any of these signs, in yourself or your children, signals a need for immediate professional counseling. Some people, conversely, feel as though they are healing, but wonder how to tell if they are making the progress they should be. Generally, professionals advise that if you feel the pain lifting gradually, are able to move forward with your life, begin recognizing the good things around you, see some evidence of your growth, feel a sense of peace with the past, and are able to form positive new relationships with others, you are probably doing just fine. If you are unsure, check to see if you have fallen into any of the common traps outlined below, which indicate a need for outside assistance.

Destructive Behavior

If you find yourself engaging in seriously destructive behaviors, beyond the natural "wildness" that often accompanies the early stages of recovery discussed previously, you need to take the necessary steps to stop yourself, no matter how "good" you may feel on the surface. If this is the case, you are probably masking emotions you need desperately to face, which only makes matters worse.

How do you know if your behavior has gone too far? If you are hurting yourself through excessive overindulgence in alcohol, food, drugs, or otherwise, and especially if you find yourself harassing or stalking your ex, or acting in any way that could be considered abusive toward any other person, seek help right now. Seriously—put the book down and go to the telephone, and call a hotline, clinic, mental health center, or other source of professional help. Many are listed in the Appendix; others are listed in your local telephone directory. People who persist in self-destruction or abuse of others end up dead or in prison. Decide here and now that this will not happen to you.

For those experiencing less drastic reactions, just understanding what you are going through can help you stop damaging behaviors and work through detrimental emotions. The key, though, is to realize that you will have to face the tougher side of your present real-life situation, and do the work it takes to get through this rocky time, perhaps on your own, perhaps with the assistance of others.

Is Your Present Pain Linked to the Past?

Psychologists often point out that pain we feel in the present time is often linked to unresolved pain we experienced in the past. Sometimes it is easier to deal with past than present events. Healing workshops often include an exercise in which present pain is linked to other situations in which participants had similar feelings. In this way, a more profound letting go of the pain can occur. For example, repressed feelings of abandonment from a childhood trauma may be awakened by a divorce. By facing and feeling and working through all of these emotions, complete healing may occur.

Counselor and author John Gray refers to such work as processing our "hot spots." He believes that besides learning to process the universal healing emotions experienced after each loss of a relationship, the act of linking current painful feelings with unresolved hot spots of the past is one of the easiest and most powerful ways to heal, process, and release the misery we feel in the present. He states that while dwelling on the hurt we feel is not helpful, using it to discover and lead to past pain we still need to heal can be very beneficial. Sharing this process in a safe environment, such as one on one with a counselor or in a therapy group, can be a significant component of healing.

Waiting Instead of Working

Too often, people rely on some outside event to spark a "sea change," to end their emotional turmoil, to make it be over, once and for all. Some expect that this will occur when they receive the final divorce decree; others believe that a move, the first or fifth anniversary of the divorce, or remarriage will mean a final ending. Yet none of these events, while they may be symbolic, will end the divorce "hangover," the unfinished emotional experience of divorce, until the lingering feelings are resolved. The key is not external events, but the internal state of mind. If you find yourself repeatedly setting deadlines, focusing on what is going on outside rather than inside, you may need assistance in bringing your interior life to the forefront and doing the necessary emotional work to create a real change in your outlook.

Are You Still Hung Up on Your Ex?

Many people find it very difficult to let go of unhealthy connections to a former spouse. Signs that a person may be hanging on to such ties include strong emotional reactions whenever you think of your ex, such as tears, sexual fantasies, or a desire for revenge; a sense that you are energized by these feelings;

feeling victimized by the divorce; obsessing about your ex and his or her new partners; finding excuses to see or contact your ex more than is necessary; a sense that the past seems more real than the present; or a feeling that your life is on hold.

Anyone may have occasional flashes of such feelings. Most of us still experience some emotional reaction when reminded of people who were very important to us in the past, who are no longer in our lives. But if these feelings occur on a regular basis, are overwhelming, or persist for months on end, you may need some form of counseling to heal and move forward. Again, if you catch yourself harassing your ex, you must get the assistance you need to stop.

SEEKING HELP IS A SIGN OF STRENGTH, NOT WEAKNESS

Do not hesitate to seek mental health treatment if you have any inkling that you may need it. The emotional effort to complete a divorce is far more complex than the legal details, yet few people hesitate to seek the advice of an attorney to get the legal work accomplished.

There is no shame, no demonstration of weakness in seeking therapy or counseling. On the contrary, it takes wisdom to recognize and admit that you could benefit from assistance and strength to seek out the help you need. The lingering pain that follows a divorce can affect your happiness, self-esteem, career, financial stability, children, sex life, ability to trust, and physical health. These are not small matters, and should not be ignored.

TYPES OF THERAPY AND COUNSELING
One-on-One Counseling

Individual work with a counselor can be very beneficial in helping a person gain specific clarity into his or her own feelings, reactions, and present situation. Especially during the "shock" period right after a divorce, many people are extremely confused, riding an emotional roller coaster that feels completely out of control. One-on-one therapy can help provide insight into your own unique set of circumstances and make sense of chaotic, conflicting feelings.

Clinical mental health counselor Kathryn Lang believes that different types of counseling, or combinations of methods, work for different individuals. "One-on-one therapy is usually more important at the beginning," she says. "Many people need to heal on their own first, to take time to recover from their anger and pain. Then group therapy can be very helpful. There are different types of divorce adjustment and divorce recovery groups available. But many people right out of a divorce are too angry, emotional, and self-absorbed to benefit from the group process. They can't see beyond themselves."

Lang has also found that different types of therapy tend to appeal to different groups of people. "Some of my patients, especially older women, find it hard to be in a recovery group. They may feel ashamed that their marriages ended. Also, people who are deeply religious and believed that marriage was supposed to be for life are often simply not comfortable sharing their feelings in a group, at least not until they have had some individual help first. Adolescents, too, who are so self-conscious and sensitive to the opinions of others, may feel uncomfortable expressing their feelings in a group."

If you feel that you or your children need one-on-one counseling, there are many ways to locate a therapist experienced in assisting families after the trauma of a divorce. Ask friends who have been in a similar situation, clergy, physicians, lawyers, community mental health agencies, family service centers, college counseling centers, school counseling offices, the YWCA or YMCA, hospitals, and clinics for referrals.

Use care in choosing a therapist. Be aware that not every counselor is right for every person. Sometimes personalities simply do not mesh, and it may take two or more tries to connect with the person that is best able to give you the help you need. Also, be sure to avoid anyone who advises you to escalate the hostility, who suggests that you are a failure, or, especially, that you should accept any type of unkind or abusive treatment. These problems are rare, but they do happen.

A course of treatment with a good counselor can give you the tools you need to get your life in perspective during this trying period, as well as provide insights on adversity and techniques for coping that can prove beneficial for the rest of your life. Most people do not need to spend years in psychoanalysis to learn these valuable lessons. A short course of counseling can be a life-changing experience.

Support Groups

Many people find that simply knowing that they are not alone in feeling crazy provides considerable comfort and reassurance. The number of support groups being established to help with all types of difficulties is increasing daily. As of 1991, fifteen million Americans met in self-help support groups every day.

Many types of groups and organizations for divorced people are available today; they provide recovery, fellowship, group counseling, or simply the opportunity to talk and socialize with other adults in similar circumstances. These include, among others, divorce recovery therapy groups, single parent organizations, joint custody support groups, stepfamily organizations, and church groups (discussed in more detail below).

Perhaps the single greatest benefit of support groups is what some call the "been-there" factor. People who have been through a particularly challenging phase of life can offer a special brand of empathy. They can help us to interpret our feelings and experiences through offering a combination of "been-there" closeness along with the distance required for perspective, since they are not friends or family members (who have preconceived notions and their own emotional investments that prevent such objectivity).

Most divorce support groups include people who are at different stages of the recovery process. Members can offer advice based on experience rather than clinical expertise, provide an immediate and real-life model for what can be achieved, and give you an opportunity to achieve the healing satisfaction of being able to help others.

Support groups vary tremendously in their focus, duration, and range of topics covered. Some deal with emotional issues alone; others address such matters as single parenting, self-esteem, letting go of the past, forgiveness, self-discovery, grief, intimacy, and anger management. Some are ongoing discussion groups with no set duration or format of specific sessions, in which new and old members come and go as they choose. Others are set up as classes, workshops, or seminars that may last for an evening, a weekend, or a set period of months or weeks. Many have a program that takes participants through several levels or stages, encompassing the issues that people most commonly face at each point in the healing process.

For example, Clayta Spear participated in an eleven-week seminar on divorce recovery that also included sessions on accepting the grief process, managing anger, building self-esteem, learning to love and trust again, discovering new opportunities, intimacy, sexuality, and friendship. Special sessions were offered for parents helping children adjust to life after divorce.

Spear's support group also taught improved communication skills, an especially crucial issue for parents who must maintain contact with their former spouses. "Communication skills are critical in all our interactions, but training is lacking in our society," says Spear, a teacher who characterized the communications training in a divorce recovery seminar as an unexpected bonus. "People are expected to know how to communicate effectively with one another, but we are never taught the techniques. I'm pleased to say that we teach communication skills and dispute-resolution techniques at the elementary level at the school where I work, and train the kids to mediate disputes without violence as early as third grade."

Support groups are becoming more and more abundant. Specific divorce recovery groups now meet in almost every community in the United States. Even small towns often have self-help groups sponsored by a local church, clinic, or social services organization. Many of the national organizations listed in the back of this book have local affiliates that conduct seminars or sponsor groups. Others provide materials and guidance to those who wish to start their own self-help groups. Some areas have self-help clearing houses or community helplines that can tell you what is available in your region. Local newspapers often list area groups. Women's centers and associations such as the YWCA host and list women's groups, while the YMCA and similar organizations provide these services for men. Friends and acquaintances, local mental health organizations, the Internet, and library bulletin boards also provide information.

The organizations that sponsor support groups, as well as churches and other community organizations, always need volunteer assistance. Many people find great opportunities for growth, as well as the chance to make new personal and professional contacts, by offering to volunteer for these groups. There can be great satisfaction in knowing that you're helping where help is needed, and many divorce recovery groups offer participants the opportunity to stay on and aid others when they have completed the program to foster their own continued growth and recovery.

Centers That Specialize in Divorce Recovery

Various mental health centers, like certain hospitals and clinics that address physical illnesses, have begun to specialize in the treatment of specific kinds of emotional problems. Numerous centers for family therapy have existed around the country for a number of years, such as the Gestalt Center for Family Therapy in Flagstaff, Arizona. As the ranks of people seeking postdivorce assistance have swelled, clinics and centers specializing in such focused treatment have sprung up around the nation. One of the most prominent and well respected is the Center for Divorce Recovery, located near Chicago.

The Center for Divorce Recovery was founded in 1994, with the stated mission of providing the highest quality of care in assisting individuals and families to recover from the trauma of divorce. Specialization is the key ingredient, says Dr. Chet Mirman, the Center's cofounder, who was surprised to learn that few therapists specialize in divorce-related issues. The Center's staff of psychologists, clinical social workers, and other mental health professionals all focus on the special needs of individuals and families going through the divorce recovery process. The Center's clients include adults, children, adolescents, and families. Many come to the center in "survival mode," and therapists work to move them from a focus on simply surviving into a thriving, growth-oriented pattern.

The Center's services, while all geared to the divorce recovery process, vary from supportive counseling to intensive individual psychotherapy to interactive groups. It also offers custody evaluation and mediation services. Clients are encouraged to use the Center's services at any stage of their recovery.

Sources of Help in the Spiritual Community

One of the most rapidly growing sources of divorce recovery assistance is the spiritual community. Churches, synagogues, and other spiritual organizations offer an ever-increasing variety of classes, seminars, groups, and programs to help those healing from divorce. While some are grounded in a particular religious tradition, most church-sponsored programs are open to people of any faith, not just members of the host church or its particular religion.

Religious faith or other forms of spiritual foundation can be among the most important sources of comfort and stability for a person facing major life changes. Religious congregations and organizations have been at the forefront of helping families cope with the aftermath of divorce and begin healing. Spiritual support can help you put things in perspective and provide practical assistance with the challenges common to divorce, and help you find forgiveness, self-acceptance, community support from others in similar circumstances, faith in a more positive future, gratitude, and a center of gravity.

Churches and other spiritual groups offer an astounding variety of resources to help those coping with divorce survive and find strength, both through spiritual perspectives and practical approaches. Church-related programs include counseling, classes, workshops, and group sessions, covering an incredibly diverse array of topics. Many offer general divorce recovery sessions that may include such topics as forging a new identity, getting the ex-spouse in focus, assuming responsibility for a new life, building new relationships, and letting go. Some are offered specifically for men or women, and others provide special groups for singles who feel that they have completed the divorce recovery process but still need to address issues related to returning to the single life. Some also offer classes or workshops that address issues that frequently arise as part of the process of healing after divorce, such as forgiveness, anger management, loneliness, and single parenting.

For example, Hillside Community Church, a New Thought church in Albuquerque, New Mexico, has been called "the seminar church" because of the many classes and programs it presents on an ongoing basis. Like many churches, Hillside welcomes people of all faiths. Its seminars range from single evening sessions to eight-week courses, provided at a low fee. In addition to a specific program on healing after divorce, the church offers classes on related topics including anger management, building self-esteem, forgiveness, and overcoming fear of intimacy. Hillside also offers one-on-one counseling with volunteers trained by the associate pastor, Dr. Susan Nettleton, who is also a psychiatrist.

Many churches provide services to entire families coping with divorce. For example, one Baptist church offers an eight-week series on divorce recovery for children, with parents participating in corresponding adult sessions. The children's program is divided into four two-week sessions, each dealing with one topic (such as how divorce feels, change, new family relationships, and where to find God when you are hurting). This program is geared toward children aged five through junior high level, with classes divided by grades.

Another Baptist church provides different divorce workshops specifically tailored to those in the process of a divorce, those newly separated or divorced, or those divorced for a period of time but still looking for resources and assistance in coping. This program brings in a broad variety of professionals to address the groups. Children's sessions are also offered for children from the kindergarten level through age eighteen.

A Presbyterian church in Ann Arbor, Michigan, provides a support group for men and women at any stage of recovery from separation and divorce, in which participants have the opportunity to share experiences, learn new coping skills, and begin the process of rebuilding their lives as single adults. It strives to provide a safe and accepting environment where participants will feel comfortable exchanging their thoughts and ideas. Topics covered in this program include understanding the legal and emotional process of divorce; grieving and letting go; dealing with anger, guilt, and rejection; and understanding how the marriage died. The classes also help participants find and experience forgiveness, build community, and create a new sense of purpose and freedom in their lives. The program leader is a clinical social worker, therapist, and pastoral counselor. This church also offers a group for couples or individuals in a subsequent marriage, so that those building new family relationships may experience support, fellowship, and education about how to build new relationships and make them work.

Many churches have Web sites on the Internet that provide information on available programs. Most church-based groups are available at low cost, with some offering free assistance, accepting donations, or waiving the usual fees for those who cannot afford to pay them.

Secular Programs Hosted by Churches   It is important to emphasize that not all of the divorce recovery programs offered by churches are spiritually based—some are entirely secular, with no more connection to the sponsoring church than shared physical space in which to meet. Quite a few of the church-supported groups are not tied to religious doctrine in any way. "The group I facilitated was sponsored by a Presbyterian church," says counselor Kathy Potter. "But there was no religious affiliation, and spiritual issues were not made a part of the program unless one of the participants had an issue with his spiritual life and brought it up in the session. The minister simply saw a need for such a group in the community."

Special Divorce Recovery Programs for Pastors   Recently, the Illinois Baptist State Association started a special divorce recovery ministry for pastors who are going through the divorce process. The goal of the program is to let ministers experiencing this transition know that there are others who can be available for prayer and support. As one pastor explained, divorce is a catastrophe for a minister. A pastor may lose his or her livelihood, ministry, and church family. Many have discovered, however, that their congregations are a willing source of support, and have learned that divorce need not be the end of a ministry.

The Illinois Baptist group hopes the ministry will develop into a support network, with the founder emphasizing that divorce is not a time to judge, but rather a time for healing, restoration, and caring. The ministry plans to expand its offer of support and assistance to other church staff members.

Divorce Care   A rather unique approach to church-based divorce support is offered through a group entitled "Divorce Care." This organization has established a series of seminars for use by independent support groups, designed to help those going through a divorce or recovering from a divorce to deal with the pain of the past and look forward. This nondenominational program has established hundreds of groups throughout the United States and Canada, all sponsored by various churches. The Divorce Care program is open to all, not only members of the host church. Each session begins with a videotape, conducted in a TV-magazine format, that features experts on divorce and recovery topics as well as commentary from people who have experienced the challenge discussed. Following the tape, a support group discusses the information viewed and what is going on in their individual lives.

Topics covered in Divorce Care include typical emotional, physical, and spiritual reactions experienced by those who have been separated or divorced. Also, sessions entitled "Road to Healing" provide members with steps to take to begin healing and finding the help each individual needs to deal with anger, depression, loneliness, new relationships, financial issues, children and single parenting, and forgiveness. The groups also offer assistance on reconciliation for those attempting to reunite with their spouses, scriptural and spiritual perspectives, and instruction on how to gain spiritual growth from negative experiences.

The Beginning Experience and Other Catholic Programs

The "Beginning Experience" is a widely available, low-cost, weekend-long program developed and sponsored by the Catholic church, but open to men and women of all religious affiliations. According to information provided by the Archdiocese of Santa Fe, the weekend program is designed to help divorced, separated, and widowed individuals make a new beginning in life. All who attend the weekend, including leaders who work in teams, have been divorced, separated, or widowed.

The goal of the Beginning Experience is to help those who have lost a spouse to find closure and to reach out to others who have experienced a similar loss. Participants should be at a point beyond the initial feelings of despair which usually follow such a loss—usually at least one year later. It is also recommended that they have the desire for a new start, separate from the spouse, and feel ready to do the requisite work to make that desire a reality.

During the Beginning Experience weekend, a trained team leads the participants through a trilevel program. First, team members speak from personal experience on specific topics. Next, participants compose private, written reflections. Finally, dialogue is shared in small groups. Confidentiality is assured so participants feel free to share thoughts and experiences.

Program literature acknowledges that the loss of a spouse through divorce is a devastating experience that alters life patterns permanently. The grief and pain that accompany the death of a marriage is considered comparable in intensity to that which accompanies the death of a spouse (though it is different). The program recognizes that both the divorced and widowed suffer a sense of alienation in a couple-oriented society; and that those who have divorced or separated face the added burden of feelings of failure and worthlessness.

Some Catholic churches and archdioceses have developed other types of divorce recovery programs. The Archdiocese of Santa Fe has established a support group called DOVES for those who have lost a spouse through death, divorce, or separation. The DOVES ministry is open to both Catholics and non-Catholics, to provide education, spiritual guidance, and sharing to help people through their grief and sorrow. The program is based on a model of three stages of bereavement and healing that encompass the recovery process, likened to the Paschal Mystery, Jesus Christ's suffering, death, and resurrection. The first, called by DOVES the "survival stage," is intended for those who have recently lost a spouse, or who have not yet come to grips with a less recent loss. The second, "healing stage" helps participants make the necessary adjustments to begin the healing process, and seeks to enable them to understand how complete healing takes place. The third, "growth stage" provides participants with tools and information for starting anew.

The ministry addresses various topics, including understanding the grieving process and coping with common emotions such as shock, denial, anger, fear, depression, and rejection. DOVES also provides practical education on learning to deal with responsibilities previously handled by a partner, single parenting, and rebuilding self-esteem.

Catholics may also face the issue of annulment of their marriages according to the church's canon law. Annulment of a previous marriage is required before a Catholic wedding may be performed. An annulment is a declaration by an ecclesiastical tribunal that a particular marriage was invalid from its inception. According to information provided by the Metropolitan Tribunal of the Archdiocese of New York, annulment does not deny that the relationship existed, nor does it imply that the marriage was a product of ill will or moral fault. It also does not have any civil effect in the United States, or render any children born of the marriage illegitimate.

Annulment is based on the premise that the consent given by both parties to the matrimonial covenant is presumed to exist until the contrary can be established before a church tribunal, and on canon law principles stating that certain conditions must be present at the time a marriage is contracted for the marriage to be considered valid. One of the partners to a marriage can petition a church court to investigate the canonical validity of a marriage (either Catholic or not), a process that is normally initiated after a civil divorce has been obtained. Tribunals are associated with archdioceses and generally investigate the marriages of those who legally reside in the archdiocese, or those whose marriage was contracted in it.

A person seeking an annulment proceeds in a manner specified by the tribunal. A representative of the appropriate tribunal advises the person about what documents are needed, and provides directions on preparing the required statements. An appointment is then arranged with a tribunal consultant who discusses witnesses who can provide statements, explains the grounds for annulment, and outlines the procedure. If there is found to be a basis for a formal hearing, a petition is drawn up, and the matter proceeds in a manner somewhat similar to that of a civil hearing, including a right to appeal a negative decision.

Those seeking an annulment in New York are cautioned that the process may take more than two years to complete; they should not plan a church wedding until the final decision is rendered.

SELF-HELP RESOURCES

For those who do not feel that they need or want to seek therapy or counseling, or who want to educate themselves before making the decision to seek counseling or to explore specific matters that may not be addressed by therapy or simply to do some solo work on personal growth, a tremendous variety of self-help resources is now available. These materials include videotapes, books, hotlines/helplines, informative pamphlets, magazines, newsletters, and the vast amount of information now available on the Internet, including informative Web sites, interactive discussion groups, newsgroups, and contacts with local organizations.

Self-Help Groups

Self-help groups can be very effective for sharing feelings, experiences, and solutions to problems. Therapists do caution that self-help groups without a trained leader sometimes deteriorate into blaming and complaint fests, which can make participants feel worse. "Groups need to be facilitated by someone who can help the participants work through what they're feeling and move beyond where they are stuck," says counselor and former group facilitator Kathy Potter. "They are a great place to share both emotional issues and practical information."

More and more materials and guidelines are becoming available for those who wish to form an effective self-help group, such as the Divorce Care program discussed above, with training for facilitators. See the Appendix for a listing of sources of such materials.

The Internet

During the past few years, the Internet has emerged as a comprehensive source of information on every imaginable topic, including divorce. Today, having an online computer is akin to having a desktop library. For those with access to cyberspace, Web sites devoted to divorce recovery issues can provide information on local and national laws, sources of professional assistance, publications, videotapes, discussion and newsgroups, and other resources. For example, one newsgroup provides a forum where single parents can swap ideas, ask others for thoughts on issues as they arise, and share information on how to solve problems.

If you are not online through a computer at home or at work, check with your local public library. Many libraries now have computers that patrons may use to access the Internet, as well as free classes on how to navigate your way through cyberspace (most people can learn the basics in an hour or two).

A great many organizations and groups devoted to divorce recovery topics maintain Web sites filled with a wealth of information. Do bear in mind that anyone can create a Web site, and some of the information you find may be inaccurate or inflammatory. I have seen many Web sites providing extremely helpful information, as well as a few offering terrible advice, such as encouraging people to play dirty to "win" a child custody battle at any cost, or to try to handle a complex divorce without legal assistance. Weigh what you read on the Web, or in print, against your own common sense, and always consider the source of the advice. Remember that your situation is unique, and you should consult a competent professional (counselor, lawyer, clergyperson, financial advisor) for specific recommendations. Check the Appendix for a list of recommended Web sites.

The Internet has also brought a new facet to communications between former family members, which may be either a convenience or a complication, depending on how it is used: e-mail. E-mail can be a quick, easy, and inexpensive way for former spouses to exchange necessary information—for example, a reminder that a child has a piano recital the weekend of a visit with the other parent. It can also be a wonderful tool that allows noncustodial parents and children to maintain daily contact. Yet it can also be abused by ex-spouses who can't let go of the past. "E-mail is different from either a telephone call or a letter," says mediator Frances Webb. "There is no back-and-forth conversation as there is with the telephone. Yet the message can be sent right now—there isn't the lag time to think about what you've said as occurs with a letter." Webb has begun to see more and more problems associated with inappropriate use of e-mail in her mediation practice. "People are using e-mail to challenge their former spouses. You have distance—yet it's very intimate, and you can really get under a person's skin," she remarks. Webb advises those who are receiving annoying e-mail from an ex to set clear boundaries on what is and is not appropriate communication, and if necessary, to use the blocking systems that allow the receiver to screen or block e-mail from certain people.

Publications

A wealth of excellent books, videotapes, and other materials that provide information on the various aspects of divorce recovery and related issues is now available. Some books, such as John Gray's *Mars and Venus Starting Over* and Anne Walther's *Divorce Hangover,* provide self-help exercises that can be extremely valuable for gaining personal insight and growth. Others, such as Judy Lawrence's *The Budget Kit* and Peter Favaro's *Divorced Parents' Guide to Managing Custody and Visitation,* are filled with forms and worksheets that help organize practical facts. Information on these and other useful books is listed in the Appendix.

One of the most unique publications now available for those dealing with divorce and its aftermath is a magazine devoted entirely to the subject. *Divorce Magazine* was con-

ceived in 1994, when founder Dan Courvette, then an associate publisher of a Canadian wedding magazine, found his
own marriage ending. Courvette realized that while there
were scores of magazines dedicated to helping couples plan
their wedding day, no periodicals existed to assist with the
complexities of a divorce, arguably the most stressful and
traumatic time in a person's life. So in 1996, he launched
Divorce Magazine, billed as "help for generation 'ex'."

The publication achieved rapid success, quickly expanding
to produce four regional editions in North America. It is a
user-friendly resource providing information, advice, and
expert guidance in the areas of law, real estate, tax concerns,
relationships, mental and physical health, children, dating,
blended families, and other issues to readers at various stages
of the divorce process. Other publishers seem anxious to emulate the magazine's success. In early 1998, Japan launched its
own divorce magazine, entitled *Liz* in honor of the much-
divorced Elizabeth Taylor.

IS IT EVER TOO LATE TO SEEK HELP
IN RECOVERING FROM A DIVORCE?

What if five or ten years have passed since your divorce and
you still feel stuck in depression, confused about your life, or
merely annoyed by your inability to move ahead at the pace
at which you'd like? Is there any point in seeking counseling
or joining a support group or making other recovery efforts
after so much time has passed?

Most mental health professionals believe that it is never
too late for someone committed to healing to successfully seek
the help they need to do so. Many, many people have found
their way out of what they believed were incurable problems,
years after the initial traumas that caused them. There is no
expiration date on pain, and it is always worthwhile to seek

help to overcome persistent misery—provided you have the sincere desire to do so.

There is an old joke about how many psychotherapists it takes to change a light bulb: only one, but the light bulb has to really want to change. The joke may be silly, but there is a lot of truth in the sentiment behind it. While most people who seek any form of counseling have made the commitment to healing by taking the first step to seek help, people occasionally go to therapy looking for confirmation of unrealistic beliefs.

Counselor Kathy Potter recalls a man who came to a divorce recovery support group she facilitated several years ago. "The man had been divorced for nine years, and still clung to a belief that he and his wife would get back together," she recalls. "He kept insisting that God wanted them to reunite and He would eventually make it happen. As we continued to talk with this man, it turned out that he had been going from group to group for years looking for support for this delusion, rather than help getting past it so he could grow and move on. The reason he had come this time was because his former wife was about to marry someone else. It was so sad, but we finally had to tell him that the group probably couldn't help him, because he was stuck where he wanted to be, hanging on to this idea." People so firmly mired in a delusion probably need a more intensive form of one-on-one psychotherapy to get beyond their problems—if they ever become motivated to seek genuine help.

Yet for those who do want to break free of the past, healing is always possible. Some fear that if they have suppressed their feelings of pain, anger, and other essential emotions for a long period of time, it may be too late to ever break free of familiar habits of denial. Professionals stress that this is not true. It is never too late to turn around and make the decision to heal and move forward. Author and counselor Diane Fassel, who has extensively studied adult children of divorced parents, advises that adults who still carry the scars of a parent's traumatic divorce can, with help and effort, heal at any point in their lives. Group therapy in which participants share common feelings seems to be especially helpful for such individuals.

Those who have been there agree. Clayta Spear had been divorced for seven years, moved across the country, revitalized her teaching career, and was well on her way to settling into a satisfying new life when she realized that although her life was great on the surface, many of the emotional issues that had arisen during her divorce were not yet resolved. "When I received a flyer in the mail promoting an eleven-week seminar on divorce and personal growth, I remembered that the therapist I had seen at the time of my divorce had recommended a divorce support group. I hadn't felt ready then to share my feelings of pain and rejection with strangers, but I know now that I still had a lot of feelings buried inside."

Until she joined the seminar, Spear did not realize that the emotion she had suppressed was anger. "I was brought up in a New England family in which anger was not considered feminine, and any expression of anger was forbidden," she recalls. "When I got divorced I kept my anger inside, and it was still there after all those years."

Spear felt awkward with the group at first, because most of the others were newly divorced or separated. But the psychologist who led the program urged her to join, both for her own benefit and to serve as an example to the others of the importance of facing and dealing with the emotional issues that come out of a divorce, whether sooner or later. "I was a living example that the pain and confusion don't go away until you are willing to confront them," she says.

Spear found the seminar immensely helpful. She managed to identify her feelings and learn how they had naturally occurred because of the circumstances surrounding the end of her marriage—rejection, loss, betrayal, and confusion about guilt. Spear also saw how her husband's refusal to deal with baggage from his first marriage had contributed to problems in their relationship. "I really learned a lot in group therapy," she comments. "The people in the group were all at different stages, and we were able to learn a lot from each other."

Like many groups, the one Spear joined included weekly sessions that combined structured activities with a chance for participants to talk and share their thoughts informally. Each session built on topics covered in previous weeks, with assignments given to be completed before the next session. Volunteers trained by the psychologist who led the group assisted by calling participants during the week to offer a listening ear and arranging social events that group members could choose to attend if they wished.

"Even though I had my career and a group of friends, so I didn't face the loneliness many people did, it was still good to be a part of a social group with common issues," Spear recalls. "The community was important, and some of the people who met in the group continued getting together socially after the seminar period." After completing her own seminar, Spear continued as a volunteer with a subsequent group. "It was really good for me to see how much I had learned and how far I had come," she remarks. "You also see the advantages and disadvantages of your own situation when you compare it with that of others. For instance, I had a much easier time than many people in making the transition to single life because I had always been independent. I had a career, friends, lots of interests. Yet the healing still takes a long time."

Like many people, Spear tried to give herself deadlines for recovery. "People have to realize that everyone is different, everyone heals at different rates," she says. "I was my own worst and harshest critic. I would advise others to be patient with themselves and to realize that even after you do feel good there will be things that cause emotional upheaval. Going through this roller coaster of emotions is very upsetting—but it's typical."

Now, Spear looks back on the years of her marriage from a different perspective. "The past will always be a part of your life," she explains. "Those years are a component of your experience. You have to deal with it and go on, but you can't just remove a block from the foundation that built your life. People have to realize that the marriage was a part of what made the life they have today."

Spear also learned that it is acceptable to retain a certain concern about the former spouse. "Even today, I still feel concerned for his well-being," she says of her former husband. "But that's just the way I am about any friend. In the seminar I learned that this is normal. The history you shared, with its bittersweet memories, is important."

Spear also gained a new perspective on the labels we tend to place on relationships. "Americans are so success oriented, we expect absolute success or absolute failure in relationships and don't recognize what is in between," she comments. "We still believe that if a marriage doesn't last forever, we've failed. It's very shameful and completely devastating in our society to fail. We need to see that moving out of a marriage is not a failure, it means you're taking another path in life."

4

Divorce and Children

EVEN UNDER THE BEST OF CIRCUMSTANCES, DIVORCE MAKES children afraid and anxious. When parents divorce, children lose their sense of security and protection. While parents often see the divorce as primarily an issue between themselves, with the impact on the children as incidental, children view the divorce as something happening to them. They see the family splitting apart, and their own identities changing.

The effect of divorce on children has been a topic of great concern in recent years. Many states have modified their laws to make divorce more difficult or to require a longer waiting period before the divorce becomes final when there are minor children involved. Undoubtedly, the motive behind such efforts is noble, but whether such steps actually promote stronger families, or only prolong the pain of families trying to end an unworkable situation, remains open to debate.

One thing, however, is certain. It is not the divorce itself, but exposure to hostility between the parents that is most damaging to children. Study after study has shown that one of the most destructive things children can experience is ongoing conflict between the parents, whether before or after a divorce. In a home where argument and discord define the prevailing atmosphere, it is far better for children if the parents split, provided the end of the marriage results in the end of the conflict.

Most young people agree that it is negative for parents to stay together if their love has died and conflict is the predominant emotion in the home, because children do not feel loved and secure in such an atmosphere. In fact, many say they wish the marriage—and the discord that was a part of it—had ended sooner. One woman, whose parents divorced when she was in high school, remarks, "It was really upsetting when my parents divorced, but it's worse to grow up in a home filled with constant conflict. I do think it's harder for teenagers when parents divorce, because there is more of a tendency to take sides. I think it would have been easier if my parents had split when I was younger, because there would have been fewer years of conflict overall."

Mediator and counselor Diane Fassel, author of *Growing Up Divorced: A Road to Healing for Adult Children of Divorced Parents*, has studied and counseled many people whose parents stayed together for a period of years after the marriage had soured, "for the sake of the children." Invariably, Fassel found that as adults, those who grew up in such homes say their parents did them no favor. Children know when parents are unhappy, and they sense the tension. All feel miserable; some even feel guilty just for having been born so that their unhappy parents are forced to stay together. Many, looking back, feel as though they were punished rather than benefited by being forced to remain in a home where the quality of life was, in the words of one woman who grew up in such an environment, "horrendous."

Like children from homes in which one parent is abusive, most report a sense of relief when the marriage finally ends. Even if there is no overt conflict between the parents, those who live with a person they consider an enemy subject the children living in such a situation to "hostile territory" in which the air is permeated with misery and unexpressed anger. When children live with parents who do not collaborate, who shut down their emotions and carry on in an atmosphere of seething hatred, the children become, as Fassel states, like "civilians in a war zone."

Parents are the most important role models for their children. Kids learn, and frequently emulate, the behaviors they observe in their homes. Children who grow up in an atmosphere of denial that encourages suffering in silence become adept at presenting a false image to the world instead of dealing with and changing the reality of a bad situation. They often emerge as adults with low expectations and a habit of hypervigilance against deception.

After scores of interviews with adult children of divorced parents, Fassel concluded that a parent's divorce was, of itself, a neutral act. Many of the people she interviewed stated that the divorce was far preferable than remaining for years in a hostile and dysfunctional home. When violence and/or fighting prevailed, most children, both at the time of divorce and in retrospect, find the split to be a blessed relief. In a peaceful home with one parent they are finally able to achieve a sense of safety.

Fassel, and most others, believe it is always the right decision to terminate a marriage that is hurting the children. Children from such homes often appreciate the courage it took for the abused parent to leave, or, even when the parents were miserable but not combative, for both to admit incompatibility and do something about it. As one divorced mother commented, "My daughter said that the divorce was the best thing her parents ever did. We had been in conflict for a long time, and she was ready for it to end."

Fassel says the key issue is not whether parents divorce, but how. In a positive divorce, there will be honesty and solutions to problems found, as opposed to denial, in which a family tries to stay together pretending everything is okay when it is not. Fassel reports that if the process is clean and straightforward, with each person's feelings honored, and parents maintain a basic respect for the child's right to a relationship with both parents, then the divorce will not have lasting traumatic or long-term negative consequences for the children.

Fassel found that even after a traumatic divorce, children may emerge with certain strengths from the experience. Such traits include independence, a greater willingness to be responsible for themselves and experience a sense of responsibility within the family, resilience and a sense of inner toughness, and a healthy attitude toward accessing and expressing feelings and emotions. They learn they can suffer, get over it, and go on with life. Many learn to take a philosophical view of life and to accept reality without self-pity, focusing on the benefits of the situation.

One woman Fassel interviewed was, as a young girl, brutally beaten by her father until she was removed from the home to be raised by loving grandparents who cherished her and gave her a wonderful upbringing. She and others with similar experiences learned that a wrenching change in their existence may result in a broader and better life as a result. Such people tend to be adaptable and well prepared to let go and move through life's changes. They learn flexibility, and grow up knowing they have choices. Those who receive counseling or therapy after their parents' divorce also learn the benefit of asking for help and professional support in times of crisis.

When the conflict in a home has escalated into violence, whether directed against the children or by one parent against the other, or both, the children *must* be rescued from continued exposure to abuse. Virtually all of the experts I have encountered agree that witnessing violence between the parents is the second most damaging thing that can happen to a child—second only to direct child abuse.

WHAT FACTORS DETERMINE HOW WELL CHILDREN WILL RECOVER?

The quality of life after the divorce is the key to how well and how quickly children recover from the upset of their parents' divorce. In addition to the key element, parental conflict, certain other factors help predict how a child will adjust. These include long-standing behavior patterns in the child (for example, a child that is hard to manage before the divorce will likely become more difficult, and require more attention from both parents, afterwards); the relative degree of change the child's life that follows the divorce (kids who stay in the same home, school, and/or neighborhood tend to do better); lifestyle after the divorce (stability of the new home, frequent and unimpeded access to both parents, financial circumstances and whether the child has to sacrifice activities or things they care about); and whether outside factors add stress to an already volatile situation. The big issue with children in divorce is not the divorce itself, but how the family relationships change.

Again, however, the relationship between the parents is the one key factor that outweighs all others. The messier the divorce, and the more hostility involved, the longer it will take for everyone to recover and heal. Psychologists caution that an unresolved divorce is never final, and that a real resolution requires closure of all of the pertinent issues. Children cannot be expected to mature when they observe their parents behaving like children—lying, making promises that won't be kept, and throwing tantrums. Parents who wrangle endlessly with an ex-spouse over money or other issues are teaching their children to be petty and manipulative. Sometimes parents also have unrealistic expectations for their children following a divorce, such as immediate and idyllic bonding with a new stepparent they barely know.

It is crucial for both parents to stay informed about what is taking place in important areas of their child's life—school, friends, interests, and health, to name a few. This depends on establishing a cordial relationship that allows for regular communication, maintaining flexibility and responsibility in visitation, and respecting rules of the other household, while not expecting that they will be exactly the same in both. Under these circumstances, most children adjust well after the initial dust has settled. While divorce is always somewhat traumatic for children, they bounce back and readjust in nearly all cases *if* the parents are able to focus on their love for them and are willing to put aside their animosity toward each other and behave in a civilized manner.

BUILDING A NEW RELATIONSHIP WITH YOUR EX

Family therapists who work with divorced couples say that some animosity between ex-spouses is normal, especially soon after the divorce. It is a part of the grieving process over the loss of a loved one. During this phase, when wounds are still raw and emotions likely to erupt, counselors—and those who have been through it—advise keeping contact minimal and businesslike. Professionals caution that constructing a workable new relationship does not happen overnight, and advise patience. It may take some time, and a fair amount of trial and error, but the effort will be well worth the work, especially for parents of young children who will need to continue to work together for years to come.

Following is a list of recommendations from both professionals and parents who have managed to construct an effective, peaceful relationship with their former spouses:

1. "Make yourself behave as you would with your banker, not your former lover," one woman suggests. "Be busi-

nesslike, not emotional, and keep the kids as the central point," advises another. A change in the way you view a person or situation—what counselors call "reframing"—can help tremendously when trying to detach from the emotional issues that make it hard to deal with an ex-spouse. Many recommend learning to view your ex in terms of a business or workplace relationship. Most of us have had to deal with people in our work lives that we don't particularly like, but must learn to tolerate and interact with in a civil manner. Many former spouses who must now work effectively together as parents have found this approach successful. Mediator Frances Webb advises former spouses trying to succeed as parents to treat the other person as a business partner or simply as a friend. "Don't talk personally with each other," she says. "Discussing personal issues ties you together and prolongs conflict. Think about how you would speak to a co-worker, business associate, or person you barely know. You wouldn't go to him to cry on his shoulder or complain. There are some exceptions, of course, but generally, people do much better if they can take the emotion out of the conversation."

2. Taking the business analogy a step further, some parents have even created a "mission statement," similar to those used by corporations, to keep their focus on the business they must address together. A mission statement is a concrete way of setting out goals, such as obtaining a good education for the children or making sure they stay close to members of each extended family. When the common goals parents share are spelled out, it can help keep the focus on the mutual effort of working effectively as coparents.

3. Put agreements, schedule modifications, and other important matters in writing. If one parent is leaving town on a trip, be sure the other has a written itinerary

so that parents can communicate if necessary. If a child has a particularly important event or activity coming up during a visit with the noncustodial parent, be sure that parent has all the information. Another tool that is routinely used in business can also help parents: written "policies and procedures" on how changes in the visitation schedule, for example, should be handled. Calendars especially for kids, such as one called "My Two Homes" (see Appendix), can also help keep track of scheduling matters.

4. Meet on neutral ground to conduct your business. Don't meet in the home you once shared, and avoid any discussion of matters concerning the children when they are present. Arranging your get-togethers in a place that is free of emotional connotations and conducive to conducting business can help reinforce the nature of your new relationship. Consider meeting in a conference room at one parent's place of business, a mutually convenient restaurant or coffee shop, or a public library.

5. Try to view your ex as the child's parent instead of your former spouse. This helps keep the focus where it belongs—on working together as parents to effectively raise healthy children.

6. Communicate with your ex only when it is really necessary, keeping in mind that you now have a business relationship. Keep communications as brief as possible, especially when exchanging children; a short and pleasant greeting is usually enough. Discuss your business issues when the children are not present, and stick to the agenda at hand.

7. When communicating use language that is clear, nonjudgmental, and brief. If the conversation seems to be escalating, or your ex is trying to goad you into argument or makes unkind comments, end the exchange immediately with a statement that you will have to discuss the matter

later, and mean it—leave or hang up. Communicate in writing, if necessary, to avoid a clash. If you steadfastly refuse to argue, your ex will, hopefully, learn that you cannot be manipulated into a confrontation. Stick to your guns on this one—and if your ex refuses to get the picture, suggest that mediation may be in order. You owe both yourself and your children a life free of this type of abuse, and that is what deliberate hostility amounts to.

8. When you exchange the children, maintain a positive, businesslike attitude. Smile and wish the children a good time, then send them on; do not exchange money or discuss issues, and above all, do not use the children as messengers for such matters. Your relaxed and positive attitude will reassure them.

9. If you learn from your child that your ex is constantly putting you down or otherwise campaigning against you, you must put a stop to this behavior immediately—it is severely destructive to the child. First, don't waste your energy worrying that your ex will turn the child against you; if you have a good relationship with the child, it will be very difficult to alienate him or her from you. Second, request mediation or family counseling. If your ex refuses, it is time to seek the aid of the court, which can order therapy or other forms of intervention (not, generally, a change of custody unless the problem is extremely severe, but rather counseling that can teach all family members how to communicate more effectively and keep the focus on the child's interests and needs).

10. Parents who are not hostile, but find it difficult to reach a workable relationship on their own, can benefit from the assistance of a counselor or mediator. One couple who went through a short-term course of counseling to improve their communication skills commented that it helped them avoid their tendency to backslide into past

hurts, and taught them to focus on the positive goal of being good parents rather than on negative issues. "It also helped us realize the crucial importance of not saying anything negative about each other around our son," the father remarked. The mother agreed. "Kids make it hard sometimes," she said. "Counseling taught us to deal with those times. For instance, he will say that I don't like his daddy. Now I just reply, 'How could I not like your daddy when he gave me you?'"

The Essential Duty to End the Conflict

Psychologist Constance Ahrons, author of *The Good Divorce*, stresses the importance of establishing and maintaining a "limited partnership" when couples with children divorce. This means forging an egalitarian relationship between parents, setting basic ground rules, and being realistic about the problems that must be addressed. Ahrons emphasizes the importance of parents keeping sight of the many good choices available for effective coparenting after a divorce and seeking professional assistance if required to establish a plan that will minimize the family's loss and maximize its gains. She urges parents who have difficulty communicating or cooperating after a divorce to look for common ground and try to keep sight of their mutual love and goals for the children.

As Ahrons states, "A good divorce does not require that parents share child care responsibilities equally. It means they share them clearly. Whatever living arrangements and division of responsibilities parents decide on, they cooperate within those limits." Ahrons found that 50 percent of the couples she studied have been able to forge some sort of cooperative parenting relationship, with 12 percent true friends and 38 percent what she deemed "cooperative colleagues." Sadly, however, this left 50 percent of the parents still in various degrees of conflict with one another.

The bottom line, to state it both harshly and simply, is that conflict between parents absolutely *must* be resolved. If parents can't do it on their own, they need the help of a mediator or mental health professional. As one psychologist stated, when parents in a high-conflict divorce cannot find a way to put their anger aside but rather insist on bringing their children into the conflict, they are abdicating one of the primary parental duties—protecting the children from harm.

Open Hostility Between Parents

"When children love both parents, then hear the parents attack one another, it can ruin lives for years," says counselor Kathryn Lang. "There are parents who still fight openly years after they have divorced, at their children's graduations, for example. I've heard of more than one instance when battling parents have ruined a grown child's wedding day."

When counseling such couples, Lang tries to get them to look at the reality of their lives. "When people who are divorcing are parents, 'til death do us part' becomes a given," she states. "People must accept this for their children. They have to let go and realize that they can't control what happens when the child is with the other parent, and that unless it's endangering the kids, it really is none of their business. The sooner people accept this fact, the sooner they can let go of their own anger about injuries of the past. People simply have to commit to not doing things that are detrimental to their children."

Many psychologists believe that the use of children to get even with the former spouse is a form of child abuse, and the greatest danger of a hostile divorce. As one psychologist remarked, "Propaganda campaigns against one parent by another *destroy* children."

What if the parents can't stand the sight of one another? Can positive parenting ever be achieved? In a word, yes. More and more parents in high conflict—sometimes with the assistance of a therapist or mediator—are finding ways to cope with their animosity toward one another so that it does not poison the children.

For those who cannot even manage to establish a minimally civil business relationship, a third party such as a counselor may have to act as a go-between when the need to communicate arises. A new concept recently put into practice by some mental health professionals who work with families in conflict is the use of a parenting coordinator. In this role, a third person who is familiar with the legal, psychological, and child development aspects of the case works to settle disagreements involving the children as such clashes occur between parents. The parenting coordinator acts as a facilitator to help parents formulate a detailed parenting plan that addresses all anticipated issues surrounding visitation, scheduling change protocol, telephone use, respect for rules and boundaries, even children's toys, belongings, and pets. The coordinator monitors visitation and suggests changes when necessary, and may also work with therapists involved with the family and even report to the court, when one parent seeks a visitation or custody change.

When parents absolutely cannot be civil to one another—or when one parent poses a danger to the other—solutions can still be reached that allow the child to have a relationship with the noncustodial parent. In many communities, there are drop-off locations where parents may exchange children in a safe, nonthreatening environment, such as the YWCA or YMCA. Some communities have places such as the Neutral Corner in Albuquerque, New Mexico, which exist specifically for this purpose. These locations may also provide space for supervised visitation, when the court has made such an order.

Other parents have worked out exchange plans on their own that don't require them to come in contact with one another, such as arranging for the custodial parent to take the child to school on Friday morning and the noncustodial parent to pick him or her up for a weekend visit when school gets out. One couple met at an intersection near a park in their vehicles. Both flashed headlights to assure the other that the right person was there. Their son was then dropped off by one at the side of the park, and the other would join him for a romp on the playground equipment, then take him home.

When children are older, parents can, in most cases, simply avoid direct contact when the child is exchanged at one parent's home. When I was in elementary school I had a close friend whose parents had divorced when she was quite young. Her mother had remarried, and my friend lived with her mother and stepfather. I always had the impression that her father and mother still felt quite acrimonious toward one another. Yet both loved their daughter, and were able to work out a visitation plan that allowed her father to pick her up and drop her off at her mother's home without direct contact. In this way she was able to enjoy her natural father's company—I recall that she always looked forward to their weekend adventures—as well as develop a warm, loving relationship with her stepfather.

Subtle Hostility

Sometimes parents who have managed to stop shouting at one another believe they have ended the damaging conflict, yet the smoldering hatred persists, and it shows. As a result, they continue to hurt their children in more subtle ways.

Anything that creates a sense of conflicting loyalties in children is very painful for them. This may range from forcing a child to choose with which parent to live to grilling a child who has been visiting the noncustodial parent about that parent's habits and lifestyle. Such messages make the child feel as though he or she must choose one parent to love, and reject the other.

One area in which parents often unwittingly demonstrate hostility is in dealing with time-sharing arrangements. Before a visit with a noncustodial parent begins or ends, check your attitude. Sometimes parents try to wish the child a good time, but the sentiment is halfhearted at best. Children pick up on this hypocrisy, and it makes them feel worried and anxious. During the transition, make a point of trying to say a few civil words to your ex—this reassures children. This is a time when it is especially easy to send mixed signals, for example, by delivering friendly words accompanied by frowns, grimaces, or deep sighs. A child as young as age four or five can pick up on parents' true moods, and suffer as a result.

Family Court Judge Anne Kass has compared such parental behavior to the movie *Sophie's Choice*. In the movie, Sophie, the mother of two small children, was sent to a Nazi concentration camp. An especially evil soldier told her she had to pick one child to live; the other would die. When she replied that she could not choose between her children, the soldier replied that if she did not pick one, both would die. So Sophie was forced to make a choice that caused her to suffer anguish for the rest of her life, and she became aimless and alcoholic after the war as a result.

Judge Kass believes that parents often force children into a similar decision that may be nearly as painful. Sometimes the message is blatant, she explains, as when a parent makes a child tell the judge with which parent he or she prefers to live. In other cases it is more subtle, with one parent moping or showing irritation when the child tries to enjoy the company of the other. "Divorcing parents need to know the most loving gift each parent can give their children is his or her permission for the children to love the other parent and accept love from the other parent," Kass states. She has observed that children who are forced to make a "Sophie's choice" often self-destruct, as Sophie did in the movie. "Theirs is the lifelong anguish of being denied what should truly be an inalienable right," she adds, "the right to love both parents."

Dealing with a Persistently Hostile Ex

What do you do when you want to make peace—or at least declare a truce for the good of your children—but your ex keeps waging war? When you have tried all the commonsense tactics for avoiding a clash, without success, then what? Professionals who have worked with such couples recommend some specific techniques that may help.

First, when speaking with your ex, watch for hot spots— those topics and habits that produced friction or power struggles in the marriage. Avoid going there if at all possible. If not, vow to keep those areas strictly businesslike; avoid the emotional action-reaction dynamic.

This can be very tough, especially if your spouse is trying to spark an altercation or escalate the ongoing hostility. It's a natural human reaction, when attacked, to fight back. But the best bet is to consistently refuse to be drawn into battle. At the first sign of hostility, end the conversation and hang up or leave. He or she may be deliberately trying to make you feel hurt or angry. Do not give him or her the satisfaction. Tell your ex that you will discuss this rationally, only when he or she is not upset, or only in writing. Some couples have to keep all communication on difficult issues in written form.

In many cases, a combination of compassion, detachment, and consistent refusal to be drawn into a war will convince a hostile ex to work with you in a civil manner. Check your own willingness to compromise on things that aren't that important, such as minor variations in visitation schedules, your own tendency to be late to pick up the children, returning the children muddy after a day at the river. A sense of give and take can make it easier for some to bury the hatchet.

For some people with extremely volatile relationships, such efforts won't be enough. Hot issues may need to be addressed in writing or through a third party, such as a counselor, mediator, or facilitator, as described above. In some cases, court intervention may be required to order the recalcitrant party into some type of counseling or dispute-resolution program, or into court for a stern judicial admonition that can shame a person into behaving himself. In extreme cases, such as if your ex becomes destructive or abusive during an encounter, it may be necessary to call the police, press criminal charges, and get a restraining order to prevent him or her from threatening or attacking you ever again.

Whether the problem is minor or severe, you deserve a peaceful life free of continuous hostility. Be sure you don't hang onto unrealistic expectations about your ex, such as believing that vicious behavior isn't really a big deal, or that hostility that has persisted for several years will eventually pass. When you are able to see things clearly, this is a sign of healing. Choose not to be attached to persistent hostility— you cannot be responsible for his or her recovery or behavior, but you can, and must, set your own boundaries. At the first sign of attack, make it clear that you will not put up with such treatment and will take whatever steps are necessary to put a stop to it.

HOW PARENTS CAN HELP CHILDREN HEAL

When parents divorce, children feel that their survival is threatened on two primal levels: safety (the physical environment is at risk) and love (the emotional environment is also imperiled). Like adults, children experience fear as the core emotion. Yet children tend to be more resilient, adaptable, and practical than adults give them credit for. Children who receive steadfast reassurance that both parents love them, an honest picture of what is going on, freedom from continued conflict between parents, and a demonstration that their physical and emotional needs will not be neglected, tend to bounce back just fine.

Young children are especially fearful of abandonment. They need repeated reassurance by both parents—through both words and deeds—that they will not be loved less, lose contact, or get lost in the shuffle. Some of the most common worries that children dwell on include, "What's going to happen to me?" "Did I cause the divorce?" "How can I continue to love both parents without hurting one?" "Are we going to starve?" "Where is my room going to be?" Some of these concerns may seem self-centered to parents, but remember, children are not miniature adults. It is in their nature to be very self-focused at certain stages in their development. Remember, too, that these are the practical realities of children's lives, on a parallel with the concerns of adults about their own homes and financial needs.

By the time adults have been through a marriage and divorce, most have seen enough of the world to know that different options and choices exist for them, and different roads may lead them to happiness. Children do not have this experience, however. Most grow up with one image of a family solidly in mind, and divorce shatters the only belief system that they know. It may take more time for children to heal, since they have to incorporate an entirely new belief system they may not be ready to absorb. Key factors in how children will be affected by a parent's divorce include their ages, how the parents handle the breakup, and how much security the parents provide in the years that follow. Children who find safe havens in the recovery process, through supportive parents and other family members, counselors, support groups, and understanding friends, will generally survive their depression and anxiety and emerge stronger for the experience.

It is very helpful if children are assisted to focus on the future, to continue to think about their dreams and make plans for their adult lives. Loss can be channeled into positive paths. One young man commented that his mother's vow never to discredit his father to the children had contributed to his ability to maintain a positive attitude.

Parental cooperation has long-term benefits for the children, as well as promoting harmony in the present. Parents who set a successful example by resolving their differences with dignity and compassion, who choose to put their children first, who can see and face their problems and work out realistic solutions, and who are willing to seek help from a third party when unable to reach their own solutions, set a fine example for children to emulate as they grow into their own adult years.

Parents can use this time as a golden opportunity to teach children, by example, about healthy ways of relating to themselves and others and weathering the inevitable storms in life. This can help children develop a sense of self-reliance and self-confidence. This is also the time for parents to draw boundaries—not to let the divorce become an excuse for unacceptable behavior. Some children actually benefit by more one-on-one attention from each parent after the divorce, especially when the problems that led to the divorce had been sapping most of the parents' energy and making them emotionally unavailable to the children.

Children are still learning how to manage their emotions, and to separate feelings from behavior. Therapists emphasize that children need a safe forum in which they are encouraged to talk about feelings of anger, sadness, worry, and guilt.

Some children can talk freely to parents or other adults in the family about such matters, while others need the counsel of someone more neutral. Children usually need to discuss such feelings repeatedly in order to come to terms with what is happening to them.

At least some aspects of this healing process need to be addressed by parents, even if children are also seeing a counselor or participating in a support group. Parents can help their children by spending some time just hanging out and communicating with each child, free from the distraction of organized activities or other people. Let your children express their feelings without fear of condemnation or punishment.

Those who work with children recovering from divorce emphasize that parents must make clear that it is all right to feel anger and to express it through acceptable outlets, but that it is never okay to hurt yourself or someone else when you're feeling angry or upset. Also, kids who learn to manage their feelings tend to find a sense of relief.

Psychologist Peter Favaro, in his book *Divorced Parents' Guide to Managing Custody and Visitation*, suggests that parents make an effort to collaborate on certain basic principles of good discipline, and to maintain consistent, high expectations for their children (such as dedication to schoolwork), delivered with extra warmth and affection during this period of adjustment. Favaro notes that while there is no harder time in parenting than moving children past suffering and into a more positive phase, this is when children rely most on parents.

While it is essential to maintain good discipline, Favaro and other child development professionals advise avoiding two common forms of punishment that do more harm than good: spanking or any form of hitting (which have been proven over and over to be ineffective, and only to increase aggression while damaging self-esteem), and withholding visitation with the other parent.

Specific Steps Parents Can Take to Help

The best source of information on how parents can help children heal often comes from the children themselves. Those who work with children after their parents' divorces hear similar stories from kids over and over when asked what they wish their parents would do to make things easier. Among the most common requests:

1. Recognize that kids love and need to be with both parents.
2. Don't turn the kids into messengers or ask them to report on what goes on at the other parent's home.
3. Don't say bad things about the other parent.
4. If you have something angry you have to say to the other parent, don't do it around the kids.
5. Don't make the children take sides.
6. Don't make the kids feel like they are being disloyal if they have a good time with the other parent.
7. Don't purposely forget to pack clothing or other things the children need when they are going to the other parent's home.

Many of these same factors are mirrored in advice from the experts. Some of the most frequently stated recommendations from mental health professionals include:

1. Refrain from criticizing the other parent, or his or her habits or lifestyle, in front of the child.
2. Ignore the child's negative comments about the other parent unless they indicate a serious problem—abuse, neglect, or endangerment. On the other hand, sometimes parents go too far toward the other extreme, gushing about what a wonderful person the other parent is. This can lead to confusion or false hopes of reconciliation.

3. Never use the child as a messenger to send money or information to the other parent. Even in an amicable situation, this makes the child feel awkward.
4. When considering a revision in the time-sharing schedule, keep the focus on the children. Remember that they are different individuals with needs and preferences that may not match your own, your ex's, or those of siblings. Compromise if necessary—it is usually easier for parents to bend their schedules than for children to make continual adjustments and sacrifices.
5. Consider the age of the child and his or her developmental stage in managing time sharing.

The Age Factor

The age of a child can make a big difference in what type of coparenting arrangement works best. Children younger than about two and a half years have a short attention span and a tremendous need to feel secure in a primary caretaker. Psychologists recommend that short but frequent visits are best for bonding to the noncustodial parent, preferably at the child's home. The noncustodial parent will have a better relationship with the child in the long run if he or she is willing to return a fussy or crying child to the other parent for comforting rather than insisting on strict adherence to schedules.

Children from toddler age to about five are becoming more independent and individualistic, but still need a great deal of security, and shouldn't be pushed to spend long periods of time away from the primary caretaker if they become anxious or upset. Some are ready for overnight visits at this age, while many are not.

Between ages six and eight, children are developing lives of their own involving friends and activities that are important to them. Parents often find it works well to participate in these activities. A child at this stage may still become home-sick if he or she is away from the primary parent for long periods of time.

Children between ages nine and twelve are developing skills in academic, athletic, and artistic endeavors and tend to be more involved in their own communities. Parents may need to be sensitive to the child's strong need for such activities, and to try to join in or schedule time away according to the stage the child has set.

Adolescents are usually even more tied up in their own complex lives, developing identities, pursuing diverse activities, and often working or dating as well. While regular involvement with the noncustodial parent remains important, it generally works best to be as flexible as possible, and to allow the kids to help work out the time-sharing plan. It is tough to force them to follow a schedule they did not create.

While certain needs and patterns are common at different developmental stages, children are, above all, individuals. Change is more difficult for some than for others. Some remarkably simple acts by parents can be tremendously reassuring to children. For example, children need a time frame for the changes they are facing. They need the answers to their questions, in both general terms (reassurance that "no matter what, you will never go hungry") and concrete issues ("you won't have to quit your Scout troop and you will have your own room in our new apartment").

How Much Do Children Need to Know?

While children generally do not need to know the intimate details of why the parents are divorcing, they should be made aware of the changes that will occur in their everyday lives, why these changes are taking place, and how these changes will affect them. For example, many mothers who have been able to stay at home or work part-time or flex-time in order to spend more hours with the children during the marriage will now be required to work full-time jobs. Kids need to know what to expect in terms of what will change in their daily lives.

Children often worry about financial issues and other practical security matters, whether they express these concerns or not. Children who are left out of the process completely may become bewildered and reach the wrong conclusions, frequently blaming themselves for the divorce. Likewise, children who are told nothing about the circumstances that led to the parents' rift may decide they were at fault. One young man, whose mother left the family, commented that he was hurt by the way his parents quietly drifted away from each other and never seemed to express what was wrong. He felt that his parents had taken the "strictly business" aspect of their postdivorce relationship to an extreme, since neither ever talked about what had happened. As a result, he did not feel free to discuss his feelings about the situation with either parent.

Stuart Berger, M.D., author of *Divorce Without Victims,* and other professionals urge parents to be truthful with children about what changes the family is facing after divorce, patiently addressing specific issues as they arise and answering questions honestly, even regarding such difficult issues as a parent who has abandoned the family. In this instance, Berger suggests emphasizing that the behavior of the parent is his or her own problem and not the result of anything the child did. He also states that telling the child she was wanted and the product of love may provide some comfort. Too much information, however, can be detrimental. Most mental health professionals believe that children should not be given detailed explanations on why the parents are divorcing (except for facts they must know, such as why they may no longer have contact with a violent parent), but should be told specifically and repeatedly that the divorce is not their fault and that each parent wants them to continue to love the other. Those who are given too many details about one parent's transgressions or the financial havoc wrought by the divorce, for example, sometimes begin to blame or even hate that parent and refuse to see him or her, as discussed below.

The question of how much to tell is always a touchy issue, especially when gross misconduct by one parent is involved, but most experts advise that it be treated in a manner similar to sex education—by giving accurate information appropriate to the age of the child. Author and counselor Diane Fassel advises parents to answer questions as they arise and to be honest, not trying to control the situation, no matter how difficult the real issues involved. Children who are lied to sense a breach of trust. For example, a child as young as three years of age can sense when more is going on than he's being told.

Fassel and other experts stress that some degree of anxiety, uncertainty, confusion, and fear of the future are inevitable in children any time parents divorce, but not knowing the reason for this pain makes it worse. Fassel wrote of one woman who was told at age thirteen, when her parents divorced, that her father needed to be free and explore his options in life. This left her puzzled, as her parents already seemed to enjoy an independent relationship. When she found out several years later that her father was gay, she was very upset—not by the fact of her father's sexual preferences, but by the breach of trust she felt from her parents' dishonesty.

Holidays and the Extended Family

Holidays are frequently a difficult time for families who have been through changes in the previous year. Children seem to be especially sensitive to emotional pain on holidays. Adults who are forced to spend holidays away from their children, or are with their children in a new context, also face tough emotional issues.

Plan well in advance so that your holidays will be marked by fun and adventure, perhaps the start of new traditions, rather than painful reflection about the past. Many people find that a brief vacation away from the family home or the location of traditional celebrations can be a good alternative. On the other hand, if your family is accustomed to spending a particular holiday with relatives, and it's possible for this tradition to continue, this can be a source of comfort and continuity.

Grandparents, aunts, uncles, cousins, family friends, and others who have been an important part of a child's life need to remain accessible to give children a sense of security. All states now have laws providing for grandparent visitation.

If your children do not have other caring adults in their lives, or if circumstances have removed some who were formerly involved, consider contacting organizations such as Big Brothers and Big Sisters, the YMCA or YWCA, or local community-based groups that can help your child interact with different adults on a positive level.

TYPES OF CUSTODY AND TIME SHARING

Numerous names are given to different types of custody and time-sharing arrangements in the law, but in reality, the differences between sole custody, joint custody, and other labels are less significant than whether parents are able to come up with an arrangement that works for the children, according to their own situations and the practicalities of life for all individuals involved.

During the 1980s, a strong trend developed for joint custody. Many states adopted laws stating a preference for joint-custody arrangements. In a joint-custody parenting plan, both parents have authority and input on major decisions affecting how the children are raised, such as education, religious training, and health care. Under joint-custody plans, one parent usually has primary physical custody, so actual living arrangements may not be that different than in a sole-custody arrangement.

Certainly, joint custody sounds good, but family psychologists who have studied families in joint-custody situations since it became popular fifteen years ago have found, not surprisingly, that joint custody works well only in situations where families maintain amicable relationships and live close to one another. Otherwise, the parents tend to fight over every decision and the children suffer more, because the conflict is intensified.

Family law attorney David B. Riggert notes that there is no longer a statutory preference for joint custody in Illinois, and he feels the shift away from joint custody is a positive change. "I used to encourage clients to push for joint custody," he states. "But now I would have to say that joint custody is really just a placebo, because in reality, the custodial parent has to make the day-to-day decisions about the child's upbringing. Whether the arrangement is joint custody or sole custody with visitation, it's important for the noncustodial parent to stay involved in the child's life, but to let the parent with primary custody make the main decisions. If I'm representing the parent who will have primary custody, and the other parent is very insistent about joint custody and this is the only issue that's a sticking point, then I may advise the custodial parent to agree to joint custody. Whether joint custody or sole custody, however, I typically urge the primary residential parent to let the other parent remain involved. If parental involvement is the issue, then custody alternatives are really two sides of the same coin."

Riggert explains that his own change in perspective about joint custody is based on numerous conversations with judges, who say that the goal of joint custody often isn't accomplished because it sets couples up for disagreement later. "I'm leaning toward believing that sole custody plus liberal visitation is the better way," he says. "Parents need to think long and hard about their custody arrangements, always remembering that stability is essential for children. Joint custody is often a feel-good thing for parents, and often has nothing to do with what's best for the child. Kids don't care about active involvement in decision making. Their concerns are more along the lines of 'Can I still go to the fair with Dad this year?' "

It is considered a given today that joint custody simply won't work in high-conflict divorces. Consequently, many of the same professionals who once stated a strong preference for joint custody now join Riggert in recommending sole custody, plus generous visitation by the other parent, to reduce the stress on the kids.

The same type of shift is occurring with regard to physical custody arrangements. Where people once believed that it was best for children to spend large chunks of time in each parent's home, with some attempting an even fifty-fifty split, those who have been involved in these custodial arrangements have often found them very difficult, especially for the children.

Riggert expresses special reservations about fifty-fifty time-sharing arrangements. "These fifty-fifty splits are especially difficult after the child is in school. I had one case in which the child seemed to be doing okay, but then he remarked that his friends never visited him, because they could not keep track of where he was. He always had to go to their homes instead. Things like that are probably tougher on a kid than we realize."

MAKING TIME SHARING WORK

One of the most essential components in effective parenting after divorce is flexibility. Custody and support agreements frequently require modification as children grow and circumstances change. What seemed to be the best arrangement at the time of the divorce may prove difficult when put into practice.

Some difficulties and adjustments regarding visitation are inevitable for nearly all parents. Ideally, parents should be able to discuss their concerns as they arise, when the children are not present, and work out a reasonable compromise. Consistency is important to children, but so is flexibility that allows for predictability in other areas of life that mean a lot to the child. Often, this just requires communication and consideration by each parent during the child's time with him or her. For example, if your daughter's basketball team has a game scheduled at a time when she was to be with you, try to make it possible for her to play rather than scheduling other plans.

In other cases, the parents need to work together to change a scheduled visit or make other adjustments. If clashes that can't be worked out persist, consider counseling or mediation. The more you can commit to doing whatever it takes to make time sharing work, the more your children will benefit. Child welfare professionals sometimes need to remind people that child custody does not mean ownership.

Children are unique individuals, and develop at different rates as the years progress. Sometimes finding the right schedule for a child requires some period of trial and error. As children grow and change, parents need to be willing to modify time sharing to adjust for their changing psychological and social needs. Inevitably, children's needs and preferences alter as they get older. The teen years are characterized by experimentation in all areas of life, and working out a division of time between two homes is no exception. It is common for teens to express a desire to move back and forth between parents' homes, and most advise that unless there is a problem in one home, it is best to allow them to do so. Since they tend to change their minds often, it is preferable for parents to negotiate a trial period for such changes, if possible, before filing a revised parenting plan with the court.

Too-frequent changes, however, can have a negative impact on a child's sense of security. Attorney David B. Riggert remarks, "Stability in the life of a child is important, and custody decisions are too often made on the basis of what is most convenient for the parents, while the controlling issue is supposed to be what is in the best interest of the child. Parents need to understand—and continue to understand as their own circumstances change—that the child's interests are paramount."

The logistics of managing a time-sharing plan can be daunting, but some simple tools and steps can help make the process easier. Planning ahead to be sure the child's schedule is clearly understood by everyone involved is one of the most important aids to keeping things running smoothly.

Mediator Roberta Beyer has developed a special calendar for children of divorced parents called "My Two Homes." The calendar is bright and cheerful, with stickers the child can use to mark upcoming events such as school activities and birthday parties, as well as the days when the child changes homes. Kids and parents have both found the calendar a highly useful tool for keeping track of schedules and important events. Beyer made a point of using bright colors and positive images in designing the calendar, so the idea of living in two homes is presented as perfectly normal and okay. "My Two Homes" is available from LadyBug Press by mail or over the Internet, along with related products especially designed for divorced families (see Appendix).

No matter how good the advance planning, children tend to forget specifics. Remind children of the visit the day before it occurs. Help them choose and pack their bags, making sure they have what they need (such as homework) as well as things that make them feel secure (such as favorite toys or books). It is usually easier on both parents if some basics, such as toothbrushes and pajamas, can be kept at each home. Some children like to have a picture of the other parent when they visit. You can help by putting yourself in your child's place—for example, by thinking about what makes you more comfortable when you travel, while at the same time remaining sensitive to your child's need for solitude, companionship, and other reactions that may differ from your own.

While there are endless variations on what works, regularity and predictability, combined with the flexibility required to keep the children at the forefront, are the key ingredients, at least until the children reach the teen years. School counselors or therapists can often help when problems arise.

Some children are reluctant to speak up if the time-sharing schedule is not working. Parents may need to watch and listen to the child for hidden clues. Even when parents have done their best to work out a schedule that seems ideal, sometimes the child doesn't adapt well. Cooperative parents should be able to work the problem out. Some recommend that the preferences of a child as young as age six, if strongly expressed, should be accommodated as much as possible, unless it appears that the child is trying to please one parent.

Rules and Discipline

If possible, children should have the same fundamental rules in both homes. Parents with similar expectations can present a united front that maintains the consistency that can effectively teach children important lessons. In reality, specific household rules and practices usually vary somewhat, and parents can explain that this is simply how things are when you spend time in different homes. But parents who are able to work together can generally put together a consistent plan that addresses major expectations, responsibilities, and limitations.

The key to keeping major rules consistent is to narrow such rules down to those that are truly vital, then being more relaxed about less important matters. For example, parents may want to work out an agreement as to bedtimes, schoolwork requirements, and basic health issues such as not skipping meals, but agree to disagree about skateboarding and television viewing. If a problem arises, both parents can then remain effective authority figures.

Counselor Kathryn Lang warns that children who do not have consistent boundaries in both homes tend to manipulate and divide the parents when they don't like something one parent is doing. "That's another reason parents need to work together, so that the kids can't take advantage of the conflict between them," she explains. "Parents need to make it clear that some rules will be different in the two different homes, and that this is okay. Consistency would be ideal, but it seldom happens. Learning that different places have different rules can actually help kids learn to be flexible."

One tough spot many parents encounter is ongoing discipline. Most recommend that punishments such as being grounded or banned from TV or video games for a period of time be suspended when the child visits with the noncustodial parent, then resumed, if necessary, on return to the custodial parent's home. It is simply too difficult, as well as unfair to the noncustodial parent, to try and carry these punishments through during a visit.

Common Time-Sharing Problems

Two common, and extremely frustrating, problems that custodial parents often face are a child who returns from a visit out of control, and, at the opposite end of the spectrum, the child who refuses to visit the noncustodial parent.

Children, especially young ones, often have a hard time adjusting from one environment to another, especially when it reaffirms a traumatic event—in this case, by underscoring the parents' divorce. This is always made worse if there is tension between the parents at the time of exchange. Parents can best cope with such behavior by ignoring it, if it is just a nondestructive release of energy; by arranging some high-energy activity after the visit that will allow the child to blow off steam; and by refraining from automatically blaming the other parent for having done something to provoke it, which is seldom the case.

When Children Refuse to Visit   Children sometimes resist or flatly refuse a visit with the noncustodial parent. It is essential to approach this situation calmly, with an open heart and mind, but also crucial to find out why. First, check your own attitude. Could you be sending your child mixed signals, telling him you want him to go and enjoy himself but showing signs of sadness or resentment? If not, assess what is causing him to balk. Often, a heart-to-heart talk will resolve the problem—children may be simply bored, anxious, or upset about having to miss a social or other event.

Young children—aged six or under—may not have the ability to carry a mental picture of the absent parent and may experience a fear of abandonment. A photo of the parent sometimes helps. Discuss the problem with both the child and the other parent. Find out if the parent is spending time with the child, if the child has the necessary things to be comfortable during the visit, if he or she is allowed to use the telephone to call you or other family members or friends, and whether he or she is able to keep up with activities that are especially important.

Parents need to be sensitive to the fact that things that may seem trivial to adults, such as being able to play with a friend, watch a favorite television show, or attend a school event, can be very significant to a child, and can impart a sense of continuity. A minor scheduling adjustment or simple reassurance may do the trick. It may be necessary to work with the other parent to make sure the children have the attention, objects, and freedom to choose important activities that they need. Plan a conversation with your ex about this, writing out what you will cover in advance, if necessary. Keep it nonaccusatory and as positive as possible, acknowledging that visits are important, and that you need to work together to solve a problem that affects the child.

On the other hand, if the child exhibits fear of the non-custodial parent or steadfastly refuses to go or explain why, there may be genuine concerns about safety or abuse, especially if the parent has been abusive toward any family member in the past. If discussions with the child and other parent do not yield straight answers you can use to resolve the problem, seek the advice of an attorney and/or mental health professional. Do be very, very cautious before accusing your ex of wrongdoing, especially abuse, because inaccurate charges can do terrible harm on many levels. If there is abuse or neglect, however, there must be immediate intervention to protect the child. Parents who suspect such a problem must take fast and appropriate action.

When children refuse to visit the other parent, the worst thing the custodial parent can do, unless there is a genuine concern about mistreatment, is to allow them to have their way. It is essential to encourage a child to spend time with both parents. Never decide to suspend visitation on your own unless there is a definite crisis (defined as evidence of severe neglect or abuse). In such a case, call a counselor or legal advisor immediately.

One extreme form of this problem, in which children flatly refuse to have anything whatsoever to do with the noncustodial parent, is called "parental rejection syndrome." Mental health professionals who have studied this common, but vexing, difficulty report that it often occurs among children who have more information than they need, such as financial details or stories of a parent's philandering. These children may exhibit a totally cold attitude toward the parent, have nothing positive to say about him or her, act as though he or she has done something terrible, and refuse to consider even a brief visit. Children with this syndrome often act very protectively toward the custodial parent. Again, children should not be allowed to shut off contact with a decent, loving noncustodial parent. Besides the obvious negative consequences of alienating a child from a parent, such an experience can disturb the child's ability to relate to others, empathize, trust, forgive, and build new relationships. Children should not be allowed to disown a parent unless the parent is violent, abusive, or otherwise dangerous. When a relationship with a parent is not repaired, the child may suffer devastating regret or guilt years later.

Therapists and counselors can work with children exhibiting parental rejection syndrome to help them get past their confusion and resistance. One technique that has proven helpful in this situation is called "therapeutic visitation," which is specifically geared toward reconciling a parent and child. Many families have seen positive results after only a few weeks of this therapy, even when the child professed utter hatred for the parent.

Special Concerns for Noncustodial Parents

Some parents feel so overwhelmed by guilt after divorce that they have a hard time relating honestly and openly to their children. Sometimes noncustodial parents, in particular, overindulge or won't discipline children because of the limited time they spend with them. Psychologist Stephen Fehr explains,

"They fear that if they are too strict, the child won't want to spend time with them, so they go too far the other way. This is especially common when the custodial parent is poisoning the mind of the child against the other parent." Yet the parent who won't set boundaries does the child a disservice, and makes the transition back to the other home that much more difficult. As discussed above, some variances are inevitable, but it is much better for the child if the major rules are the same and consistently enforced in both homes.

Noncustodial parents may also try to fill each visit with endless amusements. This can prevent the child from having the time and attention she needs to get to know the parent in the new situation and become comfortable with the change. Also, many children today are run ragged by the demands of school, hobbies, sports, and other structured activities. They may benefit most from a low-key weekend with few or no planned activities. This allows for creative, spontaneous ideas, and for the child to express what would really please him.

Parents who fall into the "Disneyland Dad" trap often do so out of guilt, born of the preconceived notion that a parent who does not spend every day with the child is a bad parent. Yet love and attention to the child as a unique individual is what is important. Overindulgence, inconsistency in discipline, and constant gifts of material goods can work against this by preventing the natural development of a sense of genuine caring.

For the noncustodial parent, there can be a noticeable advantage to having blocks of time that are designated as devoted to spending time with the children. Communication and unstructured time to simply hang out or pursue a spontaneous idea is what children and parents often need and enjoy the most. Resist the urge to overplan and schedule too much entertainment.

This is not to say that all time must be unstructured. Many children and parents enjoy participating in sports together, taking short trips to explore nearby parks or nature preserves, or taking a class together. For example, one father combined his desire to enjoy time with his children and his need to learn a new skill by enrolling himself and his two daughters (who loved the idea) in a cooking class. Broadening your own repertoire of skills and interests can also help restore your confidence and stave off feelings of inertia.

Noncustodial parents can also establish favorite routines that will give children a sense of continuity. When one father picked up his young daughter after school every other Friday for her weekend visit, he always took her to her favorite restaurant. Before bed, he read to her from her beloved *Winnie the Pooh* book, then helped her call her mother to say goodnight. The rest of the weekend was open for various activities the two would choose together, or simply spending time at home.

It is important to give children the sense that they are still a part of your world, and your family. Avoid treating them as guests when they're in your home. Ideally, each child should have her own room in the noncustodial parent's home. When this is not possible, as is often the case, simply reserving a small space that is hers alone—a corner of a bedroom, an alcove, a nook at one side of a studio apartment—can give her a sense of belonging. One woman I knew, who lived in a tiny one-bedroom apartment, took the door off a walk-in hall closet and decorated it with superhero posters, a sleeping pallet with cartoon-character sheets, and a hammock full of toys that delighted her young son.

Noncustodial parents can provide valuable reassurance when apart from their children by calling or e-mailing them on a regular basis, as well as letting them know how they can get in touch with the parent. Caring parents have worked out creative solutions to seemingly impossible dilemmas. For example, one father who moved across the country when a once-in-a-lifetime career opportunity came up still managed, with the cooperation of his ex-wife, to maintain a steady relationship with the couple's young son and daughter. He called almost every night to talk to the children briefly and say goodnight before they went to bed. He worked out an arrangement with his employer whereby he could take a four-day weekend every six weeks and travel back to the children's home city for a visit. He frequently sent games and puzzles to the children, which they sent back when completed. With so many families today having access to the Internet and e-mail, the possibilities for low-cost, daily interaction between parents and children who live in distant areas are growing all the time.

Regular contact can also help ease the loneliness many noncustodial parents suffer to a greater degree than they expected. Support groups may be especially helpful for fathers who have lost the opportunity for daily contact with their children and find that they miss this aspect of their lives more than they thought they would.

Special Concerns for Custodial Parents

Single parenting is a challenge on many levels. Custodial parents often find the logistics of having to take responsibility for all of the discipline, chauffeuring, and even play and attention daunting. Yet this can be a time to build a strong new sense of family, as parents and children work together to find a balance of communication, chores, and fun.

After a divorce, schedules tend to be more hectic for children and parents alike. It will be difficult to juggle the new family structure for awhile. To make the adjustment period easier, many recommend that certain steps be taken by the parent with primary custody. First, key family routines should function as normally as they did before, as circumstances allow—this includes such matters as rules, mealtimes, and bedtimes. Maintaining familiar rituals—or beginning new ones—around everyday activities such as dinner together and after-school walks can help children establish a sense of continuity. Children often enjoy and provide useful assistance in such jobs as renovating your home or decorating a new one.

Second, and it cannot be emphasized enough, the children must be kept free of any troublesome aspect of the relationship between the parents. Resist the urge to use them as couriers to relay even seemingly innocuous messages or child support checks between the parents.

Third, remember that affection and communication are the number one priority for children, and you can provide an ample supply of these essentials without abdicating your responsibility to yourself. Take some special time—at least twenty minutes or half an hour each day—to interact with each child one on one, to talk about what is going on and provide reassurance, and to listen to what children have to say. Be honest about the financial ramifications of the divorce. If the expensive camp children usually attend each summer is no longer an option, tell them well in advance of the summer so you can work together to find alternatives.

Parents also need to remember that the best thing they can give their children is a mentally and physically healthy parent. As long as parents are in pain and not moving forward toward healing, children suffer, too. Counselor John Gray states that the greatest gift parents can give to their children is to be an example of love and healing. Don't forget your own needs, including being on your own or with other adults. When your child is with the other parent, this can be a time to enjoy your freedom—but not the only time. You set a good example for your child if you maintain your own interests and recreation. Join a gym or a sports team, take a class, or revive an old hobby you used to enjoy.

Work schedules and child care often change after a divorce. If you find that you must make new child care arrangements and don't know where to turn, there are many sources of information and assistance. Contact local family service agencies, child care facilities, churches, the YWCA or YMCA (which provide training and babysitter certification programs), the Yellow Pages, other parents, sitter certification and registration agencies, child development departments at local colleges, and Big Brothers and Big Sisters programs, and look into after-school activities and programs offered by schools and community centers. Some national organizations provide local referrals (see Appendix).

Many children find themselves in the role of "latchkey kids" for the first time after their parents divorce. When and whether a child will be comfortable and trustworthy in such a situation depends on the age and personality of each individual child. Some kids are ready for this type of arrangement at age ten or eleven; others are not prepared at age fifteen. Follow your own instincts and judgment, but be sure that a child who is introduced to a latchkey arrangement has appropriate guidelines in place, such as access to neighbors who will be home in case there's an emergency; an understanding of safety rules such as locking the door and never letting strangers on the phone or at the door know they're alone; and a clear picture of household rules, such as whether friends are allowed to visit, which appliances may be used and which are off limits, and what to do in case of an emergency. Some parents have children call them to check in when they arrive home. Others have a friend, relative, or trusted neighbor drop by occasionally to give the children a sense of security and to discourage misbehavior.

One mistake many custodial parents make is to use the child as an emotional crutch. While it is perfectly natural and beneficial to communicate honestly with children about your own feelings, it is important to draw the line before the child begins to feel responsible. For example, it is both appropriate and necessary to explain to children that the family will need more help around the house from each member, or that money is tight and older children will need to earn their pocket money through a part-time job. But never tell a boy he is "the man of the house now." Children who hear such admonitions often take on burdens they are not ready to bear, such as feeling that they must look out for the family's welfare or be accountable for a parent's happiness. Many children worry too much after a divorce anyway, and such seemingly innocuous comments can lead to depression and anxiety.

DIFFERENT WAYS CHILDREN COPE WITH DIVORCE

Like adults, young people need to work through their grief and sorrow in a manner that is comfortable for them and does not add to their stress. While a child or adolescent should not be allowed to deny or repress their emotional reactions to divorce indefinitely, some, like adults, need a period of quiet time to go within themselves and sort out their feelings before they are ready to discuss them with others. When that time comes, some may prefer a group setting, while others would be very ill at ease in a group and prefer to discuss what they're feeling one on one. For many, an older friend, a school guidance counselor, or another adult with whom they feel safe in baring their souls can be the key to working through their feelings and progressing toward healing. One-on-one work with a counselor or other individual may lead to greater comfort in discussing emotions and eventual participation in a group.

Children themselves are often the best source of information about what does and does not make it easier for them to survive and heal after a divorce. Author Nancy O'Keefe Bolick interviewed a number of adolescents and collected their stories in her book *How to Survive Your Parents' Divorce*. She found, as have others, that children have to learn to cope with loss and manage their recovery, just as adults do. Some suffer more than others, especially those whose parents have broken the cardinal rule of not involving the children in continuing hostility.

Yet all children hurt when their parents divorce. Many feel betrayed, yet many are relieved to escape from a home in which conflict and tension prevailed, although most would still prefer, as their ultimate choice, for the family to be together and happy. Bolick interviewed two dozen junior and senior high school students and found that while all the stories were different, all had certain similarities.

Children react in a variety of ways when their parents divorce. Some, especially those who are already high achievers, become workaholic overachievers to mask the pain they are feeling. Yet the anger and bitterness still manage to creep out. In a similar vein, some assume adult responsibilities they are not really old enough to take on, and envision themselves as caretakers and protectors of the parent they see as the one wronged and more vulnerable, as well as younger siblings. This can be a problem when children do not progress through their own natural stages of growth but instead go directly into adult roles.

Children may however, benefit, from taking on reasonably appropriate leadership roles. Some learn through the experience to defend others who are hurting, and to be more compassionate and fair in their dealings with others. Like adults, children in a divorcing family often experience lingering, intense anger. Children who have options such as sports and other organized activities in which to express these feelings in an appropriate setting can grow and benefit, as well as heal.

One common area of confusion for children arises when the parents repeatedly assure them that the divorce was not their fault, yet fight with each other over issues directly related to the children, such as support, scheduling, or custody. It is important that children be made aware that even when parents are disagreeing about them, it is the responsibility of the parents to manage family conflicts and work out problems, and that the kids should not feel that they are in any way responsible for these issues.

Bolick writes about one thirteen-year-old girl whose parents have been divorced for eight years, yet still fight about her and put her in the middle of their conflicts. As a result, this girl feels that she has grown up guarding her feelings carefully, afraid of being hurt further. She also expresses resentment of her friends who have enjoyed the luxury of growing up in stable families, feeling that she missed the years of security and innocence these friends have taken for granted. She reported feeling a sense of estrangement from those who have not shared her experiences.

Recovery from divorce may be especially tough on adolescents. Just at the time when they are trying to forge a comfortable role and identity, the one place in the world that was supposed to be settled and secure is suddenly thrown into upheaval. During a time when their lives already feel disorganized, one of the few places in which teens feel a sense of structure is broken apart. An adolescent boy who would normally be distancing himself from his mother is suddenly thrust into the role of caretaker and protector for a mother he sees as abandoned by his father. Not surprisingly, adolescents often react in extreme ways to their parents' divorces. Some shut down and refuse to discuss their feelings, in the same way many adults practice denial as a defense mechanism.

HOW DO YOU KNOW IF YOUR CHILD NEEDS PROFESSIONAL HELP?

Most children can benefit from some form of counseling after a divorce. It may be difficult to distinguish between a child who is normally moody as the result of this major life change, and a child who is in real trouble that requires immediate professional attention. Teachers can help monitor a child's behavior, watching for changes and "red flags." It is a good idea to let your children's teachers know what is going on when there has been a divorce in the family.

Psychologists advise that the most common ways children exhibit that they may be having serious trouble adjusting to divorce include emotional difficulties (depression, anxiety, or acting out); academic concerns (distraction in school, underachievement, forgetting or refusing to do homework); and social problems (withdrawal from social activities, problems getting along with peers).

Generally, these problems tend to manifest most strongly during the first two years after the divorce. After that they should diminish. If they do not, professional assistance is advisable. If the child's problems are not addressed at this time, they can carry over into the adult years and cause continued difficulty, especially in forming healthy interpersonal relationships.

Danger signs to watch for in children that may indicate a need for professional counseling include ongoing anger and resentment, persistent depression, and the inability to enjoy their social lives in settings that they formerly enjoyed. Observe the child's everyday behavior, watching for changes. In young children, look for variations in their play, different eating and sleeping habits, nightmares, and physical complaints such as headaches and stomachaches. Children aged seven to ten also show variances in their daily patterns such as sleeping, eating, and hygiene when they are troubled, as well as changes in their grades, the way they interact with friends, and their social activities.

For older children—preteens and adolescents—drastic changes in patterns of social interaction are often the key factor. Do they suddenly quit sports, clubs, and other activities that formerly meant a lot? Do they withdraw from friends or school, or suddenly develop behavior problems where none existed before? The best way to assess your child's health is by talking with him—and genuinely listening to what he says. Sometimes parents coping with their own denial don't hear their children's pleas for help. Pay attention to your daily interactions and conversations. Anytime a child seems regularly unhappy or anxious, or is not functioning in her daily life, professional consultation is a good idea. Often, short-term therapy can turn a child around.

Counselor Kathryn Lang has found that in her experience, boys tend to have a harder time adjusting after a parents' divorce than girls do. "Girls tend to be more verbal and to mature faster, socially and emotionally," she notes. Lang believes that age may be a more important indicator than gender as to how difficult it will be for a child to adjust, however. "Teens and young adults have the hardest time coping with a parent's divorce, harder than people expect. People worry more about the little ones, but a five-year-old, for example, tends to be very flexible. When adolescents watch their parents divorce, they are horrified and really angry," she says. "They tend to be very protective of the parent who was left, and feel very hostile toward the other."

Lang advises that counseling may be especially important for teens, but emphasizes that some need one-on-one counseling in which they can receive private reassurance from a professional that their emotional reactions are normal, and that they will survive and recover. At this time of life people are acutely aware of peer opinions, and some are very uncomfortable expressing their feelings in a group setting.

Some children, however, do very well with the type of support they receive in a group therapy setting. According to psychologist Chet Mirman, children often experience feelings of shame, guilt, fear, and anger. Meeting with other children in a support group can help reassure them that these feelings are normal. Children can benefit greatly from talking to others of a similar age who have experienced and survived their parents' divorces, and who may be able to help them navigate and keep their sense of hope. Many schools now sponsor support groups for children whose parents have divorced, and even those that don't are likely to have guidance counselors who can be very helpful.

Other kids benefit from simply discussing their feelings and experiences informally, with peers who have been through the process. Many find that journaling is a comfortable outlet for feelings that they may not be ready to share with others.

Helping Children Succeed in Therapy

Parents can take some very helpful steps to prepare a child for therapy. Ideally, both parents should discuss the issue and agree on a mental health professional to see the child.

Both parents may need to keep notes or a log tracking the child's problem behavior or troubling statements. Keep a record of schoolwork problems or reports from teachers. The therapist may also request information about the child's and family's history, or other background information. Sometimes a counselor will request a meeting with both parents. By all means, find a way to make this work. Occasionally, one parent will oppose therapy for the child. Sometimes a meeting between that person and the therapist helps clarify why counseling is a good idea.

Children are often confused about what therapy means. It helps to reassure the child that no one thinks she is crazy, and explain that this is a health matter, just like taking care of physical health. If the child resists, explain that you're just asking her to give it a fair try, and you won't force the therapy to continue if the child strongly opposes it after a few sessions. Also realize that personality conflicts or mismatches occasionally happen between children and counselors, just as with adults. If a child professes a strong dislike of the therapist or the process, consider trying someone new.

Well-meaning parents sometimes interfere with the treatment process. Avoid the temptation to tell the child what should or should not be discussed with the therapist—the child and counselor will work together to discover what issues are important. Reassure children that what they say to the counselor is confidential, and respect this confidentiality by not asking what they talked about after appointments. Give them the time and space they need to get comfortable with the therapist. If you express your trust and confidence in the therapist, this often helps.

Also realize that sometimes therapists use techniques with children that appear to be a waste of time, such as playing games. This type of interaction can serve several purposes. It may help break the ice and establish a bond between the child and counselor, and it can tell the therapist a great deal about the child. For example, a child who cheats or can't stand to lose a game—or, conversely, can't allow himself to "beat" an adult at a game—reveals a lot about how he sees the world and interacts with others.

Often, children need only short-term therapy to get back on track. Some children, like adults, need longer to deal with the issues that are troubling them, however. Try to be patient; it sometimes takes awhile before progress is apparent.

THE SILVER LINING

Divorce, while inevitably painful for children, can have positive consequences for them in the long run, if parents are willing to keep the kids out of the conflict between them. In a home filled with tension, a divorce that puts an end to the discord is a blessing.

Counselor and mediator Diane Fassel expresses grave concern about the social stigma surrounding divorced families and the perpetual myth of the intact family. Her studies of adult children of divorced parents have revealed that many families that look intact on the outside are severely dysfunctional within. Children in such families learned warped lessons, such as the notion that suffering in silence is somehow noble. Fassel and others have found that children raised in such families tend to fare far worse than those whose parents divorce. Those who grow up in families that are "together" in name only have no models for intimacy, learn that relationships are difficult and painful, and emerge confused and disillusioned.

Children do gain strength, resiliency, and perspective as they watch their parents progress through their own recovery following a divorce. They learn that they do have options in life and that they do not have to stay in unhealthy situations, and they are likely to grow up independent, flexible, and self-reliant.

Children who share stories with others in similar circumstances also gain empathy and a sense of perspective. One fourteen-year-old stated that she considered herself lucky because although her parents divorced when she was three years old, the families remained close and never expressed hostility toward one another. Both parents remarried, and the two families continued to take responsibility for the children, demonstrating that love did not stop when the families were rearranged. In her case, the parents had made determined efforts to provide unified support, to continue to communicate with the children, and even to share family gatherings.

Many children who see their parents go through a divorce vow that they will have a different type of marriage themselves, one that will be based on mutual respect and kindness. Adolescents whose parents divorce often express a strong desire to avoid a divorce in their own marriages, and often take their time in choosing partners carefully. As adults, they tend to work hard on their relationships, demonstrate a very strong commitment to their spouses and children, and prize family in a special way.

BUILDING A NEW CONCEPT OF THE FAMILY

While there has been a backlash against no-fault divorce in recent years, and reactionary attitudes will always be heard, most people have come to accept that a family restructured after divorce is far healthier than a family that stays together despite misery, abuse, or general unhappiness in a home. Counselor Diane Fassel and others who have worked extensively with children of divorced parents stress the importance of admitting the reality that other forms of family life can be every bit as healthy, or more so, than the idealized image of the "intact" family.

Today, the whole concept of what defines *family* is evolving. No longer is a family established so much by law and biology as by choices and acts. Each family is a unique creation bound by love, not just blood. Your family includes those who share with you, support you, and treat you with kindness. A relative, by definition, is someone with whom you have a relationship and who is relative to your life. Relatives, therefore, may include friends, members of an extended family, stepchildren, former in-laws, and anyone else you have chosen to make an intimate part of your life.

Counselor Kathryn Lang believes it is essential to reinforce the notion that one parent and children living in a home indeed constitute a family. "Over and over, I hear clients say, 'We don't have a family now.' People must realize that yes, one person or two people are a family. I remind people that they don't have to wait until they are back into a traditional nuclear family again through remarriage or whatever to get on with their lives."

Like many other family therapists, Constance Ahrons feels that the terminology we use in referring to families is vitally important—and very much in need of change. She deplores such terms as "broken home" because of its negative connotations, preferring instead the term "binuclear" for families no longer living in one household. Stuart Berger, M.D., author of *Divorce Without Victims,* also advocates abolition of the term "broken home."

Many people are troubled by the term "visitation," believing that it casts the noncustodial parent in the role of guest in the child's life instead of actively involved parent. Terms such as "coparenting" or "time sharing" are beginning to replace "visitation," in the belief that such words more accurately reflect the fact that in a good arrangement, both parents remain parents regardless of living arrangements.

Unquestionably, there is a lack of appropriate terminology to describe many modern relationships. Children asked by teachers to tell the class about their families must often go into convoluted explanations, describing half-siblings, stepsiblings, stepparents' brothers and sisters, those who function as grandparents but are not related by blood, or parents' unmarried partners. Not only is the lack of labels confusing, but too often, outmoded, degrading phrases such as "shacking up" and "illegitimate children" are applied to families.

Counselor Kathryn Lang agrees that the language we use to describe families who have been though a divorce needs to be changed. Fortunately, Lang notes, children are resourceful; until new semantics develop, children often deal with awkward moments more gracefully than parents could imagine. Lang proudly describes her own daughters' response to those who commented that they came from a broken home. "They would say, 'What's broken about us? We're not broken.' "

CHAPTER

5

Legal Concerns
After Divorce

IDEALLY, THE FILING OF THE FINAL ORDER OR DECREE OF DIVORCE should be the last piece of business required to resolve all of the legal issues involved when a couple ends a marriage. In practice, however, this is often not the case, especially when matters of child support or custody are involved.

Because of this reality, when a divorce case is closed, the court that handled it retains jurisdiction to reopen the case in the future, if necessary. Many aspects of a "final" divorce settlement or decree may need to be modified later if the parties' circumstances warrant a change, and one or both of them request it. When the couple can agree on modifications, it is then a simple matter of having an attorney draft a document reflecting the agreement in the form required by the court and filing it for the judge's approval. The judge then issues an order that makes the agreement enforceable in the court, and these documents become a permanent part of the case file.

Remember, if your agreement is not reduced to the correct written form and filed with the court, it cannot be enforced. In some cases, however, this may not be necessary. For example, a childless couple I know have agreed that he will continue to carry her on his health insurance plan, because this alternative provides broader and more economical coverage than the plan offered through her job. Twice a year she gives him a check to cover the cost of the policy, and he renews it to include coverage for her. He then sends her a new insurance card which proves that she is covered.

In this case, if either person defaulted on his or her obligations, the other would know immediately and could take care of the matter informally. She has alternative coverage available from her employer, and would not consider it worth the hassle to seek enforcement. Thus, there is no requirement that they take the time to formally modify the decree. If they had children, or a less amicable relationship, however, or if his insurance were the only source of health care coverage available to her, this would change the picture considerably and they would need to be sure that the mechanism was in place to enforce their agreement if necessary.

WHEN SHOULD YOU SEEK TO REOPEN YOUR CASE?

There is often a fine line between what problems are worthy of legal intervention, and those that are best ignored or addressed by less drastic means. While no settlement is irrevocable, remember that your priority should be to heal and move forward, not to "win." It is often best to work with what you have and rise to the challenges, remembering always that you are your own best asset. Returning to court to revive the battle is a step into the past.

Remember, too, that you may be opening a huge can of worms. Your ex will likely be furious, and may use the occasion to challenge another aspect of the settlement or decree, perhaps one that you want desperately to keep as it is. You could end up in a worse position than you are now. In any case, postdecree litigation is always an emotional ordeal for everyone involved, especially children. *Divorce Hangover* author Anne Walther and many others, including lawyers, recommend avoiding a "legal hangover" if at all possible.

Yet sometimes your circumstances are such that you feel you must make new arrangements. Or perhaps your ex requests a change and you can't work out a compromise on you own. If this happens, make the time to take a long, honest look at all of the circumstances. Resolve to be generous without becoming a doormat.

Family law attorney David B. Riggert acknowledges that a divorce decree may be modified for practically any reason. But all too often, he deals with clients who return to court over and over instead of forging a workable agreement to address the underlying problem. "Sometimes I have to resist the urge to tell people to get a life," he sighs. "For example, a man recently came to me wanting to modify the support order because of a change in his income. I knew the decree had been modified before, although I didn't handle the original divorce, so as part of my preliminary work I went to the courthouse to read the docket. I saw that there had been a modification or some action to enforce the decree in court on the average of every six months over a period of eight years." Attorneys find such wasteful and repetitive litigation frustrating. As Riggert states, "These parties, instead of running back to court all the time, ought to be thinking in terms of creating an environment for themselves so that they can avoid litigation. Even though some of the issues are valid, they are spending all of their money on attorney's fees that they can't afford and not accomplishing what they are trying to achieve."

In some cases, an original divorce order or settlement agreement that seemed adequate and thorough enough at the time will, on later examination, prove to be lacking in certain essential elements. This is especially common where the divorce was accomplished quickly, or handled by an inexperienced attorney. For example, if the settlement agreement fails to address health care and life insurance costs, it should be modified. If you and your former spouse have a reasonably businesslike relationship, it should not be difficult to sit down and point out the areas that need to be addressed, emphasizing that it is in both your best interests to do so.

The question of how to divide uninsured medical expenses is another issue that is often ignored when the couple or judge formulates a final decree, and one which Riggert frequently encounters in his practice. He advises that the parenting plan should be specific on how such costs are to be handled. "The custodial parent should be sure to get a bill that accurately describes the treatment for which the cost was incurred, as well as what was covered and not covered by insurance," he says. "Then the custodial parent should provide a copy of this bill to the other parent in a timely fashion, along with proof that her or his half has already been paid. Some custodial parents save up medical bills over six months, for example, when there is an ongoing charge for something such as braces, then send them to the other parent. Then it's difficult for the non-custodial parent to come up with all of the money that is due, or sometimes past due by that time."

The Importance of Timing

The best advice is to choose your battles carefully—bearing in mind that clashes between parents over any matter are hard on the children—but to address serious issues without delay, so as not to lose your legal right to do so through "laches" (waiting too long to do anything about a problem) or "waiver" (accepting someone's behavior so consistently that your failure to complain amounts to acquiescence). Generally, if you take other steps to try to resolve these problems, such as mediation, this will avoid giving your ex any defenses to use against you if you do end up back in court.

Some people have constant problems with their exes in a particular area of the relationship—for example, late support payments or children consistently unprepared for a visit. If this type of behavior becomes a pattern, it can create a legal issue as well as signal greater problems to come for all involved. Keep records of all such difficulties. It is best to address such matters early on, through counseling, mediation, or, if necessary, modification of the custody and visitation decree.

It is equally important, however, to resist the urge to dash back to court prematurely. "Too many people return to court seeking a modification before the ink on the original decree is dry," says David Riggert. It is usually inadvisable to return to court if less than one year has passed since the original decree was filed or the last modification was made. In some states courts cannot modify a divorce decree more often than once a year, unless a true emergency such as child abuse is shown, and in others judges simply lose patience and refuse to intervene in what they feel parents should be able to work out on their own. Seek the advice of a qualified attorney if you are not sure whether the time is right to proceed.

The Same Lawyer or a New One?

Most people who seek legal counsel regarding postdivorce modification of the decree call on the same attorney that represented them in the divorce. Some may need or wish to change, however, if the original attorney is no longer available or they were less than thrilled with the outcome of the divorce. While returning to the same attorney can save time and money because he or she is already familiar with the case, it can be wise to shop around, especially if you were not entirely satisfied with the representation you received before. It is best to seek a lawyer who specializes in family law—not necessarily a registered specialist, but someone who devotes a large portion of his or her practice to family cases and is thoroughly familiar with postdivorce issues.

Remember, your lawyer works for you, and his or her duty is to advocate on your behalf. Also bear in mind, however, that the attorney's role is that of guide and advocate, not assassin. A good lawyer will seek to minimize the emotional side of the issue, and focus on finding a workable solution to a legal matter. If you feel the need to seek revenge or wage war against your ex, it would be wiser to seek the assistance of a counselor rather than an attorney.

Frances Webb, a mediator and a divorced mother, urges divorced people who are still disentangling the legal and financial aspects of their lives together to seek sound advice—and to do so cautiously. "Read all the small print when you sign something, and never sign until you know what you are signing," she says. "Don't believe something that sounds wrong or odd, just because a lawyer or banker is telling you it is so. Get independent advice from someone you trust, and make sure everything is put in writing, in a form you understand."

Webb had bad luck with attorneys during her divorce, so she cautions others about automatically placing too much trust in legal professionals. "There are some slimy lawyers out there," she says. "The first one I had not only lied to me, but came up with a bill that was roughly equal to everything I received in a child support matter for which he represented me. My second attorney came highly recommended, and was a good person, but he was in bondage to a big firm that wouldn't let him wrap up the case the way he and I wanted to. Be very careful."

Make sure you get a full explanation of everything your lawyer recommends, that you understand what is going to happen, and that you are clear on the legal parameters and how any new agreement will be implemented and enforced. Discuss fees and billing arrangements before you give the lawyer the go-ahead to do any work on your behalf. Be sure the lawyer understands where you will and will not compromise in the case, and that you both have a firm understanding of the goals you are trying to achieve.

Often, issues that arise can be resolved by agreement of the parties and simple modification of the decree, with minimal assistance by legal professionals. When the parties cannot agree, however, either litigation or mediation will be required. If you need legal assistance, information and referrals are available through local legal aid societies, bar associations, state or local lawyer referral services, law school clinics, and national organizations such as the American Bar Association (see Appendix).

Steps to Take to Avoid Future Legal Problems

Family law attorney David B. Riggert believes that many post-decree problems are the result of a failure to address all of the issues at the time of the divorce. "People need to ask their attorneys to formulate a plan that will keep them out of court. If this wasn't done at the time of the original decree, it can be done later. But people need to review the settlement documents very carefully so they can avoid the trauma and expense of constant litigation."

Riggert feels that a yearly review of custody arrangements, as well as finances and support, can be an effective mechanism to serve this purpose. "An agreement can be drafted in which parents agree to exchange information once every year or two, and then to complete their own analysis of that information by a certain date. Then, another period of time can be provided within which the parents must come to a decision if they want to request any changes," he explains. "If neither asks for a modification, the whole thing flips over to the next year. In this way, couples can negotiate a fair compromise, and bring the results of what they decide to their attorneys, who can draft an order for the judge to sign."

Riggert recently worked with a client to formulate such an plan. According to the proposed agreement, the father is to provide copies of his W-2 forms and tax returns within a month of filing each such return. The mother calculates whether any increase in support appears to be warranted, and, under the terms of the agreement, can request an increase or ask the judge to revise the support agreement if there is a 10 percent or greater change in his income. Both parents were pleased with this plan, and the judge was presumably glad to put an end to the constant litigation between the parties.

"If one person decides there needs to be a change and initiates litigation, it can be a real mess," Riggert explains. "It's adversarial, and each side may spend a thousand dollars to litigate. Much of that cost can go for discovery—the exchange of documents and information. If this is automatically required by agreement, it can save a lot of money, time, and aggravation for everyone."

This type of agreement can be especially effective if one or both parents anticipate a change in their current salaries or another aspect of their present situations. "In this community, there is a Mitsubishi manufacturing plant that is a major employer in the area," Riggert comments. "It periodically changes its production line and corresponding work schedules. One year, an employee may work a great deal of overtime, then the next year the overtime stops and his or her income drops significantly. The judges in our community have to deal with this in support modification agreements all the time. If parents know something like this is expected to happen, it can be dealt with in advance."

Many of the issues that send parents back to court, counseling, or mediation can be avoided through clear communication. Any changes in your parenting agreement should be put in writing and at least exchanged between parents, even if you don't feel that they are significant enough to file with the court. For example, if one of you is going out of town, write out your itinerary so the other parent can reach you if necessary. Important events in children's lives or changes in their schedules should also be listed and exchanged. Some books, such as Peter Favaro's *Divorced Parents' Guide to Managing Custody and Visitation*, have forms that can be used for this purpose. LadyBug Press (see Appendix) produces a special notepad called "The Mom and Dad Pad" that parents can use to exchange information in an efficient and upbeat manner, while creating a copy of the communication for their files.

POSTDIVORCE MEDIATION

Mediation has become a very popular alternative to courtroom warfare when a divorcing couple cannot agree on a settlement, particularly on issues involving children. Mediation is also becoming increasingly common as a means to reach an amicable settlement of areas of disagreement that arise after a divorce. Some divorce decrees even contain a mediation clause, providing that if there is a problem involving the children after the divorce which can't be resolved informally, the couple will go to mediation. "Going to court again should be the last resort," says family law attorney Kathleen Robertson.

Mediation is steadily gaining in popularity, and it does have many advantages in addition to saving money and avoiding hostility. People tend to be more creative and open minded in the context of mediation than in court. The process tends to be less traumatic for adults and children alike, and participants learn communication and negotiation skills that can be put to use if future conflicts arise. Mediation is a less adversarial, less expensive, and more satisfying way to solve an impasse than litigation for those who have a mutual desire to settle their differences with as little adversity as possible, but cannot do so on their own.

"The adversarial way of trying to resolve family disputes is also the worst way," says mediator and family law attorney Roberta Beyer. "It centers on blame and fault and is oriented toward the past rather than the future. In mediation, it is so gratifying to help people work things out rather than take sides in a battle."

Frances Webb has seen a great deal of change in attitudes toward mediation since she began working as a mediator in the late-1980s. "Mediation was considered wimpy then," she recalls. "Attorneys often referred to it as 'that touchy-feely stuff.'" Webb, who has a master's degree in curriculum and instruction, was creating instructional media for business and educational uses in the late 1980s. She was asked by several mediation centers in North Carolina to produce a series of instructional videotapes for training and promotion of mediation. "When I began learning about mediation, and saw how quick and effective the process could be in resolving disputes, I was awed," Webb remarks. "It was such a gentle process, preserving the dignity and encouraging the responsibility of the individuals."

Webb was encouraged by the way mediation reduced the opportunity for participants to get "stuck" in anger and by its peaceful approach. She completed her mediation training in Hendersonville, North Carolina, through a community mediation center. She has now been a mediator for a dozen years, mediating disputes in a wide range of areas including corporate, court-referred, neighborhood, and family matters.

"People in mediation finally begin to hear each other," she explains. "It's a soulful process, even spiritual, but never pretentious. It's real communication, with people responding on a gut level." Webb takes great satisfaction in watching people relate honestly to one another in a forum where power is balanced. "There is such a great relief for someone who has finally been heard," she explains. "It's different from having a counselor or psychologist listen, because in mediation you finally know you've been heard by the person who was your adversary but is now positioned as your equal." Webb states that her experience, both personal and professional, has convinced her that "without a doubt, if people could choose mediation their happiness and that of their children would be enhanced."

People who have been through different processes and compared the merits of each agree that mediation is preferable to battle. "It's much more constructive to mediate," says Becky Ralston, "to negotiate a settlement in a nonadversarial setting. You have X amount of assets to split up, and if you continue fighting over it through your lawyers, if you're not careful, you won't have anything left to fight over."

Ralston hastens to add that she also valued the services of her attorney, however. "I had a lawyer who was worth her weight in gold, who had clout in the local family law community," she says. "Therefore, the lawyers were able to narrow the issues to what we could mediate, and get to the point where we could have a fair settlement without too much fuss. She was a very ethical attorney, she had me do a lot of the legwork to save money, and she encouraged us to mediate our remaining differences."

Ralston and her husband chose a psychologist to mediate when they reached an impasse on certain property settlement issues. "The guy is a saint," Ralston remarks. "Because of the professionals who helped us come to terms, we still have a relationship on some level—we can deal with certain business we still have to handle together, and remain friendly."

Postdivorce mediation is most often sought by parents grappling with the difficulties of the relationship that must necessarily continue after the couple's divorce. In such a case, one of the mediator's primary jobs is to teach the couple positive communication skills so they can continue to work together as parents. "We help them learn a positive way to interact in the type of relationship they have now, and prepare them for better communication in subsequent relationships with others," mediator Roberta Beyer explains. She and her partner, a psychologist, often work with couples during the years after a divorce, when disputes over children occur or the need to change a custody or support order arises.

Mediation can also assist parents, stepparents, and children in resolving problems that crop up as families evolve and restructure. "We did one mediation that was really different, really exciting," Beyer remarks. "A couple had been divorced for twelve years, and their sixteen-year-old child was falling apart. The child, the mother and father, and their new spouses came in to mediate. The first session was rough, with a lot of anger and shouting. But after four or five sessions, everyone left hugging each other and the sixteen-year-old had turned around. It made such a difference that they could finally work through the resentment and anger that had been sitting there for a dozen years."

Many believe that mediation can only work when a couple is already in a civil relationship with a completely equal balance of power. Beyer, however, believes that this is not necessarily true. "People in high conflict are the ones who really need the type of help that mediation can provide," she says. "True, if there is a power imbalance along with an unskilled mediator, bad results can occur. But it is the mediator's job to balance the power, and the process itself is empowering. There is learning, and each person becomes a part of the decision-making process. And if we can't get the participants to treat one another fairly, and one keeps trying to bully the other, we have the right to terminate the mediation and send them to attorneys. We have a moral and ethical obligation to see that any agreement we help a couple reach is fair to both partners and fair to the children."

Frances Webb emphasizes that mediation is always confidential and nonjudgmental, with the sole aim of resolving a conflict. "However," she adds, "it is now being recognized—as many of us knew all along—that a skilled mediator can take the opportunity to enlighten the participants, to help them grow in some way." For example, in one mediation, Webb simply repeated the participant's own statements back to him, without commentary, but emphasizing the questionable values, so that he could hear what he was saying from the listener's point of view.

Webb emphasizes that it is never too late for a couple who has divorced to mediate ongoing difficulties. "If the conflict is there, that's the basis for the need," she states. "I did a mediation for one couple who had not had the opportunity to mediate at the time of their divorce—mediation simply wasn't available in their area then. These two people knew they could relate better as parents if they could talk out their differences and work on custodial issues. Mediation can be advantageous at any stage of a relationship."

When Mediation Won't Work

Unfortunately, mediation is not for everyone. In order to succeed at any form of negotiation, both parties must be willing to compromise, and have a genuine desire to resolve the issues involved in spite of the conflict between them. If one or both have hidden agendas or have raised the issue at hand for another purpose—such as getting even, revenge, or harassing the ex-spouse—mediation will not work.

Frances Webb recalls that when her own marriage ended, it took four years to finalize all of the issues involved in the divorce. "I wish we could have mediated, and I considered pushing the issue, but ultimately, I knew it would not work for us. The key ingredient of mediation requires two people who want to reach a resolution, and that was not true of our situation. We finally had the case arbitrated by a former judge, and he did an excellent job."

Webb emphasizes that a good mediator must be aware that some people misunderstand the function of mediation and seek to use it for inappropriate ends. "One woman called and stated right up front that she wanted to get into mediation so that she could have the mediator tell her husband a thing or two," she recalls. "I had to explain that in mediation, people come in as equals with the idea of working together to find a solution to a problem. I always reiterate that as a mediator, I am not a lawyer or counselor, and I don't give advice, legal or otherwise."

Another common problem Webb has encountered is the desire by one person to provide information to the mediator outside the mediation. "When people insist on ignoring this rule, or keep telephoning to badmouth the other person, I must tell them that I cannot do the mediation," she says. "I have to maintain control of the process and they must be willing to allow me to be responsible for the process. Through my experience, I can tell when someone is unwilling to relinquish any small amount of control, and I have to tell them that the mediation won't work." Webb tries to avoid such dilemmas by explaining in advance how the process must be handled if mediation is to succeed. "I explain that they are here to attempt to settle a problem through mediation, that mediation is voluntary, and I warn them that they might not be successful in finding a resolution. I also make sure they understand that if the mediation is not successful, all of the other options are still open, including court. Nothing said in mediation can ever be used in court—they have to sign an agreement on that point."

Dishonesty also precludes successful mediation—for example, when one person is trying to hide assets from the other. Likewise, mediation is usually not appropriate when one partner is or has been violent toward the other, because the abuser will almost never relinquish the desire to control the other. As Webb explains, "By definition, there really can't be mediation between people in such an unequal relationship—the foundation isn't there. Mediation requires two people who are committed to working toward resolution of a problem. When the power balance is very unequal—as in a violent relationship—it's impossible. Anyone who feels that he or she is not the other person's equal, who is afraid, can't make a contribution."

Roberta Beyer, and many other mediators, will not accept clients from a violent marriage unless certain requirements are met. "There must be no current abuse, the people must agree to certain boundaries such as no contact outside the mediation, and both partners must be in counseling. First and foremost, the process must be safe." Mediation requires prolonged contact between people, which can be dangerous or emotionally damaging to the victim in an abusive relationship. A good mediator will screen potential clients to determine whether mediation is appropriate for them before taking them on.

How Long Does Mediation Take?

Mediation is not an overnight process, but the results can be well worth the time investment that is required. Webb advises those approaching mediation to narrow down the issues and identify what's really important before the mediation. "I have each person write down what he or she feels the issues are, and bring in the list. I go through and consolidate the issues that both agree should be addressed in the mediation and if necessary, we all confer on the rest. Usually we get it down to two to four main issues. Sometimes, things can be resolved in one two-hour session."

While the process varies according to the people involved and the nature of the matter to be settled, a fairly standard process is followed in most cases. Beyer schedules appointments for two-hour sessions, and tries to meet with clients every week to keep the momentum going. The number of sessions that will be required depends on the people and issues in each situation. "Most couples come to as many sessions as it takes to agree," says Beyer. "We are always happy to work ourselves out of a job, and some people find that one session is enough. We use a lot of different techniques to address specific problems, but the bottom line is that it has to be a process that works for everyone involved and culminates in a fair agreement."

Choosing a Mediator

Use care when choosing a mediator. Many states do not have well-defined requirements for mediator training and qualification. Some mediators specialize, so be sure you choose one (or a team) that is experienced in assisting families. Beyer recommends finding a mediator through referrals from attorneys, counselors, clergy, and friends. She also advises asking certain questions before making a final choice. "Ask about educational background, work experience, and training. Most states have no certification or licensing procedure, and a forty-hour course is the only formal training required to join the professional organizations. One crash course is not enough to qualify a mediator without an appropriate professional background," she says.

Mediators, including Beyer, often work in teams, frequently combining a lawyer and a psychologist. "As a team, we can address all of the issues that need immediate attention," she explains. "When counselors or psychologists mediate alone, they are usually good with the parenting issues, but have trouble with the legal aspects of the property, tax, and debt matters. Likewise, when attorneys mediate on their own they may not be able to deal with all of the emotional issues underlying the legal problems. I've been working with a great psychologist in a team approach for a number of years, and we prefer this approach, although there are some very good mediators that do a great job on their own. Attention to the emotional matters involved is crucial to the overall mediation endeavor," she states.

This does not mean that a lawyer, psychologist, or other trained professional working alone cannot be a good mediator, as long as she recognizes her limitations and coordinates with other professionals by referral so that all of the client's needs can be addressed. Frances Webb usually works as a solo mediator, although she sometimes works with a partner. "The premise of mediation," she says, "is that two people have the capacity to find a resolution to their conflict without experts intervening. In divorce mediation, I always make sure that the parties have attorneys. But I advise them to use the attorney to deal with legal issues only—not for guidance on the mediation. Otherwise, it can become adversarial and destroy the purpose of mediation—that is, equal parties very capable of finding their own resolution."

UNFINISHED BUSINESS BETWEEN EX-PARTNERS

Child Support Enforcement

Recent government studies have estimated that only 58 percent of single-parent households have child support orders in place, and that of these families, only half receive the support due. In response to this national crisis, both the states and the federal government have initiated various new efforts to make parents take financial responsibility for their children. In 1996, for example, the U.S. Postal Service announced that it would coordinate with states to assist in the identification and apprehension of "deadbeat" parents by displaying "Wanted" lists of parents who had failed to pay child support in post offices.

The Clinton administration has declared child support enforcement a priority, and has worked with Congress to assist the states in developing more effective collection programs. Welfare reform legislation signed by President Clinton in 1996 included strong new measures against noncustodial parents who failed to pay the support they owed. The new law added tough penalties to those already available, including driver's license revocation and seizure of many new types of assets. All states now have provisions for automatic wage withholding, direct bank deposits, or payment to child service agencies that monitor and collect support payments. The legislation also recognized the importance to children of having access to their noncustodial parents.

To assist in this effort, the Child Support Enforcement program (CSE) is a federal/state partnership which promotes family self-sufficiency by securing regular and timely child support payments. State CSE programs locate missing parents, establish paternity, set and enforce support orders, and collect payments. CSE services are available automatically for families receiving assistance under the new Temporary Assistance for Needy Families (TANF) programs and to other families who apply for the services.

The CSE program has already begun to amass impressive results. During fiscal 1996, an estimated $12 billion in child support payments was collected, and paternity established for a million children. Almost 1.1 million new child support orders were established in fiscal 1995. Income tax refunds, lottery winnings, retirement benefits, real estate, and other property of nonpaying parents may be seized or encumbered by lien to satisfy unpaid child support.

The "teeth" provided by this new law have proven sharply effective at the state level as well. In New Mexico, for example, child support payments collected by the Human Services Department increased by 27 percent in a single month after the state revoked the driver's licenses of nearly 11,000 people who had failed to pay child support and had not responded to a six-week amnesty program that gave parents an option to pay what they owed before the penalties were invoked. Other states have reported similar increases. The message is clear: Parents must assume responsibility for the support of their children, or suffer serious consequences. State offices involved with this program are listed in the Appendix.

The federal Office of Child Support Enforcement has a Web site with links to very specific and detailed information on the laws and mechanics of child support in each state. The site is currently located at www.acf.dhhs.gov/programs. Various other federal, state, and local government offices also maintain excellent Web sites. Web locations change frequently. A search using the name of the organization, topic, or government office will usually lead you to the correct site.

Efforts are continually underway to establish new methods under the law to make child support collection easier and more efficient. When substantial amounts of child support are overdue and other attempts to collect the support owed have failed, the parent's property may be attached, and then seized and sold. This method involves placing a lien on the parent's home, car, or other property. Bank accounts may also be frozen.

One tool that is being used more and more often is a wage deduction order, also referred to as salary garnishment or payroll deduction. This court order requires a parent's employer to make payroll deductions in the amount of child support due and to pay the support directly to the beneficiary or to a

local child support enforcement office. Similar forms of garnishment can also be used to acquire payment from Workers'
Compensation checks, disability, unemployment, or Social
Security. To learn about how these options work in your area,
and to find out what enforcement devices you may be able to
use, check with your local child support enforcement office or
a family attorney. Some family court systems also have programs to assist with support collection.

If you are on the receiving end of a wage deduction or garnishment order, above all, don't ignore it. If you have not been
paying the support you owe, it is probably legitimate. The law
states that your employer cannot penalize you or retaliate
against you for having a wage deduction order imposed. On
the other hand, if you have a legitimate concern about the
accuracy of the order or other questions regarding your child
support obligations, get all of your payment records together,
then contact the agency or caseworker that issued the order.
You may also wish to consult your attorney. Mistakes do happen, and incorrect orders should be dealt with as quickly as
possible. In most jurisdictions, you must fill out and submit a
form or write a letter with attached proof of payment. Be sure
to keep a copy of all such documents for your files.

In 1992, the federal government passed the Child Support
Recovery Act. This law allows a judge to fine and even imprison
for up to six months first-time offenders who willfully fail to
pay a past-due support obligation to a child who lives in
another state. The law defines past-due support as support a
court has determined is due and that has remained unpaid for
more than one year or is more than five thousand dollars. To
use this law, a parent must go to court to have a judge determine that the support falls within this definition of "past due."

When other enforcement attempts to collect child support
have failed, and court orders have been violated or ignored,
the parent refusing to pay may be subject to contempt pro-

ceedings or civil arrest. Such harsh penalties are rarely levied unless the parent has been a true deadbeat, however, and has ignored several court orders to pay up what is owed.

Direct versus Indirect Child Support

Sometimes, a distinction is made between two different types of child support. Direct child support is money paid by one parent directly to another, or to an agency that then distributes it to the custodial parent. Indirect child support includes payments to third parties for things the children need such as school tuition, camp, braces, and so on. In most cases, direct support is best because it is easier for the custodial parent to monitor and control what is received. This depends on the parties and the circumstances, however. In many cases where indirect support is provided, some direct support is also involved.

Parents should also consider the tax issues involved in formulating a support plan or modification, with the advice of a tax accountant or other qualified professional. Child support is not tax deductible to the parent who pays it, while spousal support generally may be deducted. The parent who receives child support does not pay tax on this money as income, but taxes must be paid on spousal support (alimony).

If parents agree to a plan that includes indirect child support, it should be set forth very carefully in the stipulated agreement. Indirect support can be an effective method for making certain that the money provided for the children is in fact going to pay their expenses. For example, Tom was paying direct support to his ex-wife to maintain their two daughters, including a substantial sum that was supposed to go for parochial school tuition. He learned from his daughters that they had instead been attending public school, and were doing without such necessities as new glasses and school supplies while their mother was paying off a vacation cottage. Tom was able to obtain an order providing that he would pay tuition to the parochial school as a part of his child support. The other problems were more difficult to resolve, and he decided to simply buy things for his daughters voluntarily rather than facing another court battle with his ex. Tom advises others that in all cases where indirect support is paid, the noncustodial parent should keep careful records of what is provided.

Child Support Formulas

Every state now has a formula that is used as a starting point for determining how much support each parent will be expected to contribute to the maintenance of their children, based on a ratio that is determined by considering how much time each child spends with each parent, the number of children in the family, and each parent's income. In most states, other factors are considered, with deductions allowed for tax expenses, other child support payments, and similar necessities. The net income that is left after these deductions becomes the basis by which child support is calculated. Most support laws also have hardship provisions that are to be considered.

Ideally, the parents and their attorneys can use these formulas as a tool to help them work out their own modifications to child support agreements, depending on what works best for the individual family. Some child support agreements contain a clause that provides for the yearly exchange of information, and incremental increases in child support as the noncustodial parent's income increases, as discussed above.

Spousal Support

Spousal support, or alimony, is seldom awarded on a permanent basis today unless the recipient is elderly or disabled. Nearly all divorce settlements and decrees now consider that a financially dependent spouse has a duty to work toward becoming self-sufficient. Courts more often award "rehabilitative alimony," designed to provide a person with temporary support until he or she is able to obtain the training and other assistance required to become self-supporting.

Rehabilitative alimony is usually paid only for a set period of years, so that the dependent spouse is able to complete a course of education or training in order to become self-supporting. Permanent alimony is rarely awarded unless the dependent spouse has been out of the job market for many years, contributing to raising the children, maintaining the home, and supporting the other person's career. When a person is close to retirement age at the time of the divorce, permanent alimony may be awarded.

Rehabilitative alimony may be extended if expectations do not pan out according to what the parties had hoped. Courts try to take a realistic, human approach under these circumstances. If, for example, a homemaker who was awarded five years of rehabilitative alimony made a real effort to prepare for gainful employment, tried to find work, but met with little success, while her former husband thrived financially, the period of alimony may be extended. On the other hand, one who did not make the effort to prepare for the future will seldom gain the court's sympathy. As with any type of support modification, the judge will look at all of the circumstances, including whether there are still children at home who require care, and the person's age, education, and job experience.

In some states, the law provides that spousal support automatically ends when the dependent spouse remarries. This may also be specified in the divorce decree. Some people have tried to avoid such provisions by keeping the second marriage a secret or by cohabiting rather than getting married. Generally, these methods won't work. The effect of cohabitation may not be as automatic as remarriage, but if the supporting spouse seeks a modification and is able to show that the dependent spouse is being maintained by someone else, or no longer needs spousal support, courts won't hesitate to order it ended. In a few cases in which people have tried to keep a subsequent marriage secret, the courts have ordered the return of all spousal support received after the marriage.

Also, if a second marriage ends, support from the first is almost never reinstated. The best advice is to think carefully about marrying again if you are receiving spousal support. This is sound advice if you are supporting a former spouse or children as well. Be sure your new fiancé understands and accepts your responsibilities of time and support for your first family.

Modification of Support

Ideally, your divorce decree should provide for regular review of your and your ex-spouse's circumstances, and state the criteria that will warrant a modification of either spousal or child support payments. As with any postdivorce modification, it is always best to try to work out a solution with your former spouse if at all possible.

If you do feel you must go back to court to request a change in the terms of payment of spousal or child support, bear in mind that the one seeking modification must demonstrate substantially changed circumstances that result in a major need for the terms of the decree to be adjusted. Additionally, the change must be essentially permanent. For example, a short-term company strike or a job change that results in a minor pay cut will generally not call for modification.

Also, the factor that gave rise to the different circumstances must not have been self-induced. If a qualified, healthy adult with a college degree and an impressive résumé simply quits a job and does not pursue another, or takes a job paying very little, the court is unlikely to reduce the person's child support obligations. While the law recognizes the right to personal freedom in making career choices and job changes, the courts are taking parental duty to support children more and more seriously. The basic idea is that while everyone has the right to change careers, they must also meet their standing obligations to support their children. Needless to say, anything the court sees as a calculated effort to reduce a parent's income in order to avoid his or her financial responsibilities will not be looked on with sympathy.

On the other hand, a court will not force someone to increase their earning power to its maximum potential so that he or she can pay more support. "Ability to earn" will generally not be considered by the court unless there is evidence of a deliberate attempt to avoid financial responsibilities. *Actual income* is the key. For example, a noncustodial father with an MBA degree who leaves his career in investment banking to open a gardening shop because of a sincere desire to do something different generally will not have child support obligations lowered, but neither will the court penalize him if his former spouse comes in to complain that he could be earning more and paying greater amounts of support. If the garden shop expands into a highly successful chain, and the father is now earning ten times what he made as an investment banker, the court may or may not order support payments increased—again, depending in most cases, on a showing of need by the former spouse and children.

If either the supporting or dependent spouse receives a large chunk of money or valuable goods in the form of an inheritance, bonus, or lottery winnings, for example, this may amount to changed circumstances that will justify support modification. Again, need and other factors will be considered as well.

The necessity for increased support must not be something that was previously contemplated. If a trust fund or lump-sum payment was set up in the original decree to cover college tuition or extra payments for tutoring a child with learning disabilities, the judge may deny modification. This concept has a flip side as well. If the matter was negotiated, but not included in the decree, and the person opposing the change can show evidence that the parties agreed to waive the issue, such as college tuition, at the time of the original settlement, this can also preclude modification on the matter at a later time.

It is important to remember when seeking modifications that courts will look at the whole picture of both parties' financial circumstances and needs. Many different factors may amount to changed circumstances which justify the modification of support orders. Some things, though, are universally recognized as *not* amounting to changed circumstances that would justify modification. These include general inflation, comparative standards of living, and any deliberate acts taken to reduce a party's income. Voluntary changes generally won't support modification, as discussed above, with some exceptions. For example, in one case a man who knew he was about to be laid off from his job took the best available alternative, in which he earned less. Because the court believed that he made the change in good faith and was making a sincere effort to avoid unemployment and meet his responsibilities, his support obligations were lowered.

While temporary changes are not generally recognized as changed circumstances, some extraordinary, unexpected expenses may be subject to a special order by the court—for example, a child's need for medical treatment that is not covered by insurance. A serious illness or disability that has an economic impact on either the payer or recipient of support is generally considered to be a substantial change of circumstances.

This sounds complicated, and very often it can be. For this reason, it is best to consult an attorney any time you discuss a need for alteration with your former spouse, reach an impasse, and anticipate that you may want to seek a court-ordered modification.

Bankruptcy

Bankruptcy does not release a supporting spouse from his or her obligations or debts due to the former spouse for maintenance, alimony, or child support. Bankruptcy can be a type of changed circumstance that results in modification of support obligations, but it will not necessarily effect a reduction. For example, in one case, a father who was originally ordered to make very low child support payments because he had so many debts was ordered to pay much more in child support after he declared bankruptcy. The court reasoned that once he was relieved of his heavy burden of monthly obligations, he had more income available to support his children. Again, this was based on not only the financial factor but the family's demonstration of need. Likewise, a dependent spouse who reduces his or her debt load through bankruptcy and therefore has more available income may be subject to reduced support payments because his or her need is no longer so great.

A former spouse's declaration of bankruptcy can seriously impact the other when the debts each assumed were not refinanced in that person's name alone with the creditor. Often, creditors who made a loan or advanced credit based on two incomes will, understandably, refuse to refinance a substantial debt in the name of one spouse alone. If both have a credit history, however, each may be able to open new accounts and transfer the balance of the outstanding debt to a new creditor, in each person's name alone.

SPECIAL ISSUES REGARDING CHILD SUPPORT

As with child custody decisions, the criterion courts apply in determining child support orders is the best interest of the child. The law is based on the principle that both parents are obligated to support their children, and courts will consider the financial resources of each, as well as the physical and emotional health and needs of the child, in addition to educational and vocational needs and aptitudes. Courts also consider the standard of living the child would have enjoyed if the family had remained intact.

The Effect of Voluntary Payments

One thing that will almost never change support obligations are voluntary payments by a parent (as opposed to indirect support paid according to a court-approved parenting plan, as discussed above). Custodial parents have sometimes tried to argue that because the noncustodial parent voluntarily buys things or makes payments for children's expenses, he or she is demonstrating that he or she can be paying more in support. This argument has almost universally failed. The idea is that voluntary payments should be encouraged, not penalized.

In one case, for example, the custodial parent, the mother, sought an increase based on the father's improved standard of living. The court denied her request, observing that the father had bought a car for his older daughter, and provided insurance, gasoline, and an allowance for her, and paid tuition and transportation for the younger daughter's private school. The court said that an order might jeopardize the excellent relationship between the father and his daughters, and this type of voluntary payment is something the courts seek to encourage.

Exceptions to this general rule have been seen in a few cases. A sudden stop in voluntary payments, especially for an ongoing cost such as school tuition, may amount to the requisite change in circumstances that justifies an order increasing support so that these benefits to the child may continue.

Child Support and Remarriage

What about a person who remarries? Noncustodial parents should be aware that it is considered improper under the law to force someone's new husband or wife to support the children of his or her partner's first marriage. A court may view his or her contributions to the total household income as freeing up more of the other person's income for the first family; again, only if that family demonstrates a need for an increase.

Likewise, if a custodial parent remarries or moves in with a new partner who contributes to the support of the family, this may affect the right to receive spousal support, but will rarely impact on the other parent's child support obligations.

Courts may also consider the second family's circumstances and needs—for example, the birth of a new child. The law operates, however, according to the principle that a parent is expected to know and be prepared to meet his or her existing obligations before taking on new responsibilities. Thus, having more children with a second spouse will rarely be seen as grounds to reduce the support obligations to the first family. Above all, it is best to work this out with your spouse or with the help of a counselor or mediator rather than going back to court repeatedly. Judges lose patience and sympathy for people who are not able to find a method of making their own adjustments and return to court time after time.

Common Reasons for Child Support Modification

Child support modification commonly occurs when a child's circumstances significantly change. This may happen when a child becomes emancipated (reaches the age of majority under state law, marries, enters the military, or is otherwise no longer dependent on parental support); the child is legally adopted by a parent who assumes support obligations by virtue of the adoption; time-sharing or custody arrangements change; private school or college tuition is assessed under circumstances that indicate the child would have attended the institution if not for the divorce; or extraordinary expenses arise to provide training or supplies for a child with a special talent, gift, or opportunity. For example, in one case, a little girl received tremendous encouragement from modeling agencies, but was told that in order to pursue job opportunities, she would have to have a portfolio of professional photographs that the mother could not afford. The judge determined that it would be in the child's best interests to be able to take advantage of this opportunity, so the father, who could easily afford the cost, was ordered to provide the money for the portfolio, which did lead to modeling and acting jobs for the child.

Attorneys advise those who feel child support modification might be necessary to carefully weigh the pros and cons, write them out in detail, gather evidence of increased need, and then try to negotiate a modification with the former spouse if at all possible. Both parents can work together to write out a modified or stipulated agreement, and then enlist the help of an attorney to be sure that the agreement and order is put in the proper form and appropriately filed with the court.

Child Support After Majority

Generally, a court cannot order child support to be paid beyond the age that a child becomes an adult under the law of the state (either eighteen or twenty-one). Parents, however, can agree to extend payments for college tuition, for example, and if their agreement is properly filed and made an order of the court, the court can then enforce the agreement. For example, a detailed support agreement sometimes includes provisions for special birthday parties, a bar mitzvah or bat mitzvah, orthodontic expenses, sports equipment, travel, a car, and other anticipated costs for things both parents agree should be provided to their children. College tuition clauses are very common, and may also include provisions for books, housing, spending allowances, graduate school, testing fees, and so on. Even wedding costs are sometimes included.

Generally speaking, the more anticipated costs that can be addressed in such agreements, the better. But sometimes parents who wish to be generous forget that their own circumstances may change. For example, one well-to-do New York father agreed at the time of the divorce to pay for elaborate weddings for each of his three daughters, including receptions at the Waldorf Astoria or a similar facility. Some years later, he suffered an unexpected downturn in his business interests. As a result, he had to go into debt to satisfy the terms of the decree when the time came for his daughters' weddings. Generosity should be balanced with caution.

Protecting Your Right to Child Support

Custodial parents can take a number of steps to be sure they continue to receive child support for their families. First, don't let it slide when payments are late, are lower than they are supposed to be, or are improperly made. Address the problem calmly, but address it promptly and in writing. Otherwise, your ex may be able to argue in court that you waived your right to have payments made according to the terms of the agreement. For example, if your ex sends a check directly to you rather than to the state office, and you cash it without notifying the office and/or telling your ex that he or she needs to follow the established procedure in the future, this could amount to a waiver of your right to have the payments made through the state office, so as to take advantage of its collection, record-keeping, and enforcement services.

CHILD CUSTODY AND VISITATION

Problems that arise in the arena of child custody and visitation are probably the most emotionally wrenching and legally complex of any postdivorce difficulties. Attorneys Bernard Clare and Anthony Daniele, authors of *The Ex Factor*, compare divorced parents at odds on these issues to "two scorpions locked in the fatal mating dance."

Custody and visitation disputes, above all others, are matters parents should make every effort to resolve amicably. Yet it is crucial to remember that if you can't reach an agreement on your own, then the aid of attorneys, counselors, mediators, child support enforcement agencies, and/or the court should be sought as soon as it becomes clear that you have reached an impasse. This is not the time to try self-help remedies.

Parental kidnapping or denial of visitation rights can lead to loss of custody or criminal penalties. As discussed previously, the failure to pay support can lead to wage garnishment, seizure of assets, and in extreme cases, charges of contempt that may result in jail. A strong system is in place almost everywhere to help parents who need assistance in enforcing their rights. The only time self-help measures are appropriate is in a real emergency, such as when one parent is reasonably certain the child is being abused or neglected by the other.

Time Sharing and the Law

The Relationship Between Support and Visitation Rights

One of the most controversial areas of postdivorce law is that of the relationship between a parent's duty to pay child support and the rights of both parent and child to establish and maintain a relationship. Some courts issue "linkage orders," which link support obligations to visitation rights by providing that support may be suspended if visitation is blocked, or that a parent who does not pay support will lose visitation rights. Many judges simply refuse to issue these orders because the ultimate effect is to punish the innocent party—the child.

The Custodial Parent's Duty to Facilitate Visitation

Custodial parents are sometimes unaware of the weight and seriousness with which courts view visitation rights. Parents have an affirmative duty under the law not only to comply with the terms of the custodial order, but to encourage visitation between the child and the other parent. A custodial parent who maliciously or vindictively thwarts visitation by the other may be fined, ordered to pay attorney's fees incurred by the other to enforce his or her visitation rights, or even held in contempt of court if a valid court order is repeatedly disobeyed.

Family attorney David Riggert explains, however, that the use of contempt powers of the court to enforce custody and visitation orders is frequently misunderstood. "People often mistakenly believe that if the ex doesn't abide by the specific terms of a custody or visitation order, he or she will automatically be found in contempt of court. This is not necessarily true. The judge must look at whether the violation was willful and intentional. The intentional or malicious aspect of the violation may be difficult to prove unless there have been many incidents and previous orders that have been violated."

In most cases, when one parent seeks enforcement of an order, the judge will first issue an "Order to Show Cause," and set a hearing that will require the other parent to come to court and state whether he or she has a legitimate reason for violating the terms of the original order. If both parents show up, the judge is likely to issue a new order and remind both that they must comply. Then, if that order, too, is disobeyed, a contempt order may be issued. "People should not always expect to get a contempt citation on the first court appearance," Riggert states, "although many do misunderstand and expect that this is what will happen. The judge will want everyone to come in and find out what is going on before taking drastic measures. Not all judges will find contempt and enforce sanctions at the first hearing. Although there are different standards in different states, a finding of contempt is often accompanied by a 'purge' order, which allows the violator to cure the problem before serious sanctions are applied."

In some extreme cases, an order of protection, similar to those issued in domestic violence cases, may be issued to the noncustodial parent. These orders, like those that provide for automatic arrest of an abusive former spouse who comes within a certain distance of his or her ex, are self-triggering. Generally, they provide that if visitation rights are interfered with by the custodial parent, she or he can be arrested.

The ultimate sanction for interference with a parent's visitation rights is a change of custody. When a custodial parent demonstrates, over and over, callous disregard for the court order and his or her child's welfare, a judge may change primary custody, or in extreme cases even declare that parent unfit and award sole custody to the other. This is generally a last resort, however. Courts have wide latitude to come up with creative solutions to these problems, as always, keeping the best interest of the child a foremost issue.

Parents Who Do Not Honor Visitation Rights   When the noncustodial parent refuses to spend time with the children according to the time-sharing plan, or in some cases refuses to see the children at all, this can be devastating. There is really no effective judicial remedy for this type of neglect.

Some parents, especially those who were very hurt by the divorce, need to take some time alone completely away from the family in order to sort out their feelings and regroup. As a practical matter, the custodial parent can try to explain this to the children, while at the same time maintaining nonthreatening contact with the other parent, such as occasional cards or letters to update him or her on the children, perhaps including recent snapshots. In such cases, many absent parents do return after a period of time on their own.

Time-Sharing Modification   As discussed earlier, most visitation or shared custody arrangements will have to be modified at some time simply because children and their schedules and needs shift as they grow and change. This is another reason it is vital for parents to establish a workable business relationship to deal with these inevitable changes.

Parents who are able to cooperate can usually work out written agreements for time-sharing modification. If the changes are minor or may be temporary, it is probably not necessary to file a new, formal agreement with the court. If they are major, however, it is best to go through the customary process of modifying the existing parenting plan and filing the new agreement and order so that it is legally enforceable. Again, if parents are able to do this amicably, and then enlist the help of an attorney to make sure the right documents are filed, the cost and effort will be minimal.

In their book *The Ex Factor*, family law attorneys Bernard Clare and Anthony Daniele advise parents who are faced with a recalcitrant ex to apply what they term the "stretch plan" to try to facilitate agreed changes in support, visitation, or custody matters without having to involve third parties or the court. First, they recommend maneuvering for a face-to-face meeting. Face-to-face meetings allow for eye contact and a more focused conversation than simply discussing the matter by telephone. Clare and Daniele emphasize that such a meeting is essential even if it requires travel, because it stresses the importance of a former couple's status as coparents.

Second, the attorneys recommend that both parents agree to set certain parameters. Most important, assent to keep the conversation focused on the child or children and their needs, not on yourselves. This is where the emphasis belongs. Third, they recommend that parents discuss child contact, not visitation schedules. This makes for a more positive approach, in which parents are cast in the roles of two people attempting to resolve a problem together rather than adversaries. Clare and Daniele caution parents against the tendency to be self-centered, to manipulate, or to threaten the other, and to stay centered on the fact that the purpose of the meeting is to negotiate and reach a solution about what is best for the child, not the parents.

When parents do reach an agreement that involves significant changes, it is important to reduce it to writing, have an attorney or court advocate review it to make certain it is in the correct form and includes all of the necessary points to be addressed, then file it with the court. The steps required to complete this vary among the jurisdictions. In some places, judges may call both parents in for a brief hearing, generally to satisfy themselves that the parents agree and have covered all the necessary bases. Whatever the process, the written stipulation is essential, in order to minimize any confusion that may arise in the future. If the terms are unusual or questionable, such as splitting two siblings between homes in different states, the court may call for a hearing to make an independent evaluation of whether the plan is in the child's best interest.

Court intervention in a plan both parents have agreed to follow is rare, but it does occur in some cases where special circumstances are present. For example, most psychologists and other child development professionals agree that the best visitation plan for an infant is for the noncustodial parent to spend time with the child in the custodial parent's home. Small babies tend to be very sensitive to disruption of their

eating and sleeping patterns, and tend to suffer anxiety if separated from the primary caretaker, usually the mother, for
extended periods of time. Parents may need to be educated
about the importance, for example, of returning an infant to
the arms of its mother if it cries or becomes upset, even during the period of time allotted for visitation with the other
parent. When parents attempt to force babies to bond with a
person under circumstances that frighten or upset them, this
may actually thwart the natural bonding process and result in
a strained relationship later.

Going to Court on Time-Sharing Issues In David Riggert's
practice, when parents come in seeking custody or visitation
changes, his first step is always to ask them why they are
seeking the change. "Often, parents want the court to order
the other parent to be a better mother or father, to spend more
time with the children, or perhaps to order visitation to be
changed to days that are more convenient for the custodial
parent. I have to tell them that this is not the court's job, and
the standard, the bottom line, is always going to be what is in
the best interest of the child."

Although visitation rights may be modified whenever a
change would serve the best interests of the child, custody
may be more or less easy to modify depending on how much
time has passed since the initial decree or any prior modification. In Illinois, for example, the criteria for custody modifications differ according to this factor: If less than two years
have gone by since the time of the last judgment, the parent
seeking to change custody must allege that the present environment seriously endangers the child. When more than two
years have elapsed, the court must find not only a change of
circumstances, but also evidence that the change the parent is
seeking would be in the best interest of the child. The higher
standards of proof demonstrate another reason that it is

preferable for parents to work out modifications on their own without requiring another trip to court.

If the parents are not able to work out their disagreements, and one files a petition seeking a change in time sharing, the court will, as always, begin by looking at the best interest of the child. The judge will also review the current plan and order, the history of the relationship between the children and both parents, and other facts and practical aspects of the situation. The court will then make an independent evaluation based on the circumstances and facts as they are presented.

As with support, the parent seeking a time-sharing modification must show substantially changed circumstances, as well as convince the judge that the proposed change is in the child's best interest. Judges have been known to chastise those who rush into court without first making every effort to work it out with the other parent, as well as those who come to court too often. Problems commonly arise when the lifestyles of the two parents are very different, and the custodial parent does not approve of something the noncustodial parent is doing in the presence of the child. When courts see such concerns as legitimate—for example, when the noncustodial parent or someone else in his or her home is abusing drugs in the presence of the child—supervised visitation may be ordered. Other cases are more difficult—for example, when the noncustodial parent is gay and has a lover in the home when the child is present.

As always, the court will decide each of these cases depending on all of the circumstances involved and what it deems to be in the child's best interest. It is rare today for courts to make such orders as forbidding any contact between a child and a parent's gay companion, but such conditions are occasionally directed when the court finds, for example, that the child has expressed great discomfort in that situation.

Occasionally, a parent who simply resents the fact that the ex has started dating again will attempt to obtain an order prohibiting the other parent from bringing the new boyfriend or girlfriend around when the child is present. Unless he or she can prove that this person poses some danger to the child, courts will not intervene in such matters. Those who still have such strong feelings about the ex should take a close look at their own emotional states and perhaps seek counseling to move on and disconnect from the past.

Child Custody Changes

Attorneys Clare and Daniele describe custody modification as "one of the most important and far-reaching postdivorce decisions any parent can make." Courts generally will not order a change of primary custody unless there has been a "substantial and material" change of circumstance—and the change must be in the custodial parent's circumstance. A noncustodial parent who suddenly had a windfall and bought a big house cannot ask for a custody change on this basis alone, as some have been known to do.

As always, the focus is on the children, and courts are well aware that a custody change is often very disruptive to a child unless it is a carefully reasoned decision that both parents and the child have jointly made after careful consideration. When one parent opposes it, courts generally will not order custody changed without proof of serious, factual elements indicating that it is necessary for the child's well-being.

New Families and Custody Changes   Family attorney David Riggert finds that custody and visitation problems often arise when one person remarries. "The custodial parent who marries again must keep in mind that it is still important to include the noncustodial parent in the child's life," he explains. "A stepparent should not be cast in the role of replacing the noncustodial parent—for example, by allowing or instructing the child to call the new parent 'Dad' or 'Mom.' This issue is occasionally the basis for litigation."

When a custodial parent remarries, especially if this brings new children into the family, a period of stress and adjustment is inevitable. It is not unusual for a child whose custodial parent has remarried to express unhappiness about the situation to the noncustodial parent. Most experts believe that the best approach for the noncustodial parent to take in such a situation is to try to investigate why the child seems severely upset, and to counsel patience and flexibility.

Of course, if the noncustodial parent suspects that abuse or real endangerment exists, then intervention through legal channels may be appropriate. This does happen in some cases, and should be confronted immediately if the evidence is there. If a child simply complains that he or she does not like the new circumstances, it is generally best to allow some time to pass, and monitor the situation, while maintaining regular contact with the child and encouraging her to be patient and try to adjust. One way parents often make the situation worse is by demonstrating their own anxiety about it.

Occasionally, a real problem does exist in the new home, and a custody change is warranted. For example, if the custodial parent's new spouse is alcoholic and abusive to the child, a custody change will generally be ordered. The burden of proof is always on the parent seeking the custody change. Therefore, it is important to work through legal channels to get an independent investigation or evaluation as soon as possible. In such cases, a court will generally appoint a guardian *ad litem* and/or attorney to represent the interests of the child.

Stability is important to children, and frequent changes in time sharing can be very upsetting. The court will usually not intervene in a working arrangement unless it perceives a genuine threat to the child from the noncustodial parent's behavior or another very strong reason to order a change.

When Is a Custody Battle Worth It? Although it is almost always best to avoid litigating over a child, sometimes returning to court is a necessary evil. Before you embark on a custody battle, ask yourself, "What am I fighting for?" Be sure your answer reflects a genuine belief that this is what is best for the child, and not for a purpose that serves your emotional needs.

Sometimes the benefits of a custody fight do outweigh the emotional costs. If you are the custodial parent, and your spouse is challenging custody for an inappropriate reason (any reason that is not focused on the best interest of the child), such as to try to force you to relent on a financial issue, you need to fight back and put a stop to this behavior now, for the sake of the child. Sometimes this can be done through mediation, attorney negotiations, or another less traumatic method.

If you are the noncustodial parent and know that your former partner has a problem that seriously endangers the child—such as severe emotional difficulties; abusive behavior toward you, the child, or a new partner in the home; alcohol or drug addiction; or exposure to a new partner who is abusive or addicted—then litigation to gain sole custody is warranted and appropriate.

The first priority in a custody case is to keep the focus firmly fixed on the child, and then to accomplish the litigation as rapidly, and with as much finality, as possible. While litigation between parents is always distressing, final resolution of a custody dispute brings relief to the child or children involved. It can put an end to those emotions that inevitably plague a person whose future remains uncertain—confusion, anxiety, even anger.

The second essential ingredient to a successful custody case is finality. Make sure all issues in dispute or anticipated to arise in the future are addressed, and see that the final plan is geared toward avoiding further litigation. Repeated custody litigation is agonizing for children—it burdens them almost beyond endurance and can result in problems that will affect them for life. It is far better, if litigation is the only choice, to get it over with permanently.

Once a child knows what his living arrangements will be for the foreseeable future, he can relax, adjust to the new situation, and begin to heal. Children need some sense of stability and predictability. The necessity of even the most restrained and efficient custody litigation can cause a child severe stress, however, and any child who has been through such a process may need counseling or therapy to fully heal.

What Happens in a Child Custody Case?   If you must go to court on a child custody issue, be aware that the judge will probably talk to the child alone, in his or her chambers rather than in the courtroom. If one parent has tried to poison the child against the other, this will usually come out. It is best to simply encourage the child to tell the truth about how she feels, because nearly all children will, anyway.

When custody is contested, the court will often appoint one or more professionals to assist in determining what is best for the child, such as a guardian *ad litem* to protect the child's legal interests and a mental health professional to assess the child's emotional stability and to help determine what type of custody arrangement would be best for him. These evaluations may take some time, so don't expect a rapid conclusion to a custody battle.

How do judges make the decision on what is truly in the best interest of the child when a custody change petition is before them? This varies, of course, according to state law and the individual sensibilities of the judges involved, but most consider certain common factors. "In Illinois, courts look at, among other things, eight factors that are listed in the statutes in determining the best interests of a child, both in making the initial determination and when one parent seeks a change," explains family law attorney David Riggert. "One of these factors is the willingness of each parent to facilitate a close relationship between the other parent and the child. If a parent suspects that the other is abusive or otherwise dangerous to the child, he or she needs to see an attorney and get into court immediately rather than simply withholding visitation."

Riggert advises parents to think carefully about how any actions they are contemplating will affect their children. "In addition to the eight statutory factors, the courts may consider anything that affects the child. It's all subject to interpretation by the judge." He emphasizes that stability is recognized as a very important issue in the lives of children. "For example, many people become very upset if their former spouses begin cohabiting with another person. But this fact alone is not enough to warrant a custody change. Illinois has case law recognizing that shuffling a child back and forth between parents may not be in that child's best interest. Far too often, parents are looking at their own feelings or resentments against the ex instead of keeping the focus on the child. No judge will approve a modification for the best interest of the parents." Many jurisdictions now have mandatory mediation before a formal custody proceeding, both during the divorce process and when a change of custody is later sought.

When considering a custody change, courts vary in the elements they consider most important. Some states, as described above for Illinois, have a list of factors which can be taken into account. In others, it is up to the judge to consider each family on a case-by-case basis in determining what would be best for the child. Judges are individuals, with different values and priorities. Also, it is very rare that just one factor is involved in a custody dispute.

Nearly all judges, however, give great weight to the issue of continuity. Virtually all recognize the importance of working to minimize disruption in a child's life. If life with the custodial parent has been continuous and stable, a custody change is unlikely unless the other factors involved are very significant. Indications of continuity include the child's ability to maintain a continuous relationship with friends, school, home, and regular visits with the noncustodial parent. On the other hand, if the custodial parent is constantly moving, changing homes and jobs and requiring the child to uproot from school and friends, this may indicate a lack of stability. The court will look at the entire environment, not just physical changes. As Clare and Daniele state, "Stability is a function of parental attitude, not of geography." This is especially true when circumstances such as military service requiring frequent moves are involved. Conversely, a major factor may be a custodial parent's interference with visitation rights.

Custody modification proceedings are always traumatic for a child. If there is any way to avoid the necessity of a court procedure, through mediation, counseling, or other methods, this is what is truly in the child's best interest.

Children's Preferences   Many judges will give more weight to a child's stated preference regarding custody changes in a postdivorce proceeding than in the original hearing. At the time of the divorce, everyone must try to predict the future. At a subsequent hearing, after the parties involved have had time to settle into their new lives and assess how the arrangements are working out, they have a better perspective on what is and is not making sense. A child's preference will be considered as an important element, but will rarely be the deciding factor.

Helping Children Recover After a Custody Battle
According to Stephen Herman, M.D., author of *Parent v.*

Parent: How You Can Help Your Child Survive the Custody Battle, key factors that bode favorably for a child's recovery after the trauma of a custody battle include:

1. An end to *all* litigation between parents—not only custody battles but conflict over money and other issues as well.
2. The opportunity for the child to enjoy an ongoing, fulfilling relationship with both parents playing an important role in the child's life (unless a truly dangerous situation makes this impossible).
3. The end of all nonlegal hostilities between the parents, or any conflict that puts the child in the middle.
4. New, positive lives and relationships for the parents. If parents are fulfilled in their work, interpersonal relations, and other important areas of life, they will be better parents and role models for their children, and less likely to hang on to the past.
5. Psychotherapy—ideally, all children whose parents engaged in a custody battle should have some counseling.
6. School personnel who are supportive and caring— informed teachers, school support groups.
7. Parents who keep the child and his best interests number one in all of their choices, and remember his needs every step of the way.

SPECIAL LEGAL PROBLEMS

Relocation and the Law

Many people experience a need or desire to move to a new home or to a different area after a divorce. This can be a great way to make a fresh start, but can also result in headaches, especially for parents. A parent's desire to relocate often brings conflicting legal rights into the picture. On the one hand, in America we prize a strong right to travel and live wherever we like. On the other, parents also have a unique set of rights and responsibilities, and the right of reasonable visitation with a child includes the ability to do so without having to undertake great expense or inconvenience.

What is fair when one parent wants to relocate? There are no easy answers, and every situation is unique. The right of women to have equal opportunities to achieve a successful and fulfilling career, and the expectation under modern law that they must do so to provide for their own support and a major part of the support of their children often make relocation desirable or mandatory. Custodial fathers face similar problems. Parents who remarry must also consider the career and preferences of their new family members.

Some states now have laws regarding when parents may and may not relocate without first obtaining the consent of the other parent or, alternatively, court approval. Many are currently revising old laws to make them more workable. For example, Illinois recently changed its laws to modify a provision that said a custodial parent could move anywhere in the state without the permission of the other parent or the court (for example, allowing a Chicago parent to move to Cairo, requiring a six-hour drive, but forbidding a Quad cities parent to move across the river to Iowa) to provide that a parent must have permission if the move is more than one hundred miles from the other.

If you are contemplating a move that you think might anger your ex, check with a legal advisor to learn the current law governing relocation in your state. Parents who are able to communicate well and maintain a good rapport in the interests of their children can usually work out a solution satisfactory to both, through changes in visitation schedules, sharing of transportation costs, lowered child support payments to offset such expenses, and other compromises. Parents who wish to reach an agreement but can't do so on their own may wish to enlist the help of a mediator, since very specific, focused issues such as relocation can often be quickly resolved in such a forum.

If you are the custodial parent and must go to court to obtain approval of the move, be prepared to show that it is in the best interests of the child, that it is being done for a legitimate reason and not to make it more difficult for your former spouse to maintain contact, and if the children are in favor of the move, note this as well. Remember that the court that makes the initial custody decision at the time of the divorce retains jurisdiction over the case to make any subsequent changes. Therefore, if one or both parents have moved since the divorce, it will be necessary to return to the court in which the original decree was granted to hash out this or any other problem that comes up later, or to take special steps to have jurisdiction over the case transferred by that court to another. Some parenting plans that become a binding part of the decree contain their own restrictions on relocation.

Remember, parents who move without following the mandates of the decree or the applicable law may face severe penalties. Also, if one parent removes the child from the region without informing the other of his or her whereabouts, he or she may be subject to civil or criminal penalties for parental kidnapping. Be sure you understand your rights and responsibilities before making a move that your former spouse may oppose.

The Aftermath of a Violent Marriage

Many of us tend to think of domestic violence as a phenomenon associated with two people living under the same roof, something that ends as soon as the couple in a violent relationship splits up. Unfortunately, this is not necessarily true. As many as 75 percent of those who escape violent marriages are still plagued by a hostile ex.

Violent marriages are almost always one-sided, with one person abusing the other physically, emotionally, sexually, or in a combination of ways with the goal of establishing complete control over him or her. The dynamics are completely different from the combative marriage in which the partners often fight, usually verbally. Relationships characterized by ongoing domestic violence are not the same, and the ending, while always desirable, leads to a postmarriage situation that must be handled in a different manner than the aftermath of a healthy marriage.

This is often the time that an abusive spouse becomes enraged that he or she can no longer control the former partner, and escalates the violence. This may take the form of property destruction, stalking, harassing, vandalizing, threats, or direct attacks. Abusive partners who are allowed unsupervised visits with their children often use the children to try to regain control over the former spouse—for example, by disappearing with a child for several days after the scheduled visit was supposed to end.

Obviously, such behavior is extremely destructive and unhealthy for divorced individuals, and absolutely devastating for children. Nothing is ever accomplished by harassment and violence. Couples who cannot even talk to one another without allowing the intensity of their anger to drive them into a rage should simply stay away from one another and communicate through attorneys.

Domestic violence is a plague of astonishing proportions today. Fortunately, more and more services and sources of help have become available to those (primarily women, but some men as well) who need assistance in escaping the hold of a brutal spouse. Those who break free of an abusive spouse have already shown remarkable strength and courage.

Safety is the paramount concern for those who have left a violent marriage. It may be necessary to obtain a temporary order of protection and/or a permanent injunction against an ex-spouse. All states, and nearly all larger communities, now have domestic violence coalitions and other groups to assist family violence victims and their children in staying safe and free. Call the National Domestic Violence Hotline, staffed twenty-four hours a day by trained volunteers, for information and assistance in locating a group in your area (see Appendix).

Court advocacy programs, police, family law attorneys, counselors, and social service organizations can also provide referrals and assistance for those plagued by a violent ex. A simple safety plan can be developed with materials provided by these groups, and it can save your life. Most of these organizations also sponsor group therapy or counseling, or can refer you to sources of professional emotional support.

People who have suffered abuse over a period of years may face additional difficulties in adjusting to a new life. They may have a severely distorted perspective of their choices and the reality of their lives. Those who have been told over and over that they are stupid, worthless, ugly, incompetent, and other vicious lies tend to internalize these negative ideas, even though they may know intellectually that they are not true. Those who have been severely abused may suffer from posttraumatic stress disorder. Abusers also tend to keep their spouses isolated and control family finances, so many emerge from the marriage with little or no work experience or financial know-how.

Special help is also available to those who need assistance in overcoming such problems. Local coalitions and shelters can provide information, assistance, and support groups of others who have faced similar issues. Some vocational rehabilitation counselors specialize in helping abuse victims build new lives.

Sometimes abusers manage to maintain control over their partners during the divorce process and bully them into signing an ill-advised agreement. If this happened to you, remember that the decree can be modified, and that anything you signed under duress should not be legally binding. This is especially important if the fact that you were abused was not addressed in the divorce case, particularly if you have children. Consult a family attorney or a professional affiliated with a domestic violence organization or court advocacy program if you feel that you were victimized in this manner.

As discussed above, mediation is generally not appropriate when one partner has been abused, because there is an unequal balance of power and the required contact with the abuser could be dangerous or otherwise damaging. Attorneys or other legal advocates should generally handle all communications between the parties following a violent marriage.

If your former spouse (whether violent or not) keeps calling, following, or otherwise harassing you after the divorce, call the police. All states now have laws against stalking, and many have laws against telephone harassment as well. If necessary, you can obtain a restraining order and/or permanent injunction prohibiting him or her from contacting you in any manner, or setting strict limits if child visitation is involved. More and more courts are beginning to recognize that spousal abuse *is* child abuse, and are either denying visitation rights to a parent who has abused the other or restricting visitation to supervised settings. A family law attorney, court advocate, or someone at a domestic violence coalition can advise you on how to best use the resources available in your area to protect yourself and your children.

Many communities now have specific provisions for supervised visitation or the exchange of children without contact between parents, such as special centers, family service agencies, or facilities within the YMCA or YWCA. The laws of some states now contain a presumption against joint custody where one parent has been abusive toward the other.

Custody orders may be modified for good cause if the abuser proves he or she has stopped the criminal behavior, has sought treatment, and is committed to building a healthy relationship with the child.

Explaining to children why they cannot spend time with a parent is an especially delicate task. Most experts agree that children need to know the truth when one of their parents has been abusive to the other—and most are already aware, even if they never directly witnessed the abuse. For their own safety, and their emotional need to understand the reality of the family situation, kids need to be made aware of the facts (but not necessarily the details) of why their parents' marriage must end. At the same time, it is important not to elaborate on what an evil person the other parent is, even if it is true. Most professionals advise telling children the basic facts in this situation, emphasizing that the problem is between the parents and not the fault of the child, then saying no more about the abusive parent unless it becomes necessary due to changing circumstances.

One young man whose parents divorced after many years of a volatile relationship, including violence, said that he still feels a great deal of anger toward his father. Yet by late adolescence, he had learned to channel his disappointment and frustration into positive outlets, such as working on his own to get a scholarship to a boarding school he wanted to attend. He also stated that being away at this school helped him gain perspective, and remarked that while he had a hard time discussing his parents' divorce he urges others to go to someone they trust for advice. He is also looking ahead to his career, and has vowed that he will marry later and that his marriage will not be like that of his parents; above all, it will be free of violence. He advises children in violent homes to call the police when the violence begins.

Children who have witnessed abuse may need special counseling or group therapy. The same organizations that help abuse victims recover often offer programs for children, as well. While those who have escaped a violent marriage face a special set of problems others do not, they also seem, as a general rule, to recover from the trauma of the divorce more rapidly. Although they may, like others, feel ambivalence about the end of the marriage and miss the good times, they also see the stark contrast between living in fear and living in peace. When people who have been imprisoned by a brutal partner discover the joy and potential a new, safe life brings, they usually blossom.

Child Abuse

A parent who has abused his or her child should not be allowed to have unsupervised contact with the child. As discussed previously, there are various alternatives available in most communities to allow supervised visitation in a comfortable setting.

Parents who deliberately and callously use their children as weapons against their former spouses are also child abusers. The emotional damage this type of behavior does to a child cannot be overstated. Parents who badmouth the other; use their children as spies or messengers of threats; or use them as pawns to punish the ex by not showing up for visits, returning the children late, or otherwise manipulating the former spouse by misusing the children should be held accountable for such behavior.

It should go without saying that casting false accusations of abuse against the other parent is among the most reprehensible acts a parent can commit, and the most painful for the children. False accusations also have far-reaching effects that impact other children. Each claim must be investigated. In many areas, the people and resources available to substantiate alleged child abuse cases are scarce. While time and money is wasted on ferreting out false claims, the real victims go on suffering.

Child Abduction

The law takes child abduction very seriously. Parental kidnapping can lead to an FBI investigation and criminal arrest, plus termination of visitation rights. In most jurisdictions, child snatching is a felony, even when the parent does not cross state lines.

Sadly, abduction of a child by the noncustodial parent happens frequently. While most child abductions occur within the same state, it has been increasingly common for a parent to snatch a child, flee to another state, and try to settle there and get a court order awarding custody. In response, all fifty states have now adopted the Uniform Child Custody Jurisdiction Act (UCCJA).

The UCCJA is a federal law which mandates cooperation between states when a child is taken from one state to another. Its purpose is to eliminate having two conflicting child custody orders entered by courts in two different states. Under this law, a parent who moves with a child to another state and goes to court seeking any type of custody modification—and the attorney of this parent—must inform that court of any existing or pending child custody order or action in any other state; therefore, any advantage the parent may have had by taking the child across state lines is removed.

Before the law was enacted, a parent could snatch a child, move to another state, and file a petition for custody in that state's court. Under the UCCJA, if a parent attempts this, the new court will immediately determine whether another court has jurisdiction over the custody matter, and order the case returned to that court. The UCCJA also provides that a parent whose child has been taken to another state no longer has to travel to the state where the child is located in order to enforce her or his rights. The parent can petition for custody enforcement in the local court, where the original decree was entered, or where the child has resided with the custodial parent for six or more consecutive months. This discourages "forum shopping" and the confusion that arises from involvement of more than one court in trying to govern a custody matter.

If you are the custodial parent and the other parent takes off with the child or does not return at the appointed time, it is important to take action immediately. Call your attorney or your local child welfare agency. It does not take long for an abducting parent to travel a great distance, making it more difficult to catch up with the child and straighten out the custody dispute.

When the noncustodial parent sees strong evidence of neglect or abuse, a provision of the UCCJA allows him or her to refuse to return the child to the home state. The standard is abandonment or a true emergency that requires prompt legal action to protect the child's safety and welfare. In such a case, the noncustodial parent should seek court intervention and the advice of an attorney immediately.

International Abduction

If you fear that your child might have been taken out of the country, contact the Office of Citizen's Consular Services at the Department of State in Washington, D.C., or the U.S. embassy or consulate closest to the place you believe the child was taken. If you have the child's passport or none has been issued, contact the State Department. If you fax it a copy of the court order showing that you have primary custody, it can prevent issuance of a passport to the child. Again, it is important to move fast in such a case. Law enforcement sources stress that the first twenty-four hours are crucial.

Parents who abduct their children often make threats to do so first. If your ex threatens to snatch the child, take this seriously and contact the police and your attorney immediately. You may be able to get a restraining order that allows for immediate arrest if the child is not returned to you according to the schedule set out in the order. If you fear international abduction, the steps outlined above to prevent the child from getting an original or second passport can be implemented based on a threat as well as an actual kidnapping.

Grandparents' Rights

More and more, the law has begun to recognize the importance of the relationship between children and their grandparents. Virtually all states, either through a statute or as a part of their common law, recognize the rights of children to have access to their grandparents and the rights of grandparents to spend time with grandchildren. In most states, grandparents may go to court to get a visitation order and then enforce it in the same manner as a noncustodial parent. Powerful lobbying groups such as the American Association of Retired Persons (AARP) are working hard to make sure that the importance of grandparents is not overlooked. The AARP publishes a brochure for grandparents outlining their rights (see Appendix).

6

Practical Matters: Health, Work, and Money

NEW EXPERIENCES AND CHALLENGES ALWAYS SEEM TO ARISE more rapidly and in greater numbers during the period following a divorce. Men who had their meals prepared and laundry done, first by a mother and then by a wife, must now learn to cope with these responsibilities. Women who relied on their husbands for yard work and home and auto repairs must now learn to take care of these chores or hire competent people to do so. Just coping with the practical, everyday changes in life can seem overwhelming.

Yet these challenges present an opportunity for learning. The key is to ask questions without worrying about appearing stupid. The only foolish question is the one that does not get asked. The willingness to ask for help and to admit when you need assistance is a characteristic of wise and successful people. Do not hesitate to request information and aid from family, friends, advisors, or organizations. Now, more than ever, you need sensible guidance, especially in areas that can affect your future, such as finances and insurance. Ask friends for referrals, and line up the competent experts you will need to consult.

Divorce inevitably produces stress and upheaval in virtually all areas of a person's life. The aftermath of such a life-changing event can be both frightening and enlightening, providing the impetus to refurbish and streamline old lifestyles and habits. Careful thought, choices, and planning can help you turn the postdivorce rebuilding process into an opportunity to improve yourself and your surroundings, rather than allowing it to become an overpowering ordeal.

HEALTH

After divorce, many people experience profound changes in their day-to-day patterns of living. Those who were used to having another family member prepare their meals, or those who customarily cooked according to the needs and preferences of others, often find their eating habits changing. Many people also experience trouble sleeping or variations in sleep patterns. Stress, as well as practical changes, can disrupt habits and distract attention from important health concerns, leading to an increased likelihood of illness.

During this period of upheaval, maintaining your health should be a priority. Taking steps to alleviate stress and attend to your well-being can be both physically and emotionally healing. This is an ideal period for personal renewal. Now is the time to reassess your personal style, and to get in good or better shape. As with any other time you are facing stress, good nutrition and exercise are especially important. Take special care not to fall into bad habits, as we all tend to do when we are stressed. The key is to know yourself, and to tailor the changes you will make to meet your needs.

This is a perfect time to find your own balance between rewards and indulgences and explore new ways to increase your physical strength and stamina. For example, if you love to cook, you may want to consider enrolling in classes to learn how to make something special you never had time to try before. If you enjoy dancing, but haven't felt you could take the time to join a class or group, do so now. A short getaway—at a spa, camping with friends, a weekend exploring museums in the city or hiking in the country—can bring a tremendous sense of renewal.

Do see a physician if you plan to begin a workout regimen that is a drastic change from your customary level of physical activity, and attend to any health issues you may have been neglecting. The inevitable stress of coping with the aftermath of a divorce can cause both physical and emotional illness, and leave your resistance to disease lowered. If it has been a while since you've had a physical, get one.

Stress

Many people experience significant stress as they try to adjust to new responsibilities, frustrations, and life changes after a divorce. While stress is sometimes brushed off as an inevitable part of modern life, severe stress can cause serious physical and mental damage. Indications of stress may include headaches, abdominal pain and other digestive disorders, chest pain, dizziness, and other serious symptoms that should not be ignored, whatever the cause.

Fortunately, most stress-related problems can be treated effectively by counseling, medication, lifestyle changes, or some combination of these approaches. The key is prompt diagnosis and treatment, because prolonged stress can have life-threatening consequences. People under severe stress are at far greater risk for auto accidents, substance abuse, suicide, and homicide.

Innumerable sources of help in handling stress are available today. Books, classes, mental health providers, and seminars teach valuable coping skills and techniques that can be used whenever a stressful situation occurs. Many of the most effective treatments for stress are free and available to all who know how to use them—meditation, deep breathing, physical exercise, and writing in a journal.

Lorraine Parker, D.C., is a chiropractor and nutritionist who teaches classes on stress management. She explains that certain physical reactions occur when a person experiences stress as a result of either positive or negative life changes. "The physiological reaction to stress is a throwback to our primitive ancestors," she explains. "When modern humans were developing, people would encounter a threat, such as a wild animal, and experience physical reactions including a release of adrenaline, increased heartbeat, muscle tension, and breathing changes. This prepared them to either fight or flee. In their world, they would have to follow through with one behavior or the other, expending tremendous physical energy in the process. Afterward, they were exhausted and would sleep for a long time, then awake restored. In today's society, the fight-or-flight reaction may be triggered as many as twenty times a day as we encounter stressful situations, but we can't go through the steps that expend the energy to release the tension, because we need to maintain our lives according to modern norms and practices."

People adjusting to the life changes that follow a divorce are often extremely vulnerable to this dangerous accumulation of stress. "Stress is caused by changes or frustrations in life, and divorce is full of both," she remarks. "The people who suffer the most from stress are those who feel they have no control over their lives. For example, some people are surprised to learn that it is not so much the high-powered executives who get severely stressed as their secretaries. The executive can mull over a report all night—then take it to his secretary and say, 'I need this typed in an hour.' The secretary has no control."

Parker states that people trying to adjust to changes after a divorce often feel a similar lack of control, and encounter frustrations that trigger stress over and over each day. "A single mother may have to get her children up and ready for school, then rush to drop them off, then fight traffic to get herself to work, then deal with the pressures of the job, then arrive home to find that the child support check didn't come on time. People under these circumstances feel they don't have the opportunity or time to deal with the stress. It would be healthiest to drop everything and run around the block a few times, but instead we keep the energy all inside," she explains. "This causes enormous wear and tear on the body."

One thing that can help break this cycle of stress is achieving some small measure of control. "If you can gain a sense of better control over any little portion of your life, this will help," Parker explains. She also emphasizes that exercise and good nutrition are absolutely essential for anyone coping with a stressful situation. "Exercise is important both physically and psychologically, to dissipate that buildup of energy from the fight-or-flight response," she says. "Everyone needs to find a physical outlet." Likewise, good nutrition is important to both body and mind. "High stress compromises the immune system," she explains. "The likelihood of illness increases just at the time people can least afford to get sick. People need to be more diligent about caring for their health to avoid illness. It's important to eat balanced meals with varied types of protein and complex carbohydrates, and to avoid excessive junk food."

Parker adds that this does not mean giving up treats. "Rewards and treats are good in moderation—if I couldn't have cheesecake or Haagen-Dazs ice cream once in a while, there would be no point in living!" she laughs. "But the key is moderation. It may be tempting to eat a whole pint of ice cream instead of dinner, but this can cause all kinds of problems, including that familiar sugar rush that makes you feel even more flighty and irritable."

Parker also believes that a regular dialogue with others facing similar challenges can be very helpful in alleviating stress caused by a particular source. "Support groups can really help deal with the problem head-on," she says. "It helps a lot to discuss your feelings with those who have experienced the same thing before. I'm aware of many types of divorce groups of different sizes and formats—groups for kids, prayer groups, classes, all types of programs."

Parker believes that the key to dealing with stress in a healthy way is learning to cope with it. "You can't avoid stress; it happens in a situation like divorce. But you can develop positive coping mechanisms. Some people turn to negative coping tools, such as excessive alcohol, overeating, doing nothing but watching television all the time. It's important to channel the energy that comes from stress in more positive directions. This can also give a person a sense of control over his or her life." Parker advocates exploring new hobbies or activities that are not related to work or other daily stress-producing activities. "For example, I wouldn't advise someone working in the computer field to take a computer-related class," she says. "He should take a class in something like painting or swimming, to provide a respite from the rest of his life."

Parker also emphasizes that stress management training is becoming more and more available as the debilitating effects of stress are being widely recognized. "I teach a stress management class through a continuing education program at the local university, and another thorough a junior college," she states. "Corporations, HMOs, and hospitals also offer stress-management programs. There are also classes and self-teaching materials available on relaxation and meditation techniques that are very helpful. Like stress, relaxation is also cumulative. Simply taking ten to fifteen minutes each day for guided relaxation can make a big difference, and there are tapes for this available in any bookstore."

Parker also points out that simple pleasures and fun are essential. "Buy yourself flowers, do something that makes you smile," she advises. "Do something silly, take some time to play, pet a cat or dog—this can be very calming; it actually lowers the heart rate and blood pressure. Take a warm bath with candles and a glass of wine, go for a walk, even blow bubbles. I keep a jar of bubbles from the dimestore—the kind with a little wand—on my desk. There are many simple and inexpensive ways to deal with the stress that we all have to face. It's often just a matter of getting into the habit of doing this for yourself. But it's essential—it's a major part of taking care of your health."

MONEY AND FINANCIAL CHANGE

Divorce inevitably brings change in each partner's financial life, living arrangements, and work situation. Economic instability can contribute to the stress and craziness after a divorce, especially for women, who still suffer more financially in most cases. Yet this can also be a time of learning about and establishing a plan for a sound financial future.

Credit

It is especially important that credit matters be cleaned up and finalized as soon as possible. Anything that wasn't addressed before the final decree was filed should be dealt with now. Remember, the terms of the divorce decree stating that you or your spouse will assume certain debts are not binding on your creditors. All creditors should have been contacted and debts refinanced, if possible, prior to the divorce. If this was not done then, however, it should be done now. Generally, a creditor cannot hold you responsible for debt your spouse incurs after your divorce, but can seek payment for anything that accrued before the date of the final decree.

If either party in a marriage does not have an established credit history and an independent income of his or her own, creditors may be unwilling to refinance the obligation in that person's name alone. This is understandable, since creditors may have relied on two incomes or one person's long history of good credit in making a loan. An alternative to refinancing credit that was acquired jointly during the marriage but apportioned to one spouse in the settlement is to transfer the debt to a new account held singly by the individual spouse. If you are both able to acquire new credit accounts in your own names, consider making such transfers and closing the jointly held account as soon as these transfers are final.

If you have not had credit in your own name, it is essential to establish it now. Even a long history of joint credit activity during the marriage does not necessarily mean you have an individual credit history, if accounts were in your spouse's name with you listed as a cosignator.

On the other hand, if the two of you, or even if your spouse alone, incurred credit problems during the marriage, you may have a blight on your own credit record, depending on how the account was set up and paid, and other factors. If you suspect this may be the case, get a copy of your credit report from one of the reporting agencies such as Equifax or TRW. These reports are free if requested after you have been denied credit, or available for a charge of approximately $10.00 at any time.

If you worked throughout your marriage, or had any credit accounts prior to or during that time, you should have at least some credit established in your own name. If not, most people can get "instant" credit with a department store or gasoline company, and begin to establish a personal credit history.

Building credit in your own name is not difficult; on the contrary, one reason for the soaring rates of bankruptcy filings is the tremendous ease of acquiring credit today. Get a credit card or two, but use these tools with caution if you are not familiar with the treacherous world of charge accounts. It is amazingly easy to amass astronomical levels of debt without realizing that you are doing so. Tread lightly as you build your credit rating, bearing in mind that credit problems can persist for years.

Even those who work hard to realistically assess their financial capacities after a divorce may find that they are unable to meet the obligations they have assumed. Others simply feel overwhelmed, at a loss as to how to manage a new and unfamiliar set of financial responsibilities. Help for these problems is available through the Consumer Credit Counseling Service, a nonprofit organization that helps people avoid and solve financial difficulties. The organization has a thousand offices throughout the United States, Canada, and Puerto Rico, and provides services at low or no charge. The CCCS counselor can help you assess your situation, develop a budget, and work out an effective plan to pay off bills.

If you have a severe credit problem, the CCCS can work with your creditors to establish a debt management program, in which the representative negotiates a revised schedule of payments and works out a realistic plan by which you can pay off your debts and still have enough on which to live. To find out about the CCCS office nearest you, call 1-800-388-CCCS (2227).

Building a Sound Financial Future

Budget counselor Judy Lawrence has worked with innumerable people to help them rebuild financial security, gain an understanding of the financial realities of their lives, and avoid the pitfalls that commonly arise after a divorce. "Everyone needs to develop and create some kind of a budget or spending plan," she states. "It's important to know what you have, and what you can handle financially. Even those who received a big financial settlement in their divorces need to be careful, consult the right professionals, and hold off on major decisions until things have stabilized."

Most people find themselves facing the more practical problem of how to make ends meet when they have to cover all of their expenses on their own. "It is important for everyone to learn how to manage their money effectively, especially those who didn't handle the finances in the marriage," says Lawrence. "You need to know how to get started, what you have, and where it goes."

This process involves three primary steps, Lawrence explains. First, she instructs clients to complete a worksheet of yearly expenses—the periodic charges that come around less often than monthly, and can knock a person for a loop if he or she hasn't planned for them. "This is a very critical first step, to get an overview of things that really add up but are overlooked because they are not billed monthly. Things such as insurance bills, auto maintenance, school pictures, propane refills, tuition."

Next, Lawrence counsels clients to list monthly expenditures, both fixed and incidental, each month. "Then you plug in the first set of expenses and get a realistic picture of what your costs are going to be so you can plan things out before the month begins. If you won't have enough money, you can look at the incidentals." Lawrence explains that there are three ways to cut these expenses: "Eliminate it, cut back on the cost, or get creative and resourceful, such as by making a gift rather than buying one."

Lawrence has found that many people have a hard time estimating their incidental or nonfixed expenses because they don't really know where their money goes. "That's why the third step is so important—tracking your expenses."

In her many years of budget counseling, Lawrence has found that those who track their spending on a regular basis universally spend less and save more. This process can also help ferret out hidden or unanticipated costs that many people fail to consider simply because the costs are unexpected or they don't arise on a regular basis. "Especially with children, these costs can really add up. A child who plays an instrument may go through $100 a year in reeds. One that rides horses often has expenses for riding lessons, entry fees, costumes, and a variety of other charges. Soccer teams recruit parents to go along as chaperons for out-of-town matches, and then there are the costs for motel rooms and meals." Lawrence has created a workbook called *The Budget Kit* that provides an easy way for people to accomplish these three steps, as well as a pocket-sized book called *The Money Tracker* that provides an immediate place to write down expenditures.

The Money Tracker also contains sections to record splurges and victories over near-splurges, and to note the user's emotional reaction to each event. "It's a gentle way to learn about the emotional part of money," Lawrence explains. "We all have strong feelings connected to money, although we don't always realize what they are. By keeping track of these feelings, as well as spending patterns, you can tune into what's going on with regard to what you are thinking and feeling when you spend. Using your different senses—the kinetic act of writing and the visual act of noticing what you record—helps you bring up information from a subconscious level." *The Money Tracker* also provides tips and success stories from those who have gained insight and control over their spending habits.

"There are different ways to put things together," Lawrence acknowledges, "but there are several advantages to using this type of tool. If all the information is there, you have everything you need in one place for budgeting, taxes, and other financial records."

The Budget Kit also contains a section for keeping track of child support payments and visitation records, as well as writing down essential information about your ex and your case—job information, Social Security number, court order number, and so on—that may be required for child support enforcement. "One of my clients had a constant problem with her ex paying child support late, often with a check that was no good," Lawrence recalls. "So I included a place where people with similar issues could develop a record to take to a judge or child support case worker, and to remind them of the information they need to have for enforcement."

Lawrence states that it is often hard for people to think of all the details they need to record, and tools such as *The Budget Kit* do the thinking for them. "But when you make the effort to fill in the information, this also boosts your sense of control," she comments. "There is something about using pencil and paper that feels different than using a computer. Although *The Budget Kit* and many other programs are available in CD-ROM, I advise people to begin by using the traditional paper method, then going to a computer if they choose." Lawrence believes that the manual act of putting down the information, like putting together a puzzle, helps people better understand the basic concepts, and triggers brain functions that are not accessed when a computer is used. Her theory has received support from a computer science and finance teacher, who told her that he always starts his students with *The Budget Kit* book for that reason, before moving on to the computer version.

Workbooks such as *The Budget Kit* are also a handy way to keep essential records in one place in case of emergency. "One of my Florida clients told me she keeps her past and current copies of *The Budget Kit* in her 'hurricane box'—the metal box with essential records she can grab quickly if she has to evacuate," Lawrence remarks.

Organizing your financial life is also tremendously empowering. "When you get the full picture put together, it gives you a sense of control," says Lawrence. "It allows you to be proactive about your money, rather than reacting when the bills come in. You will be able to see your choices about how you can make your financial life workable."

Lawrence believes that the key to making wise choices, both in finance and in other facets of life, is to pay attention and stay conscious of your actions and decisions. "Especially after a divorce, when people feel overwhelmed, it is easy to slip into autopilot or denial," she explains. "That's when emotional spending kicks in. People need to maintain a focus on what is important for healing, on getting back on their feet financially, and remember that they are role models for their children."

Lawrence feels that the latter is especially important. "Kids need to see a model for staying centered, to learn what it takes to make their own decisions and not get caught up in outside influences," she says. "For example, the family should sit down and plan what the children will need to get ready for school, instead of just spending a day wandering around the mall, buying on impulse."

Yet in spite of her role as a budgeting guru, Lawrence is quick to emphasize that such planning should not be about deprivation. "The key is balance," she stresses. "Don't get into this mode of concentrating on what you and your kids can't have. Instead, be wise, conscientious consumers. Find ways to disconnect from the media bombardment that makes children, and adults, want so many things they don't really need or desire." Some families, she explains, have chosen to limit TV viewing, cancel mail-order catalogues, or even stop the newspaper to control the onslaught. "Awareness of your priorities is the key," says Lawrence. "Look at how your money is being spent, look at your priorities and what is important to you, not to others. Think it through."

When You Need Professional Advice

If you were married for a long time—and especially if you have children—your financial life is likely to change drastically after a divorce. Accountants, financial planners, and bank officers can help you map out your financial future and cope with changing day-to-day demands.

While Lawrence believes that the most important component of gaining financial independence is the work you do yourself, she also strongly advises turning to professionals for certain services that require expert advice. "I encourage people to meet with a professional planner, consultant, and accountant during the divorce process to be sure all financial concerns are being addressed to meet their needs. It is also valuable to meet again with these experts during the first year after a divorce," she says.

Taxes can be an especially important area to address. "Taxes can be very complicated, and it really helps to have an accountant make sure everything is in order," Lawrence advises. The way you structure such matters as investments, retirement accounts, the sale of a home, and other everyday changes can have important tax consequences before and after the divorce. The advice of a good tax accountant is well worth the cost.

Also bear in mind that if the IRS should discover any shortfall in payment during the years of your marriage, it can go after both spouses to collect on the debt. The IRS, however, also recognizes an "innocent spouse rule," whereby a spouse who can prove he or she knew nothing about the activities of the other that led to the debt may be released from liability. If you find yourself subject to a demand by the IRS or any other taxing agency, immediately seek the advice of a tax attorney or accountant experienced in these matters.

DIVORCE AND WORK

People often become distracted from career concerns during a divorce. The period that follows can be an excellent time to take stock of your work life and either infuse your present job with new energy or consider making a change.

A word of caution: Resist the urge to change jobs impulsively. Work changes always add to stress, even if the change is positive. Change may be risky. Also, your work associates can be a good source of support and stability. The best way to proceed if you are sure you want to make a change is by careful consideration, then slow, step-by-step progression.

Divorce often impacts a person's occupational life, especially that of women who were out of the workforce as mothers for all or part of their married lives. These women, often called "displaced homemakers," may emerge from a marriage ill equipped to earn enough to become financially stable on their own. A forty-year-old woman who married young and devoted her energies to raising a family may leave a marriage with about the same employment skills as an eighteen-year-old—but with far greater responsibilities. Yet, as discussed previously, spousal support, when it is awarded at all, is almost always temporary unless the recipient is elderly or disabled. This legal principle is based on the notion that all competent adults should be able to support themselves after a reasonable time has been allowed for "rehabilitative" education or training.

The occupational and financial aspects of the time after divorce can be both exhilarating and terrifying. This may be an ideal time to consider a new direction or a career change, but survival must be the first priority. Many people need to further their educations or obtain the assistance of a vocational counselor in order to reestablish themselves in a satisfying work situation.

Today, there are many sources of such assistance. Colleges, professional organizations, community service centers, and other organizations offer career counseling and placement services, and sponsor career fairs and seminars. These individuals and groups can assist with vocational evaluation, training and retraining, résumé development, career coaching, and vocational rehabilitation services. Innumerable sources of help exist for those in a career transition. A perusal of the adult education materials from any community will reveal numerous classes for both practical training and personal growth.

Many communities also have special programs for those with particular needs. For example, in Santa Fe, New Mexico, a program called Women in Transition offers free workshops for single mothers and other women facing personal, financial, or employment challenges as a result of divorce, widowhood, or other changed circumstances. The focus is on assisting women in developing goals, establishing a positive self-image, and making the required preparations to enter the workforce.

Women in Transition takes a unique approach. "There are other programs to help displaced homemakers learn job skills, but the ones I am familiar with are not organized like ours," says Anita Shields, director of the Women's Resource Center at Santa Fe Community College. "Many focus on job hunting, résumé writing, and interview techniques. We deal with self-esteem and building healthy relationships first." The essential goal of the workshops, Shields explains, is to help women gain self-esteem and learn to be in charge of their lives, so they can discover where they want to go and how to get there. "Then they are motivated to pursue their new goals."

Women in Transition has grown to serve a broader group of participants since its inception in 1985, when it focused on displaced homemakers (women who have been in the home and out of the workforce). Shields states, "Everyone facing a transition into single life after marriage experiences trauma and grief, even women with successful careers and financial stability. We teach that the grief process doesn't happen overnight. Most people take between eighteen months and four years to work through it completely, depending on how much grief there is."

The program encompasses twenty-four hours, flexibly set up to accommodate participants' schedules. At the end, each woman receives assistance in taking the next step that is right for her. "The help we provide varies, according to each individual's needs," Shields explains. "Some go on to take specific courses at Santa Fe Community College, some go into job training programs, and others get free career counseling from Student Services. The women also share an incredible amount of information among themselves."

Shields believes that this group camaraderie is one of the program's most important aspects. "There is so much support and encouragement among the members of every group—sometimes I think I could leave these thirty or forty women in a room by themselves, and they would end up in the same place as they do at the end of the class," she laughs. "So many people think that they are the only ones going through this. When they find out that they are not alone, it is such a relief. A lot of long-lasting friendships and smaller support groups form after the program." Women who have been through the class also return on the first day of each new workshop to give testimonials. "It has changed lives," Shields remarks. "And the women always emphasize that life is a continuing work in progress, that they are on their own journeys, not that they have 'made it.' "

Kathy Potter, a career counselor who has also facilitated divorce support groups, has found that clients who come in for career counseling after a divorce are almost always coping with issues related to their home lives as well. "People often seek help on the career issues first, because these issues can seem less personal," Potter explains. "But most of the time, other things are going on, too. There is a ripple effect—like throwing a stone in a lake. A change in a person's relationships affect his or her job situation, and vice versa." Potter feels that career issues that arise after a divorce are some of the most complicated to address, for numerous reasons. "For women, even those who have good careers and were not completely dependent on their husbands for income, the idea of being totally self-supporting can be very challenging psychologically," she explains. "Then there is the issue of reacting to the loss and coping with the grief. For those whose husbands just left, or those who left the marriage themselves before thinking things through, there is often a delayed reaction. It takes awhile before the impact of the change hits, but when it does, a person's work life is inevitably affected."

Potter explains that any ending, even one that is very positive, such as leaving an abusive marriage, includes the loss of something, if only daily predictability and the continuity of a life that is a known entity. "There are three stages to any ending or change," she says, "a beginning, a middle, and an end. The middle stage is the hardest place to be, because people are uncertain where they are headed; they're in limbo. Facing the unknown can create tremendous anxiety." This is also the stage at which grieving the loss is essential if it hasn't yet taken place. "It's really difficult to work on career issues, solve problems, and make sound decisions about changes until you have dealt with these emotional issues," Potter explains.

Potter works with many women who face significant difficulties with low self-esteem or great anger after a divorce, as well as people who are caught up in battles with former spouses over issues related to their children. "It's harder to put resentments, anger, and conflicted feelings behind you if you have children," Potter explains, "because you will be tied to that person forever. There is always the potential for conflict—as well as a place to find similarities and build a new kind of relationship with your ex." Potter and her former husband were able to focus on their mutual love for their children and remain friends after they divorced. "We would go to the kids' soccer matches together, and people thought that was strange," she recalls. "But we both care about our sons, and we will always have them in common, so why not?"

Potter, like other mental health professionals, emphasizes that divorced parents should work hard at finding a way to establish a civil relationship to avoid hurting their children as well as to be able to move on with the other aspects of their own lives. "I realize that this may be one of the hardest things people have to do," she says, "because the kids symbolize so many things about the relationship. But parents can't let themselves fall into the trap of using the children in a battle to hurt each other. More than overt hostility, I see a lot of passive-aggressive behavior expressed through their actions with the children, and this can be worse. For example, a parent will say one thing, and then behave in a contradictory manner—acting respectful and friendly to the ex, then always bringing the kids back late or early from a visit. This is terribly confusing for the children—it sends them mixed messages. Parents have to remember that whether they like it or not, they are role models for their kids, and such contradictory behavior really confuses them."

The anger that comes from waging this type of war can also have a profound effect on a person's ability to do his or her job. "If someone is battling with her ex, she can't focus on what she needs to do at work," she explains. "She will often take out that anger at work, although the source of the emotion is at home. Generally speaking, family problems are part

and parcel of work problems." Sometimes clients exhibit
problems so severe that Potter refers them to a counselor who
specializes in dealing with the underlying issue. "If someone is
in an abusive relationship, or addicted to drugs or alcohol
and still using, I can't help him much with his career issues
until he gets help in that other area," she says. "As a career
counselor, I can't respond to all of these major issues.
Sometimes people are looking for a quick fix, but the goal of
counseling is to work with the entire person who has a specific problem at this time in life that he or she needs assistance
in working through."

Potter does emphasize that an effective career counselor
has to work with the whole person. "I let the client lead the
way, but if the issue seems to be one that I am not qualified to
help with, I'll refer the client for counseling on the particular
issue—and either continue working on the career issue at the
same time, or suggest that we continue our work when the
client has received some relief in the other area." Potter esti-
mates that about 90 percent of the clients who come to her
have other issues besides career alone. "People go to counseling focused on one problem—they get caught up in what is at
the forefront without seeing the other issues."

She emphasizes that there is seldom a quick fix, and making a major transition is always a process. "This is what I
enjoy, though," she explains. "People come in because they
want to work on a transition of some kind, and while there
are commonalities among clients, every situation is different.
We explore what is going on and create a process the particular person can use. I hear fascinating stories, and I learn so
much from people."

Potter acknowledges that women more often face financial
difficulty after a divorce than men, and believes that it is generally best for a woman to take the necessary steps to maximize her earning potential as soon as possible, rather than, as

some advise, to hold off on seeking greater earnings so that she will get more support from the ex-spouse. "There are exceptions, of course," she states. "But usually, the best advice is to do what you need to do now, in order to get on with your life. If you're in doubt about a financial support issue, get the advice of a good attorney."

Potter also advises against making drastic career changes too soon after a divorce. "I would never tell someone to shelve their dreams forever, but people do need to be practical first," she says. "Look at your short-term needs as well as your long-term goals. For example, if someone has a dream of becoming a ballet dancer, I would advise her to consider taking classes and continuing to work toward that goal, but to keep working at her day job while she's at it."

Potter's work often involves the process of getting to the root of an employment problem that has a deeply disguised cause. "I had one client," she recalls, "who came across as very sweet, on the surface. But there was some body language that didn't match. She had been able to obtain job interviews, but she wasn't getting the job offers. As we talked, she confided that she had been in a difficult relationship, had been through some drug problems, felt discriminated against in the past because of her ethnic background, and had developed a sense of herself as a victim. There was a lot of anger buried inside of her. She was totally unaware of what she was conveying nonverbally."

Potter feels that bringing out such feelings can be a crucial step in getting a handle on what may be causing job-related difficulties that don't seem to have explanations. "I don't mean this in the sense of the talk-show, tell-all mentality," she explains. "But people need to say more to an empathetic, objective listener whom they trust." Potter also finds that when people make statements to such a listener, they are often surprised to hear what they have said when it is repeated back to them. "People make casual comments that reveal a lot," she explains. "For example, a man once said to me, 'I would do anything to get out of this job but the work I do is really interesting . . .' He had no idea of the possible contradiction he was expressing, or obviously feeling," she said.

Potter uses different techniques to draw her clients out. "Sometimes it's like the analogy of the elephant in the living room," she remarks, "that everyone pretends is not there. Everyone has been avoiding something that seems so obvious. Once you realize and acknowledge that the elephant—the problem—is there, then you can discuss it."

Potter believes that the life change that comes with a divorce is often the "elephant," the obvious factor that triggers a desire to rethink a person's career. "Divorce forces most people into some self-assessment," she explains. "People may not be able to see things clearly during this time, because there is so much changing in their lives. In career counseling, we help them take off the blinders. Sometimes they see things just a little bit differently, and sometimes they find a whole new world."

One tool Potter finds especially helpful for those in career transition is the Myers Briggs Type Indicator (MBTI) assessment instrument. "This is a tool that helps people clarify in a concrete fashion who they are in the world, how they interact with others, how they take in and make decisions about information, and how they structure their lives. It's about naturally dominant ways of seeing and doing things that can help people understand why they react to events and actions the way they do." Virtually no one to whom Potter has given the MBTI has been very surprised by the results. "Most say, 'Yep, that's me all right' when they read the descriptions of their personality type. A lot then say, 'Gee, this helps explain why I'm no longer married to Joe' or 'Now I see why that job at IBM was such a good fit for me.' The instrument takes things you may already know about yourself and puts the information in a workable format. It also indicates where your blind spots might be."

Potter is quick to emphasize that the MBTI doesn't explain everything about a person. "People are individuals; we're very complex, and no assessment instrument can explain everything," she says. "But the MBTI can outline certain dominant characteristics that can help you make sense of why it was difficult for you to live with a certain person or work in a particular job. If you're trying to live your life in a manner that is not in line with who you are, the incongruity will deplete your energy and take a toll in other ways as well."

While such assessment instruments are not useful to all individuals, for most, Potter believes, they can be a very useful tool for self-knowledge. "Knowledge, especially about who we are and how we interact, is power," she explains. "The information from these self-assessment tools, and the MBTI in particular, can confirm certain things about you that you probably already knew but may have considered personal shortcomings instead of your perfectly natural traits. For example, a lawyer who is having a hard time working in litigation may be one of the personality types that finds interpersonal conflict difficult to handle. Having an explanation for something like that can help us make wise choices in both careers and relationships."

The MBTI is a written questionnaire on values, preferences, and attitudes that is fairly fast and inexpensive to complete. It is most effective when administered by someone certified to interpret the results, so that accuracy is ensured and the subject's questions can be answered when the results are discussed. There are also books and Internet sites, however, that provide the MBTI and instructions for scoring. Many counselors, therapists, college counselors, and employers also provide the assessment at little or no cost. If you are contemplating a career change or looking for new job ideas, the Myers Briggs Indicator can be a valuable tool and a source of insights about yourself and your natural abilities.

Potter, like other mental health professionals, believes that the time required for self-assessment and healing after a divorce varies, depending on the individual. "Most people need something tangible to mark the transition—a ritual or ceremony works for some, for others journaling helps, and some need counseling. But what happens inside you is what matters."

"People have to come to self-acceptance and understanding on their own time," she explains. "Those who decide to work on themselves will get where they're going when they need to get there. Often, they seek help when they feel stuck. The good news is that by taking the step of self-assessment, the process has begun. Once they've opened the door, it may swing back and forth, but it won't be completely shut again."

Potter finds it especially rewarding to help her clients find resources within themselves they were unaware existed. "Often, when people ask what to do about a particular problem, such as the loss of a job, I ask whether they have confronted a similar situation before, and what they did about it," she explains. "Many people have faced the same or a comparable situation and dealt with it successfully. They are often surprised to see that they have handled life as well as they have, that they have remarkable coping abilities, resources they don't know about. They often know what's the best thing to do, what works, but at the time I see them, they are blocked. I've read a person's résumé, or listened to their stories, and remarked, 'You know, you really are amazing'— and had them burst into tears. No one had ever said anything like that before, and they had considered themselves such failures, yet they have survived and accomplished some truly remarkable things." When we change the way we look at a situation, counselors call this "reframing." This can be a powerful tool for adjusting the way in which we view our past achievements, as well as our present circumstances and our future potential.

7

Planning and Streamlining Your New Life

T HE PERIOD OF TIME AFTER A DIVORCE IS, FOR MANY, A TIME of rethinking and restructuring virtually all areas of life, whether by necessity or design. Many people, especially those who were married for a long time, find it difficult to forge a new image of themselves as single persons, and to see time alone as a blessing. "People need to realize that there is a positive side to being alone," counselor Kathryn Lang explains. "Also, often, if a person takes a realistic look back at the marriage, she realizes that the person she was married to was emotionally unavailable, so her life isn't really that different and she is, in fact, in a better place now. She can make choices and changes."

Yet Lang acknowledges that gaining such a perspective is very difficult for some people. "So many people have such a fear of being alone, such a fear of abandonment and betrayal," she states. "They can't see the future, can't visualize any new partners who would want them. Their perceptions are distorted by the past relationship, especially if they were put down by their former spouses. Yet when people realize that they have already been alone for years, by being with persons who were emotionally and sometimes physically unavailable, the light turns on."

One way to combat loneliness is by reframing the way you view time spent by yourself. Instead of asking, "What will I do with myself?" ask, "Now that I'm free and don't have to do things someone else's way, what would I like to do? What do I enjoy doing? What new things would I like to try?" Perhaps you've wanted to join a readers' or writers' group, but thought you didn't have the time. Maybe you've thought it would be fun to take a photography class, pick up season tickets to the theater or opera, work on a political campaign, check out the music at the new blues club downtown, join a gym, or play some golf. Think about what you've longed to do in the past, pick up a newspaper, and find out what's going on that you would like to try. If you don't want to delve into a new activity on your own, look for a club or group that sponsors trips or classes in your area of interest. Or call a friend who might like to join you.

This is also a good time to reach out to those "couple friends" you want to keep close. Many people feel awkward when friends divorce, and although they want to maintain the relationship with one or both people, they aren't sure how to proceed. Take the initiative, and those friendships that are meant to endure will find a new form. Some people feel that they must wait until they are dating again to enjoy the company of couples. This is not so—the rigid social structures of the past are almost completely extinct. Most couples are pleased to include single friends in social events.

Consider the new identity you must forge, and what you want it to be. This is when you should take stock of your new choices, options, and desires. Reevaluate your goals. This may be the right time to revive an old dream or discover a new one. Reflect on what your passions are. What things still hold the same magic for you that you experienced as a child? What were you dying to do during your marriage, but felt too busy or constrained to try? Ask yourself, what do I really want in life? A different kind of work? Travel? That biology degree— or perhaps architecture? Is the Victorian cottage near the park still my dream home, or is a low-maintenance apartment in the city near the shore a better option?

BALANCING BOLDNESS
WITH GOOD TIMING

The philosopher and poet Goethe said, "Whatever you can do, or dream you can, begin it. Boldness has genius, power, and magic in it." It is no wonder that such encouraging words are so often quoted, or that so many have found inspiration in them. Taking the first step toward a cherished goal can, quite literally, set you on the path that will change your life.

But remember, Goethe advised a bold beginning, not a blind leap of faith. He also said, "To put your ideas into action is the most difficult thing in the world." The most effective leaps of faith are those with a solid backing and a carefully planned landing.

Many people feel a wild sense of exhilaration after a divorce. They feel free, renewed, ready to take on anything the world has to throw their way. By all means, take advantage of this energy—but proceed with some degree of caution before embarking on irrevocable life changes. You may be functioning as a "loose cannon" at a time when you feel the greatest certainty you have had in years. Counselor John Gray warns that when you are in pain and confused after a divorce, this is not always the best time to trust your instincts. As I was often admonished as a child, "Look before you leap!"

Some transitions can be accomplished in five minutes. Others rightfully require five years to come to complete fruition. If you feel a sudden overwhelming urge to paint the living room, go ahead—if you decide next week you hate it, you can paint it again, and be out no more than a few hours and the cost of a couple of cans of paint. There's no great risk in this sort of endeavor. On the other hand, people sometimes make drastic changes without first thinking them through, then find themselves still reeling from the aftershocks of the impulse ten years later. Do you really want to march into your boss's office and tell the old geezer what he can do with this penny-ante job? Maybe—but think it over first.

If you find yourself feeling a strong call to make a significant alteration in your life, spend some time on careful consideration before you commit to changes you won't be able to reverse. Listen to your heart, your head, and your intuition. Be sure you're making a proactive choice, not a reactive mistake. Wait until you feel the time is right. Realize that you have many choices, and that your initial impulse may or may not be the right one. Think about your options and alternatives for proceeding into your new life.

In his outstanding book *Callings: Finding and Following an Authentic Life,* author and teacher Gregg Levoy advises, "Rather than asking 'Who am I?' we might ask, 'In how many ways can I be myself?' Rather than asking 'What is my place in the world?' the question might be better put, 'In how many ways can I experience a sense of belonging to the world?' "

When you are sure that you want to make a drastic alteration in your life, when the time you have spent in quiet reflection, active dialogue, and other forms of assessment yields an unequivocal "Yes!" then it is time to begin. Given the reality of your financial situation and current responsibilities, you might not be able to make the changes you want all at once, but setting goals and taking the first step can provide not only a motivating direction but a powerful beacon to pull you through the inevitable down times.

I once worked for a corporation that had, as one of its motivational mottos, "Yard by yard it may be hard, but inch by inch it's a cinch." This is very sound wisdom. Start taking those little steps toward the edge of the shore, but wait until the time feels ripe before you make a headlong dive into uncharted waters. Make sure you have a realistic picture of your life as it is in the present before you make new commitments.

GRATITUDE AND SIMPLICITY

The time after a divorce is always a time of reflection, of taking stock, and of planning new directions. It provides an ideal opportunity to carefully consider the blessings in your life, as well as the things you would like to change.

Many people today are seeking more meaning and less clutter—physical, emotional, and spiritual—in their lives. The current desire to simplify is hardly surprising in a world glutted with sensory overload, media-driven consumerism, and unrewarding excess. Many are seeking to pare down their lives to enjoy more quality and less quantity.

Simplicity, as most use the term today, does not mean austerity. Rather, it means taking the time to make thoughtful choices about the things, people, and activities in your life, instead of habitually acquiring more and more unnecessary and unwanted stuff that ultimately becomes more of a burden than a blessing. It also means seeing beyond yourself to consider not only your own desires, but the needs and future of the earth and its other inhabitants.

People seeking to simplify their existence do so for a variety of reasons, most often to achieve a better quality of life, to become more environmentally responsible, to enhance the spiritual aspect of their lives, or a combination of these goals.

The period of transition presented by divorce can be the perfect time to reassess your own needs and desires and consider adopting a daily pattern of living more in line with your authentic values and goals.

Many books are now available on simplifying life, and I have listed some of these in the Appendix. Do bear in mind that the ideas these books present are flexible, and that some will likely resonate more with your individual sensibilities than others. All contain wisdom from which you may be able to glean insights on how you may want to simplify and refocus your own priorities and mode of living.

Budget counselor Judy Lawrence, along with Jane Bluestein and SJ Sanchez, recently coauthored *Daily Riches: A Journal of Gratitude and Awareness.* Lawrence believes that the time after a divorce is a time to actively seek silver linings. "It may not be possible at first," she says, "but with healing, most people can look back and be grateful for something that came out of the whole experience."

Lawrence constantly encounters people who found a part of themselves they would not have discovered without going through the divorce. "It brings a gift of perspective," she explains. "Through the pain comes transformation. For those who can be flexible enough to shift their thinking, divorce can crack open old beliefs and open you up to new thoughts, people, circles, and experiences."

More and more tools are becoming available to those seeking to refocus on life's gifts, even those gifts that are packaged within adversity. *Daily Riches,* for example, is designed to help readers focus their thoughts and perceptions in a positive direction, reframe negative events in terms of growth and the benefits they allow, and consider alternatives to scarcity consciousness and victim thinking. It is divided into twelve sections that include brief, inspiring stories from others who have weathered tough times to emerge better for having done so. *Daily Riches* also includes quotations, suggested activities, and pages for journalizing.

Sarah Ban Brethnach's best-selling *Simple Abundance,* along with various companion volumes, has also helped innumerable people reassess their lives and realign their perspectives toward a focus on the abundant gifts and blessings that can easily be obscured by life's daily challenges. *Callings,* by Gregg Levoy, will prove especially useful to those seeking to find a new, authentic direction in life following the upheaval wrought by divorce.

These three books are just a few of my personal favorites among the dozens of excellent guides for self-direction available today. Peruse the shelves of your local library or bookstore, and try a few on for tone and fit. Not all will grab you, but with so many fine volumes currently available you will be almost certain to find something that will offer you a sense of comfort, peace, reassurance, and guidance in redirecting your trying present toward a richer and more rewarding future.

Sometimes shifts in attitude and outlook, along with new insights into life, come to us in the form of synchronicities—those remarkable occurrences that go beyond mere coincidence, yet are easy to miss if we are not attuned to their possibilities. In *Daily Riches*, the story is told of a woman who was seeking a new relationship, but having little success in drawing the right sort of person into her life. She had decided to clean out an old, cluttered shed at the rear corner of her property, on the advice of a feng shui consultant who offered guidance for restructuring her home according to the ancient Japanese philosophy that equates the harmony of our surroundings with various other aspects of life. When she began working on the shed, she pulled away an old piece of carpet that had covered a window. Then she noticed a sign in the window that warned, "Keep Out!" Although she had lived in the home for twenty years, she had never realized the sign or window was there. Tearing up the sign, as well as uncovering the window, became a symbolic act. She continued refurbishing the shed, including adding a "Welcome" sign to the door, and a short time later found herself in a new relationship that was, as she described it, "More supportive, richer, and respectful than I ever could have imagined."

GETTING ORGANIZED

Judy Lawrence believes that clearing out and reorganizing possessions can have a powerful effect on a person's psyche. She now serves as a professional organizer, in addition to her other endeavors. "This work evolved as an offshoot of my financial consulting," she explains. "A woman who had hired me to help organize her financial files went through a difficult divorce, and a major lifestyle change. She and her husband had been quite well-to-do, living in a five-thousand-square-foot home and entertaining regularly. After the divorce, she moved to a home about half that size in a different state. Many of her possessions were still in boxes in the basement after she had lived there a couple of years. Her therapist recommended she hire someone to help her organize these things, so she called me."

Lawrence explains that people can become overwhelmed by their possessions. "After a divorce, getting your things in place can feel like a priority," she says. "But do wait until the timing feels right. Some people need to put it off for awhile— sometimes months or even years—until they feel ready to face it. There are so many other things going on, so much to assimilate and deal with. But when you are able to clear old things away, it gives you a great boost. Until you take care of your possessions, there is a subconscious nagging that drains your energy. One of my clients commented when we had finished a huge job—in her case it took a full week—that she felt as if fifty pounds had been lifted from her shoulders."

Lawrence advises those who feel ready to face the task, yet see it as an overwhelming burden, to seek help. "Call a relative, a friend, or a professional organizer," she suggests. "They can help you deal with the emotional aspects as well as the work." Be sure to choose someone with a good sense of empathy, who will assist you in making decisions without trying to make them for you. Lawrence feels that her background in counseling has helped her in this facet of her work. "To help someone effectively, it's necessary to be able to tune into people," she comments. "It's a job that has to be done by bits and pieces, and there will always be a big pile of papers and household stuff that only the person who owns it can make the decision on whether to toss it or keep it and how and where to file it."

Even if you're fairly well organized on your own, the time that follows a divorce is a prime opportunity to regroup and be sure you know the location of things you may need for various practical purposes. If you do not already have your important documents in a safe place, organized so that you are able to quickly put your hands on what you need, this is an ideal opportunity to get these matters in order. Vital documents should be stored in a safe-deposit box at your bank, or in a fireproof box or filing cabinet at your home. If you have children, make sure to keep the basic information on your former spouse, such as his or her Social Security number. You may need this information for tax matters, children's school records, or support enforcement.

Be sure that you attend to practical business matters. Have you acquired all of the important papers required to finalize the property settlement? Things such as deeds to property, evidence that bank and credit accounts have been closed or transferred to one name only, car titles? If not, take the necessary steps to finish this business.

If your children do not have Social Security numbers, contact your local Social Security office and have them issued. The numbers will be required for various purposes, including dependent tax deductions, school records, and, possibly, enforcement of support orders.

Take a final look at your divorce documents before filing them away. Are all the loose ends taken care of? For example, if you were awarded the family home in the divorce settlement, your spouse should have signed a quitclaim deed relinquishing his or her legal title to the property. Insurance, retirement, and investment documents should all be revised with the assistance of the agent, trustee, or administrator to reflect the provisions of the decree. Wills should be changed promptly.

YOUR NEW HOME

Kathryn Lang, a licensed professional mental health counselor, works with many people who are at various stages in the divorce and recovery process. "When you get divorced, your life is displaced," she explains. "This is especially true for the person who leaves the home. The one who stays in the home, usually the woman, keeps some familiar structure. In a new home, everything is new. It's especially helpful if children can stay in the home they know."

Whether you're building a new home in a new house or apartment, or restructuring the old one after your spouse has departed, creating a new home environment can be one of the most uplifting and symbolic, as well as one of the most daunting, duties following a divorce. If you haven't yet faced the process of sorting out and rearranging your belongings, set a timetable for completing the task and, if you don't want to face it alone, enlist the help of a close friend or family member with a positive and supportive outlook, or consider hiring a professional organizer. An independent organizer can provide practical skills as well as emotional support, and can remain objective, since he or she is not emotionally tied to the situation in any way.

Whatever route you decide to take, if you are in a new apartment and still living out of boxes after six months, or still facing empty closets and gaping reminders of your spouse's absence in the family home, it is time to take action. Your surroundings can have a profound effect on your emotional health.

Living alone after years of living with another is a huge adjustment for some. Many people, especially men who leave the family home, are at a loss as to how to establish a new, comfortable dwelling. While it is important to keep budgetary constraints in mind, resist the temptation to sign a lease on the least expensive place available; consider that you will want to bring friends and eventually dates to your home. If you have children, consider their need for some space to claim as their own. Also, bear in mind the proximity to their school and other locations important to them, such as a community center where they like to play basketball with their friends.

On the other hand, some underestimate their financial responsibilities, especially if the other spouse paid the bills, and overcommit to a new home beyond their means. This adds to stress and the sense of being overburdened. Try to reach a happy medium. Sprucing up need not be expensive. A few house plants, several gallons of paint, and a couple of flea market finds can transform your abode into a new nest that is entirely your own, and many people take great pleasure in this ritual.

Acquiring new furnishings for your home, whether it is at a new location or in the same place, can give you an emotional lift. Surrounding yourself with things that reflect your own taste and preferences can help symbolize the new life you're building.

Again, it is important to watch expenditures, but with a little imagination, some paint, and a few carefully chosen treasures you can transform a dwelling without overspending.

RITUAL

Since ancient times, people have followed rituals to symbolize major life transitions, to mark progressions from one phase of life into another, and to provide reassurance to a person facing a challenging passage that it is a normal part of life. Although modern society has abandoned many of the ceremonies that were once common in nearly all cultures, we still have social customs to celebrate birth, marriage, and graduation, to observe holidays, and to mourn death. Yet there are no established rituals to mark the end of a marriage or the beginning of a new family afterwards. As a result, many people report feeling bereft when facing such significant transitions. "No rites of passage exist to help mourn the losses, to help healing, to help solidify newly acquired roles," writes Constance Ahrons in *The Good Divorce*.

Many therapists who work with people recovering after a divorce believe that ritual can be a crucial part of the process. Ahrons states, "I'd like to see us get to a time when a parting ritual for divorce is part of our culture." Fortunately, there does appear to be a growing trend, as divorce becomes more common throughout the world, to mark the occasion, not with mourning but with the recognition that it is an important life passage that can lead to positive new beginnings.

Rituals may be in the form of a shared ceremony or a private event. I recently participated in an unusual celebration designed by a woman who enjoys attending Renaissance Faires. She regularly posts on an Internet newsgroup for Faire enthusiasts, where regular subscribers get to know one another, exchange information, and plan to meet at the Faires. When she arranged a party at a Faire near her home to celebrate her new life on the day her divorce was to become final, she asked cyberfriends from the group to join her in a toast to her freedom at a set hour on a Saturday afternoon, adjusted for time zones around the country. A group of us who follow the newsgroup were attending the Georgia Renaissance Faire in costume, and gathered to raise our glasses at the appointed hour. Others across America and even a few overseas did the same. Photos were taken and mailed to her to mark the occasion.

Lynn Peters, a jeweler and the owner of a graphic design company, came up with a unique idea several years ago when she noticed her old wedding band collecting dust in a drawer. She now runs a business called "Freedom Rings: Jewelry for the Divorced." "The idea came from my own divorce," she explains. "The ring laid in the drawer for three years. One day I realized what a waste it was, and decided I should recycle it." She decided to invite a group of friends to join her in a ceremony to smash the old ring, which she would then fashion into a new piece of jewelry. Thus a new tradition was born, complete with a humorous yet encouraging "vow," supportive friends, and champagne to celebrate the new beginning.

Peters's own divorce was difficult, and included a courtroom battle. Yet when it was over, she felt a lack of finality. "One day the decree just arrived in the mail. I remember thinking, is this it? After all this time and misery and bullshit, is this all there is to it?" Peters feels that she never really put the divorce behind her until she went through the ritual. "When I bashed the ring, I released the past, and recreated a symbol of freedom with my old wedding ring."

Peters decided to offer the ceremony to others, and a poll of her divorced friends revealed great enthusiasm for the idea, as well as an amusing collection of anecdotes about what usually happens to old wedding rings. "People pawn them, give them away, throw them in the nearest sewer or lake—or at the ex!" Peters cringed at the waste of precious metal and gem-stones and saw the need for a healthier outlet for both the jewelry and any lingering anger. In her Freedom Rings ceremony, clients smash the old ring with a sledgehammer on an anvil, preparing for meltdown into a new design. In the process, many exorcise a few lingering emotional demons.

Levity and laughter are inevitably a part of the event, but Peters is quick to respond to those who accuse her of trivializing divorce. "It's a fun way of dealing with a serious issue," she explains. "The humor is very healing, and the jewelry becomes a symbol of recovery, confidence, and feeling good about being single. Some clients say a few words before the ceremony; occasionally there are tears. But in the end, the focus is always on making a fresh start with a positive outlook."

According to Clayta Spear, who was one of Peters's first clients, "Going through the Freedom Rings ceremony with my friends present was really an experience. It provided a ritual that was therapeutic for me, and the opportunity to do something creative with my lingering anger and sadness. I still had my ring and my ex-husband's, and I wanted to turn them into something positive, something entirely new and beautiful. We designed a pendant using the gold and a pearl from the Philippines. The rings and the pearl represented two of the most dramatic and important times in my life, and I love the final product—it's an original, and people always notice it." Other Freedom Rings clients often speak of similar feelings, noting the sense of release provided by the ritual, and the symbol of transformation embodied in creating new jewelry from the old rings.

Others have created personal rituals, such as M. Carol Curtis, who held a "wake" on the date of her wedding anniversary. She donned clothing from the time of her marriage, lit candles, and put on music from the era. The fact that the clothes no longer fit well served as a physical reminder that many aspects of her old life during the marriage were restrictive and no longer fit the woman she had become. Curtis also created a collage with pictures symbolizing both the positive and negative sides of her marriage, which she later burned in her fireplace. Now, to replace the celebration of her wedding anniversary, she enjoys a special day with her daughter each year to mark the date she resigned from her job to become a full-time mother. "We have the opportunity to create rituals that suit our special situations and ease our transition into a new life," she says.

SOCIAL RECOVERY

Divorce, for most, means a restructuring of many aspects of your social life. It is important to remember that you have a whole array of options you may not have considered before, because you were comfortably ensconced in the role of being half a couple. You may have to remind yourself that other people can and do have active, full social lives that include going out on their own, in groups of friends, and in groups based on common interests through clubs, tours, and classes.

Many recently divorced people find their first foray into the social world unsettling. Venturing back into old social circles inevitably brings discomfort as you present yourself to those who knew you as part of a couple, in the role of a newly single person that may be awkward for both you and them. Exploring new social territory is sometimes easier, but in a new scene you are on your own without the comfort of a familiar support group.

Going out in the company of one or more trusted, supportive friends can help ease this transition. It will take time to settle into your new role as a single person, and this is to be expected. In her book *The Best Is Yet to Come*, Ivana Trump advises the recently divorced to steel themselves for the first time they will run into the ex-spouse out with a date. This is the time to remember your pride, keep your dignity, and refuse to let your ex ruin one more moment of your life.

Above all, don't let the fear of awkwardness or embarrassment keep you home when you feel ready to get out and pursue your social life. On the other hand, some people have a tendency to leap into a new dating relationship they don't really want simply to have a social escort. This can play havoc with fragile emotions. Try to cultivate the ability to enjoy going to events on your own or with one or more friends, both male and female.

Ivana Trump describes the first year following divorce as one in which it is wise to plan for intense recuperation. She advises planning the holidays in advance and taking active steps to lock in a program to do something enjoyable. A weekend away with close friends can be pleasant, and may turn into a yearly ritual. Several single and divorced women I know routinely share Thanksgiving dinner together, sometimes on their own and sometimes in the company of children, dates, or other friends, including couples. Entertaining can be a positive experience if it is not turned into a stressful ordeal. This is probably not the time to plan a sit-down dinner for two dozen people. An informal buffet in which you prepare familiar favorite dishes, a pot luck, or a cookout, however, can be an opportunity to enjoy and renew supportive friendships.

Trump advises those making the transition after divorce to continue with some of the traditions and rituals they have enjoyed throughout their married lives. For example, Trump continued to host a weekend getaway she had long sponsored for female buddies, as well as a Christmas luncheon to which she invited old friends of both genders. As many others do, Trump found that those who have been through a divorce can be especially supportive during this time.

FRIENDS

When two people divorce, many others outside the immediate family are affected. Family members, especially in-laws, along with friends, co-workers, and other members of the couple's community will also experience emotional reactions to the couple's decision to divorce. They may offer theories, feel confusion, and attempt to help in ways that may or may not be effective. Inevitably, the old network that was in place around a couple will collapse. Some friends are almost always lost, adding another trauma to an already difficult situation.

Many people feel great embarrassment and regret at having to tell others about the divorce. Yet this can also be an opportunity for valuable transition and growth. The friend who solidly stands by you through all of the upheaval, who listens and supports you, is a true treasure. Those who scurry away at the first sign of trouble have shown their true colors, as have those who viciously turn against you or seek to escalate the animosity between you and your former spouse.

Friends often react in strange ways when a couple divorces. Sometimes a good friend will withdraw just when you need her the most. There may problems in her own life that account for odd reactions. Is she in a shaky marriage? Still recovering from a divorce of her own? Sometimes a friend's divorce simply hits too close to home, making it difficult for the person to offer companionship or support.

One word of caution: Occasionally, friends do take sides when a couple divorces, or become overly judgmental, critical, or otherwise contribute to continuing difficulty between you and your ex. If you encounter such attitudes, this is the time to correct the problem or to move on. One kind of friend you do not need is the person who insists on saying and doing things that prolong your ties to the past and inhibit your ability to move forward. It may be cathartic to commiserate with a kindred spirit and have a good wallow now and then. But those who constantly harp about what a rotten and awful person you were married to, or put you down for having chosen such a loser, or who fuel the fire of any continuing controversy with your ex, are not helping you heal. If a close friend behaves this way, tell her or him what you do and do not need. True friends with your best interests at heart will comply with your wishes. Those who refuse are not worthy of your friendship.

Do make the effort to take the steps to maintain ties with friends who are important to you, both for continuity and support during your time of transition, and to establish new social networks. One of the most common ways divorced people meet new companions is through married friends.

Friends can be a treasured source of support as you face this transition. Those who ask how you are and genuinely listen, who offer to be there to talk and help you with practical matters such as sorting out old possessions, who offer specific assistance such as baby-sitting for a day, who tell you you're doing great (or can do great when you're not) and invite you along to fun activities are the people to gather around you now.

In most cases, a few old relationships will fall by the wayside when a marriage ends. Be philosophical about this—there will be casualties with any major life change. Some friendships, just like some marriages, are wonderful for a time but are not destined to last forever. Those with close bonds usually remain friends, while others progress naturally to an end. Think about jobs that ended, and the accompanying vows between friendly co-workers to keep in touch—vows that got lost in the inevitable reshuffling of lives and people.

Some, like Ivana Trump, report that they did not lose any true friends, only a few acquaintances who were really no loss. Divorce often separates the wheat from the chaff where friends are concerned. Old friends who stick by you can offer steadfast encouragement and the foundation of history, plus ties with the positive aspects of your past. New friends are valuable in another way, by teaching you about the person you are becoming. Trump and many others advise those who have divorced to reassure friends of both partners that they will not be required to take sides. She suggests that you ask them to keep confidential information to themselves, as even innocent gossip can be detrimental to maintaining a positive relationship with your ex.

Friends and family members often feel confused when someone close to them goes through a divorce. They want to help and provide support, but aren't certain how to go about doing so. Don't hesitate to tell them what you do and do not need. Most people still grappling with the transition from married to single life experience times when they want to talk about the divorce or the ex and times when they don't. Even your closest confidants, who have the best of intentions, cannot always be sensitive to how you feel.

Seek out the company of friends who offer good-natured companionship, regular communication, and a willingness to help you find the information that you need. Avoid those who constantly offer unsolicited advice or talk too much about the past, or who treat you as a victim. Learn to be assertive in a pleasant way if someone starts offering opinions or initiates the subject of your divorce when you're not in the mood to talk about it. Simply tell him you'd prefer not to discuss it at the moment. Anyone who becomes huffy or pushy in response is not behaving like the type of friend you need right now.

John Gray cautions that friends often rush those recovering from a loss to move on too quickly, acting out of compassion because they hate to see their friends suffering. These well-meaning people may also think, as you may as well, that you are being self-indulgent if you're not completely over your loss within a few weeks. Gray cautions that intellectually, you may feel ready to move on, when the heart still needs a few more weeks of grieving and healing time.

The restructuring of a social network is an essential step in recovery after a divorce. Some people become so embarrassed or overly concerned with the opinions of others that they let this public part of the divorce pass too quickly, either turning their backs on friends or, in an opposite reaction, depending on friends to rescue and do the emotional work for them. The key is to pass through the critical time with as much grace as possible and then begin to rebuild. It often takes an unexpectedly long time to make peace with the network, but things will eventually settle into place.

FAMILY

Family members are often at a loss as to how to react or behave when one of the family divorces. Divorce affects an entire family emotionally. A parent may be frightened for her child when he or she loses a mate, on a number of different levels. Parents worry about how their offspring will cope emotionally, how they will survive physically, and how the divorce will affect them financially.

Parents, naturally, tend to take the side of their own children in a divorce. This is to be expected, but some parents take this form of loyalty too far, by encouraging the child to fight instead of settle on disputed issues, or by constantly putting down the former spouse. Of course, a good wallow with plenty of emotional unloading can be cathartic in the early stages after divorce, if it eventually ends or evolves into humor (one of my family member's especially unpleasant ex-husband is still, twenty years after the divorce, referred to as "Fang"). The key is not to let genuine hostility or bitterness persist for too long; the divorced person should be encouraged not to become stuck and to move forward to focus on the positive aspects of a new life.

If a parent or other family member repeatedly insists on stating what a monster your ex is, find a diplomatic way to let him know that you realize he means well, but this hostile rehashing is not what you need. The best method is to jump in right away if someone starts in with a barrage of criticism against your ex (or against you), and tell her that you don't want to discuss the past.

Those who were close to their in-laws find it very difficult to lose these extended family members with a divorce. This need not be the inevitable result. Many people find that if they can make peace with their past, they can maintain a new type of friendship with former in-laws. This is especially important for families with children, who need the loving influence of adults who have been important in their lives, especially during times of upheaval.

CHAPTER

8

Dating, Remarriage, and Blended Families

IN THE EARLY STAGES FOLLOWING A DIVORCE, MANY PEOPLE SWEAR that they will never again want anything whatsoever to do with members of the opposite sex. For most, these feelings gradually mellow and they find their interest in dating returning. For others, however, the choice to live without a romantic relationship becomes permanent, and they are able to establish happy and fulfilling lives without one. Others have close and loving relationships but do not remarry. Still others find that they miss the sharing and commitment of the day-to-day intimacy with a spouse, and are anxious to marry again.

All of these choices are perfectly fine and healthy, so long as they are just that—choices. Those who remain alone out of bitterness and unresolved anger, rather than a conscious decision that this is the route they wish to take, have not completed the emotional process of divorce. It is important to take it slow and explore different opportunities and avenues, but to do so within a healthy set of boundaries.

Another common response to the fresh pain following divorce is to quickly dive into another serious relationship.

John Bradshaw believes that this is one of the most damaging steps that can be taken, because the new relationship is based on neediness rather than on choice, and is used to mask painful emotions that should be faced. Those who remarry or recommit quickly out of an unbearable need to escape loneliness are cheating themselves, as well as their new partners, out of the grieving and healing that must necessarily precede the healthy entry into a new committed relationship.

Of the two extremes, the latter is the more dangerous, because those who rush into another relationship do both themselves and their partners a disservice. Moreover, in a healthy person hostility tends to dissipate more quickly than dependence. According to psychologist Mel Krantzler, these extreme attitudes are mirror images, both based on fear. He and other professionals emphasize the importance of time without a partner to renew a sense of self-worth, let feelings heal, and learn to be whole and content on your own.

"People who go into a new relationship too soon after a divorce take the same problems with them," says counselor Kathryn Lang. "In the long run, it usually doesn't work well. Often, two dependent people get together, and you end up with two halves trying to be a whole." After her own divorce, Lang slept with only one pillow on her bed for a time, to remind her that she had to heal and rediscover her own identity before becoming part of a couple. "I realized, in hindsight, that I'd never learned who I was before. I needed that time alone to discover my wants and needs, to figure out who I was." Lang waited ten years before marrying again. "I was a lot more cautious the second time around," she remarks. "I believe that it is really important to know who you are and to be whole before you can have a healthy relationship."

The question of when the time is right to start dating again after a divorce is one with no definite answers. John Gray states that when you are able to think of your ex without pain and in a peaceful way, this is a signal that you are ready to get involved with someone new. The point where people are ready to begin dating again varies. Most know instinctively when the time is right. Unless you dive into an intense new relationship immediately upon splitting from your spouse, or five years have passed and you still have no desire to spend time with the opposite sex in any capacity, you're probably doing fine by following your own natural inclinations.

Once you have cleared away the old attitudes and detritus of your former relationship, you will likely reach a point at which you feel strong enough to risk your heart on a new one. Many people reenter the dating world far better prepared for these risks and rewards after they have been through a marriage, providing they took the time to learn and reflect on what they want and need, their expectations and dreams, where they will bend and where they will not.

Defining the point at which to stop looking back and turn to face forward can be a fine line. While it's important to be aware of what you learned from the former relationship, it's not so good to constantly compare new partners to your ex. Sometimes people find, as they try to start fresh, that they can't leave persistent thoughts of the ex in the past; they still have to grapple with leftover guilt, anger, and other unresolved emotions that serve as obstacles to forming new relationships. This may be a sign that you're not ready to date, or that you need some assistance in completing your resolution of these lingering issues.

Psychologist Mel Krantzler, who has written extensively on divorce recovery, believes that it is crucial to wait at least two years after a divorce before marrying again. He states that most people go through four phases of reacting to the opposite sex after a divorce. This process, according to Krantzler, involves both mourning and rediscovery. In the first "walking wounded" stage, people are dazed, fearful, and disoriented.

This is when the extreme reactions occur—either wanting to find a new partner immediately or never wanting anything to do with the other gender again. Krantzler and others advise that such feelings are normal, but that if they last more than six months, you may need therapy to move on to the next stage.

In the second phase, people are ready to test the waters. Krantzler calls this the "sex is everything" stage. This is both an exciting time and one of confusion and uncertainty, especially for those who have been out of the dating game for many years and feel unsure of current customs. The transition from married to single is always an adjustment, and for most it occurs naturally over time. Krantzler and others emphasize that this is a time to be enjoyed, and that the attraction of someone of the opposite sex is great medicine for a wounded ego. The whirlwind abates for most after a while, however, when people feel ready to move on to a more settled life.

Krantzler refers to the third stage as "come close but go away." This phase is often a natural progression from the previous time of social reentry, and occurs when you connect with someone special, but still feel ambivalent about becoming involved in an intimate relationship that could lead to a commitment. Krantzler and other counselors urge some risk taking, and remind us that there is no gain without some peril. Many people experience a series of fairly short but intense relationships during this phase, accompanied by unavoidable emotional upheaval. This is natural, and usually a positive experience in the long run if people avoid one of two common traps: marrying or living with someone too soon, or becoming involved with someone who is married or otherwise unavailable so you don't have to deal with the issue of commitment. Either of these steps can lead to emotional disaster.

Krantzler calls the final stage "intimacy without fear," in which one is prepared for deeper emotional involvement. At this time you may wish to be alone and take stock of what you really want and need, in terms of a partner as well as in the other facets of your life. Those who are reasonably happy with their lives overall are more likely to find a healthy, rewarding relationship with an equal partner, so this time for regrouping and reflection can be crucial. This is the point at which people come to realize that they must create their own happiness, not depend on a partner to "make" them happy, Krantzler explains. During this stage, people are most open to meeting someone special, perhaps when they least expect it, or discovering a surprising source, such as a person they knew in the past.

DATING

The first foray into the world of dating after divorce can be tricky. Author Erica Jong remarked in her memoir *Fear of Fifty* that after each of her three divorces she felt like Margaret Mead among the tribal cultures when she reentered the changed world of mating and dating. Yet the basics never vary—communication, respect, and consideration remain the foundation for all good human relationships.

Often, people tend to give their hearts away too easily, or to take the opposite approach and be so closed down and protective that they are unable to get beyond the most superficial relationships with others. This is not surprising, because most people are very vulnerable when they first begin exploring romance after a devastating end to a relationship that was supposed to last forever. Handle yourself with care.

Attention from a member of the opposite sex can be utterly intoxicating at this time, especially if you have lacked such appreciation in recent months or years. Enjoy and revel in this attention, but do try to keep it in perspective. Realize that it takes time to become comfortable with the new person that you have evolved to, and that some of your innocence has inevitably been lost. It takes time to regain your ability to trust.

For most people, the best way to reenter the dating scene is through pursuit of your own interests. If you take a class, become active in a professional organization, volunteer with a community service group, play a sport, or go out to events with friends, you are bound to meet people of both genders who share some of your interests. Fun should be your goal at this point—not finding a new marriage partner. Those who come on as desperate or predatory often scare potential dating partners away before any relationship has time to develop.

Seek out companions, both for friendship and potential romance, with whom you can enjoy activities of common interest, have pleasant conversations, and laugh. Keep your standards high; expect respect and courtesy and eliminate from your life any people who do not treat you in that manner. Those who are unkind, controlling, and, especially, abusive in any way have no place in your life. Now is the time to make the commitment to respect yourself first.

Sex

The issue of sex often presents an enticing, yet forbidding jungle to those emerging from a long-term, monogamous relationship. Many of the baby boom generation have been out of the dating scene since the free-wheeling days of the "PPPP" era—"postpill preplague." Before the scourge of AIDS brought this epoch to a close in the mid-1980s, dating and sex were completely different than they are today. Many divorced people of both genders now have to face not only the awkwardness and uncertainty of reviving a social ritual they assumed was behind them when they married, but also learn the practicalities of a whole new world involving condoms, HIV testing, and today's etiquette when becoming involved with a new partner.

Another complication arises from the fact that many people emerging from a marriage have not had satisfying sex, or sex at all, for months or even years. A phase of great excitement about new sexual frontiers, accompanied by a strong desire to enjoy new freedom and experiment with new partners, is normal. But those who embark on a phase of sexual experimentation do need to be cautious on several levels. A negative experience or a harsh rejection can set back recovery, hurt your self-esteem, and make you hesitant to begin other relationships. Again—and it can't be emphasized too strongly—the practice of safe sex is essential. It is not at all uncommon for women to carry their own condoms today; don't be shy or hesitant to do so. Many new couples discuss their sexual histories and arrange for HIV testing before they become physically intimate. Talk to single friends, your physician, or someone from Planned Parenthood or an AIDS prevention/information center if you feel awkward about this or need advice.

Some people feel great guilt if they allow themselves to indulge in a promiscuous phase. It is important to keep these flings in perspective, and remember that for most, this time is indeed a phase that will come to an end as the excitement wanes and casual relationships start to seem empty. For most, the phase of sex for its own sake eventually gives way to more meaningful intimacy in a committed relationship. This period can also be very satisfying for those with a rebellious nature who feel a need to symbolically say "to hell with the old marriage" and all the constraints that went with it.

Rediscovering your desirability and the exhilaration of romance can be a wonderful adventure. Attention and flattery can help rebuild self-esteem and launch the confidence that is essential to recovery. Learning to navigate the dating waters in a new era, with its accompanying thrills, rejections, and excitement, can be a great source of growth. A time of post-divorce friskiness can help restore confidence. It can be a shared connection that soothes loneliness, and a stepping-stone to a time when one will be ready to build more solid and loving relationships. Many look back on one postdivorce fling that holds special meaning, especially if it involved another person in a similar state. A fond and delectably naughty memory can be a talisman of hope and change.

For many people, however, especially women, casual sex poses a dilemma. "I know I'm not ready to get into another involved relationship, but I really do want sex. Yet I can't have it without all this emotion and feeling, and that always gets in the way," one woman complained. "It's like my heart and my sex organs are directly connected; if I sleep with someone, that's it—I'm in love." Those who do choose to take pleasure in their sexual freedom need to understand the risk of physical intimacy, and be careful not to jump into another committed relationship too early. And those who offer themselves sexually in the hope of winning a commitment can easily end up hurt.

As a matter of common decency to your partners, be sure you are honest about your intentions. If either person misperceives a casual encounter as the start of a serious relationship, rather than simply a romp, it can lead to pain and guilt.

One essential proviso to keep paramount no matter what your sexual proclivities: There is only one reason to have sex, ever, and that is that you really want to enjoy sex with that partner. Anyone who expects sex as "payment" for a date, or demands it after a certain number of evenings out, is not worthy of your attention. People today must understand that *no* means *no*. Of course, some may cajole and beg, but then take no for an answer, and this can be a great ego boost. The key is gracefully accepting that another person is not ready for sex. One who will not is not playing fair, and should be dumped.

You should realize that your first few sexual experiences after ending your marriage may not be the greatest of your life. Many people feel shy and awkward during this phase of rediscovery. This is perfectly natural; don't worry about it unless many months and numerous encounters have come and gone and you still can't relax.

A promiscuous phase that goes on indefinitely may be a sign that you are not moving forward. Sex, like other sources of distraction or defense mechanisms, can be used to avoid facing the grieving process that must come before real recovery can be achieved. Any source of pleasure enjoyed excessively can be misused to suppress the feelings that are important to face. People use sex, work, food, and even sleep to avoid confronting painful emotions. Enjoy this celebration of freedom, but stop for a reality check if a year or more has passed and you still have no desire for any but the most superficial relationships.

The first real relationship after a divorce is believed by some to be a central passage in the healing experience. Many encounter a "bolt of lightning" romance in the midst of sorting out the pain and doubt that follow a divorce. Therapists sometimes refer to this as the search for the romantic solution, and like a period of promiscuity, this "grand passion" can be a healthy transition.

The first serious relationship is usually experienced as a sudden intimacy, which will probably be temporary. It can affirm the existence of love, restore self-esteem, and distract a person from depression, anger, and ambivalence that seem to be persisting too long. The end of this connection is an important time of transition as well, in which many people become more philosophical that the end of a relationship does not mean the end of the world. It may be followed by more casual relationships or another serious relationship or two, eventually leading up to one that feels different, special—"the real thing."

Introducing Children to a New Partner

One of the most awkward aspects of reentry into the world of dating is how to balance and mesh dating with parenting. Most experts advise taking a casual, natural approach, in which the fact that a parent is seeing new people is not kept secret, but is a separate part of the parent's life. Most agree that children should not be introduced to or included in activities with the new partner until the relationship shows signs of becoming at least somewhat serious. Children sometimes form swift emotional attachments, and become confused or hurt if a relationship—even one the parent viewed as casual—does not last. The best bet is to tell them when you are seeing someone, but leave the introductions until later.

Likewise, the people you date should be told early on about your children, for several reasons. Some people simply don't wish to become involved with those who have children, and if you are a parent, you need to know this before you become attached. The people you date also need to know that your children come first, and that they must be prepared for the logistical realities of dating a parent, such as the need to cancel at the last minute if a child becomes ill. Honesty is always the best bet, both for a healthy relationship and to avoid later difficulties.

Honesty, say the experts, is also the best way to cope with your children's natural curiosity about your adult relationships—within reasonable boundaries. Most believe that a child's questions about sex should be answered in a straightforward manner, but within the context of the parent's own sense of privacy. It is worse for children to have too little information than too much, as most have vivid imaginations and may be frightened by sights or sounds they can't identify.

When you sense that a relationship is becoming serious, your children and your partner will need to spend time getting to know one another gradually and naturally. Blending new people can be a long, often challenging process. Trying to force or rush it can lead to insecurity, anxiety, or suspicion.

Stuart Berger, M.D., author of *Divorce Without Victims*, suggests introducing partners to children in settings where there is low pressure and little interaction required. An evening at home where strangers sit around the living room staring at each other can be extremely awkward for everyone involved. Instead, plan a group outing to the zoo, a sporting event, an outdoor concert, or other recreational activity that allows for interaction, but also gives everyone something to talk about and a place to focus their attention.

Berger and others who work with blending families caution that despite the best efforts of the parents and new partners, children sometimes refuse to form any bond with the new person. They may sulk, remain intransigent, even profess utter hatred for anyone a parent brings home. This is often the result of continuing denial of the divorce or a persistent fantasy that the parents will reconcile. Berger advises that the parent should not sacrifice an important relationship because the child professes to dislike the person, and notes that children sometimes experience devastating guilt in later years if they believe a parent stayed alone and suffered a lonely life because of them.

Instead, most professionals advise talking with the child about the problem, and listening carefully to her objections. Occasionally, legitimate concerns are revealed, such as unkind or abusive behavior. In most cases, though, children can find only inconsequential things to complain about, such as the person's appearance, petty habits, or that he or she compares unfavorably to the absent parent. Some children who are extremely upset even though the parents have been divorced for several years may be hanging on to unrealistic expectations that prevent them from healing, and need some form of counseling or therapy. Berger has found that kids nearly always come around eventually and establish a relationship with the new partner that is at least civil, although some take as long as a year to do so.

Those who have been through the process advise parents that if children seem cold to new partners, don't push them and above all, don't worry—confusion and reluctance is quite natural. Talk to your children about the new person, ask them to give him or her a chance, and acknowledge that you realize this is odd for them. Do draw firm limits on any rude or unkind behavior; remind children that they are not allowed to treat anyone cruelly.

Small gifts from a new friend can help children warm up to them. The key is to limit such presents to little expressions of goodwill—a snack, a CD, a pack of sports cards—not substantial or expensive gifts that can lead a child to think that the person is trying to buy his affection.

Children adjusting to a new partner in a parent's life need constant reassurance that this friendship, and any subsequent events that may follow, will not change the parent's love for them. Emphasize that it is good and natural for both of their parents to go on to build new lives.

REMARRIAGE

It takes time before most people are fully able to trust another partner again after divorce. This is normal. Look around at others in good relationships, and remind yourself that it can happen. But don't get too anxious. The best things come in their own seasons. Take your time; date casually for awhile before committing to another partner. When you do get into another relationship that you feel may be special, accept it for the gift that it is, and take it slowly. See how it weathers the ups and downs of life. Do you continue to respect and admire the person through their difficult times? Do they support you through yours?

As the familiar proverb states, "marry in haste, repent at leisure." Sadly, with each remarriage, the likelihood of another divorce increases; the risk is higher among those who marry less than two years after the previous divorce. As Abigail Trafford writes, "Successful remarriages are built on successful psychological divorces." About 20 percent of those who remarry do so within less than a year after a divorce. Not surprisingly, most of these people end up repeating past patterns since they have not yet stepped back and broken out of old emotional habits. Even those who swear they will marry someone nothing at all like their former spouses often marry a carbon copy of the ex without realizing it.

To have a successful "emotional divorce," you must become aware of the baggage you bring out of the marriage. People often remarry quickly because they are seeking rescue, when in fact the most essential need is to learn to rescue themselves. Some people must experience a very negative remarriage and a second divorce before they realize the importance of going through this psychological process.

Does this mean that people with two or more divorces under their belts are doomed never to get it right? Of course not. Nothing that leads to learning and growth is a failure, and everyone faces different life experiences. Outside factors, including age, economic status, cultural influences, social groups, and upbringing play a large part in how we make our choices and decisions. The important point is to realize that the choices are there; it is never too late to take charge of our own growth and emotional development.

People who have been through one or more divorces, combined with other life experiences and general maturity, are less likely to stay in a bad relationship. They know themselves better, and know that although ending the relationship will be painful, they will survive and can move on. Many such people enter subsequent relationships with a far greater appreciation for the importance of equality and sharing in a marriage. They also have a strong sense of their own individuality, and have simply developed more skills in sharing their lives with a mate. They realize that a successful relationship is a mixture of individuality and shared closeness, and know that marriages have their ups and downs which, if weathered, build stronger couples. Such people are also likely to confront problems more quickly, rather than allowing them to get to the point of no return. Those who have been through therapy or counseling once are also more likely to seek it again when they see something in their lives getting out of control.

The majority of those who divorce do remarry again at some point—75 to 80 percent, according to one study. Another found that 85 percent of men and 75 percent of women marry again within three years after a divorce. One couple, both partners previously divorced, announced their upcoming marriage with wedding invitations that invited guests to celebrate "the triumph of hope over experience."

Most of those who succeed in subsequent marriages do so because they have taken the time to heal from past disappointments and have come to terms with the reality and mistakes of the past. The more self-aware you are, the better your chances of having a satisfying, lasting relationship with another. Those who do the work to get the former marriage in perspective and wait until they are fully recovered and settled into new lives of their own before committing to a new partner have a much better chance of success.

No matter how much soul-searching a person has done, and how much contentment he or she has achieved, anxiety about commitment when contemplating remarriage is very common. While it is always important to pay attention to your gut reactions, do realize that such feelings are often brought about by the persistent fears of repeating the mistakes of the previous marriage. This is natural. If you experience these feelings, don't discount them, but don't panic, either. Take your time and assess them as objectively as possible (with the help of a counselor, if they persist).

Also bear in mind that no rules are absolute, especially in the untamed region of human emotions, and no behavioral models fit everyone. Psychologists acknowledge that people experience and react to life in different ways, depending on personality, past experience, and innumerable other factors. Take heart in the fact that while divorce rates for subsequent marriages are higher than those of first marriages, many, many people do find a soul mate and achieve lasting happiness in a third or fourth marriage. Often, such individuals find that they must go through crucial life passages before being ready to truly commit themselves to a lasting lifetime relationship.

Author Erica Jong writes in her memoir, *Fear of Fifty*, that when she found herself single at the age of thirty-nine, after her third marriage ended, with a child and an entirely new set of circumstances to face, this became the most critical period of her life—the one in which she became mistress of her own fate. Jong acknowledges that she went through a wild phase immediately after this divorce, in which she tried to suppress the pain she experienced, and ended up enduring a headache that lasted six months until she finally realized that her body was sending her a message that she needed to feel the pain and accept it as a sign of blocked self-knowledge. By sheer will, Jong, who had spent nearly all of her adult life married, learned to change a tire, shovel snow, stack wood, and eventually build a peaceful relationship with the father of her child. Jong writes that she was only able to achieve a marriage with a satisfying balance of power between equals after she had come to a place where she was not afraid of being alone, in which she could treasure solitude and feel secure in her ability to provide for herself and her daughter. It was then that she was ready when she suddenly met a man she describes as "a soul mate and a friend."

Choosing to Stay Single

After taking the time to reassess their lives after a divorce, some people come to the conclusion that marriage isn't for them, and this, too, is perfectly normal. Counselor Kathryn Lang believes that the likelihood of a person remarrying often depends on whether he or she liked the state of marriage itself, rather than the quality of the marriage. "It depends on the individual," she explains. "Some feel constrained by marriage. To others, family is extremely important."

After completing a divorce recovery seminar that included sessions on assessing participants' future goals and dreams, Clayta Spear concluded that she would not marry again. "I've always been independent, and I don't believe you have to have a man to be a whole woman," she says. "I am open to new relationships, and I've dated casually. It would be nice to have the love and understanding of a partner, but it's not something I require to have a happy and fulfilling life. I know now that I can go on living a meaningful life just for myself and with the support of devoted friends."

BLENDED FAMILIES

More and more children today are growing up in two homes with two sets of parents and siblings. Variously called "blended families," "stepfamilies," or "binuclear families," these households are becoming extremely common. Yet for each child coping with this type of situation, the changes and challenges that accompany it can have a profound impact. Children must accept new authority figures; adjust to different rules, lifestyles, and personalities; and share space, time, and parental attention they may have considered sacrosanct. The lessons a child learns from a successful blending of families can significantly enrich their lives, but will inevitably involve some period of disruption and adjustment at first. Even adult children may become jealous or possessive when a parent announces the intention to remarry.

Any time a new person comes into a home, especially a home that was restructured by divorce only a few years before, some degree of upheaval is inevitable. When, for example, a custodial mother remarries, her children may see the new husband/stepfather as an intruder in their space, a competitor for their mother's affections, another adult whose orders they will have to obey, and an inferior replacement for the father they may still be hoping will one day return. It may mean a change of residence, new stepsiblings, even a change of school and neighborhood.

The key in introducing such changes is to move slowly, phasing in the transitions gradually. Parents need to realize that children are often naturally resistant to another set of changes in their lives, and may take out their resentment on the new person. Try to keep things as relaxed and easygoing as possible. Reassure children that certain fundamentals, primarily your relationship with them, will *not* change. Children crave predictability, especially after having been through the upheaval of a divorce.

Virtually all of the professionals who work with stepfamilies emphasize the importance of casting the new spouse into a different role than that of parent. Children should never be instructed to call this person "Mom" or "Dad." While the authority of a new adult in the home should be respected, and household rules enforced (generally by the biological parent with the support of the stepparent), drastic change should be minimized as much as possible, for the good of all involved.

Stepparents usually find their own unique role in the child's life, and efforts to force artificial roles almost inevitably backfire. A stepparent who moves in with a set of strict new household rules is courting disaster.

Family therapists who work with blended families say that one key is for the adults to work together to compromise and reach a workable agreement on how the home is to be run, set reasonable boundaries and ground rules, stick with the plan, and back each other up if resistance occurs. Direct orders to children, such as to do chores, homework, or go to bed, should come from the biological parent, at least during the adjustment period. Most agree that while expressions of direct authority and any form of discipline should come from the biological parent, a stepparent must have the authority to enforce rules in the other parent's absence. The new family member is advised to let the relationships develop naturally, and not to try to buy affection or take bonding efforts to unnatural extremes. Instead, a combination of respect for privacy and individual differences, along with shared activities that all enjoy, usually leads to a natural evolution into a new family.

The early days of adjustment can be very trying, however. It is easy for children to fall into the habit of idealizing the absent parent and making unkind comparisons. Biological parents often have to do a great deal of teeth-gritting to avoid the temptation to criticize the other parent. Sometimes children use constant praise of the absent parent to appease their sense of guilt over a growing fondness for the stepparent. It is up to the natural parent in this situation to remember his or her leadership role, and to present the event as a positive opportunity to enjoy the love and companionship of a person in a new and different role—not a substitute or replacement father or mother.

When both of the partners in a marriage are marrying for a second time, the situation is often made more complex by the need to blend two established families. One who marries a partner with children is getting a package deal, in which several people will be required to adjust to a brand-new home, inevitably involving a number of transitions. This effort can be emotionally, logistically, financially, and practically daunting. Stepsiblings also have to make difficult adjustments. Physician and author Stuart Berger warns that clashes between those who are close in age are especially common. He advises parents to let the kids try to reach their own solutions to problems as they arise. Of course, one child should never be allowed to bully another, and brawls or other destructive behavior must be stopped. But petty squabbles usually resolve themselves.

At this time parents also need to be sensitive to situations that may make a child feel left out, used, or self-conscious. For example, a child who is not athletic should neither be left out or forced to take part in a family backpacking excursion. Plan activities that all can enjoy, and emphasize that each can pursue other adventures on other occasions. Older children sometimes become very frustrated when they perceive that they are expected to serve as on-call baby-sitters. Counselors emphasize that the key factors to successful family blending are communication, respect, privacy, and space. When these principles are kept at the forefront, most families eventually blend well and thrive.

The good news is that most blended families do just fine in the long run, even though the initial period of adjustment can be extremely rough. The bottom line is that if the parents are happy, this is what is best for the children.

As with any situation involving a balancing of human quirks and personalities, seemingly small issues can take on great importance. Stuart Berger advises parents and stepparents to be sensitive to little matters that may be tremendously important to a child's sense of stability. Small routines, such as having a particular toy, blanket, or pajamas every night may seem trivial to an adult, but a child needs predictability and security. Stepparents often must call on their reserves of patience and persistence to remain loving toward a difficult child, but the rewards will be worth the effort.

Both family psychology experts and those who have weathered the blending of a family point to a few, relatively simple key factors that can maximize chances of success. Those most frequently mentioned include an emphasis on compromise and respect between all family members, patience, humor, forgiveness, respect for personal space and privacy, clear rules, open communication with special attention to listening among all in the home, tolerance for petty differences, and time for children and biological parents to spend maintaining their own special bonds. It is important for the adults in the family to remember that if they set the tone for the expected attitudes and behavior, children will usually follow.

Constance Ahrons, author of *The Good Divorce*, an excellent book with a wealth of information for those working to successfully blend a family, advises that people should avoid unrealistic expectations of the ideal, *Brady Bunch* instant family. Caring relationships take time to evolve, and expectations of immediate bonding can lead to disappointment and difficulty. Ahrons notes the advice provided by Emily and John Visher, founders of the Stepfamily Association of America, who teach that if the stepfamily relationships are allowed to develop as seems comfortable to the individuals involved, then caring between steprelatives has the opportunity to develop naturally.

Some family therapists have found that having unrealistic expectations is one of the most common problems stepfamilies face. People seldom stop to consider what a complex and enormous adjustment it takes to blend a family. Everything from deep emotional ties to the number of people sharing a bathroom is in a state of upheaval. As Stuart Berger writes,

"Stepparenting is not for the timid at heart." Perfect harmony from day one is not a realistic hope. Stepfamilies must cope with all the everyday problems biological families encounter—plus the need to forge bonds and make practical adjustments—without the benefit of a shared history to cement the individuals together.

Yet those who consistently call on their reserves of patience, love, tolerance, and humor come to reap incredible rewards. While the time it takes for families to become comfortably bonded varies, it is not uncommon for one to three years to pass before a family feels completely at ease together. Berger advises new stepparents to look for common ground and shared interests with their stepchildren. He reminds the family to try to laugh often, relax and not worry about minor frictions, and to keep things in perspective.

The Other Parent

The noncustodial parent can also help with the child's period of adjustment to a newly blended family by encouraging him to accept the new situation, and by providing reassurance that the new development is positive and that both parents will still be actively involved in his life. One warning that is often heard from those who have worked with stepfamilies is to be prepared for the common tendency for remarriage by one spouse to arouse new conflict with the ex. Ahrons advises avoiding abrupt changes in schedules and patterns as much as possible, so that the former spouse has time to adjust to the new arrangement as well.

New partners are well advised to stay out of any conflicts between their spouses and the ex, and never to try to compete with the ex either in the eyes of the partner or the children. This is a new relationship that is different on all fronts. Work and play with other family members to build new traditions, rituals, adventures, and memories. One note of caution: It is best to wait, if possible, until the first couple of years of adjustment have passed before adding a new child to the family. While this can be a magical blessing for all, it can also cause more stress if the household is still reeling from recent mixing.

Space and Privacy

Human beings are, by nature, territorial creatures. We all crave a place to call our own. This sense of refuge is especially important for someone experiencing difficult changes. Ideally, each child should have his or her own room in each home. When this is not possible, however, children should be able to have some space that is all their own. Let them help decorate and arrange their things in their own niches. This doesn't require a great monetary investment—a little paint, fabric, and garage sale treasures or cardboard furniture, as well as some of their existing belongings, can help each child claim his own territory.

Be sure to make very clear to all who must share a living space that the privacy of others is to be respected absolutely. This is important to everyone, but there are times in life when it is especially vital. Adolescents tend to be extremely protective of their privacy, and a breach of trust can cause a devastating setback.

Yet teenagers are also very curious about others, and the temptation to snoop may be nearly overwhelming. For example, in one blended family where the wife's teenage daughter had to share her room with the husband's daughter during her visits, the parents provided a second bed, but required the two girls to share a dresser. When the visiting daughter left her diary on top of the dresser, the other couldn't resist a peek. Her stepsister caught her in the act, and the trust that had begun to build between the girls was abruptly shattered—and not mended for months. Looking back, the parents realized that this could have been prevented by a little more creative use of existing space, such as a stack of banker's boxes covered by a tablecloth to create a private dresser for the visiting daughter. Parents who are sensitive to these issues can minimize the chances of a disaster.

Instant Parenthood

A childless person who marries a parent is faced with learning a whole new set of skills that may be completely unfamiliar. Experts advise people in this situation to take the time to learn these skills, just as they would other essential abilities. Read some books, take a class, and educate yourself about children, their development, and their behavior. Remember that children are not thoughtful, considerate, or grateful by nature, and shouldn't be held to the same standards as adults in these matters.

Children often fear that a parent who remarries will transfer the affection normally reserved for the child to the stepparent, and this can cause a great deal of insecurity. It is especially important for a stepparent to realize that there is a special bond between the biological parent and child, and to give them some time alone. Biological parents also need to acknowledge this fear, and make a point of reassuring their children that they have plenty of love to go around.

With all the concentration on the children and their adjustment, parents sometimes forget that they, too, are in the process of a major life change that needs some attention. The new couple needs to care for their relationship as well, by carving out some time for themselves through, for example, a traditional honeymoon on their own and a weekly night out. The stepparent, too, should be allotted some space in the home that is wholly his or her own.

Increasing Support for Blended Families

As blended families are becoming more and more common, an increasing number of services and products geared toward such families are cropping up. Therapy and support groups, counselors with a special focus on blended families, books, and programs are becoming abundant. Stepfamily seminars, support groups, and classes help families improve communication and build solid relationships. Stepparent groups meet to educate themselves, share solutions to problems, and encourage state legislatures to pass new laws protecting their rights. Some groups also advocate in other arenas, and lobby judges to take a more enlightened view of stepparents and children's ties to them. Some such groups are locally based, while others work under the umbrella of national affiliates such as the Stepfamily Association of America (see Appendix).

Sometimes families do everything right and still face insurmountable difficulties. This may be due to one member's significant emotional or behavioral problem, extreme personality conflicts, or other individual factors. For those who have persistent problems, a family counselor can help blended families learn communication skills and address their trouble spots, so the children can regain the essential elements of their security within the new family: support, boundaries, structure, and consistency. Fortunately, more and more family counselors and support groups specializing in stepfamilies are becoming available to help families overcome these difficulties and build good relationships. The Stepfamily Association of America, local mental health organizations, groups such as Parents Without Partners, churches, social service organizations, and individual therapists can make recommendations and referrals. Sometimes family counseling for everyone is needed; in other cases, one family member will need special attention.

Building a stepfamily can be an arduous process, but the rewards for perseverance are great. Those who study stepfamilies have found that living in such a setting can provide positive lessons, including how to accept and grow to love people different from yourself, how to adjust to a new and unknown environment, how to form alliances with potential competitors, and how to establish new and meaningful family bonds.

When Blended Families Split

Stepparents who divorce often face a wrenching situation. Under traditional legal systems, stepparents had few, if any, rights to continue a relationship with stepchildren. Today, however, all fifty states have either statutes or binding case law dealing with custody, visitation, and support by stepparents. The American Bar Association has drafted a model law addressing stepparent rights that has been adopted in its current form or in a modified version by many states.

Courts have wide latitude to facilitate special arrangements to establish continued relationships between stepparents and stepchildren, if it is beneficial to the child—always the key factor. In rare cases, custody may even be awarded to the stepparent instead of the biological parent, when there is a strong showing that this would be far better for the child.

9

Good News and
Words of Wisdom

A S MILLIONS HAVE DISCOVERED, SOMETIMES TO THEIR PROFOUND surprise, divorce can mean an opportunity for a fresh start, for the discovery and building of an authentic life, for renewal and restructuring priorities, for setting out in pursuit of old and new dreams. People who have survived war, disabling injury, disease, terrorist attacks, and all manner of tragedies have been heard to remark that their divorces were the worst thing they had ever been through—and yet they made it.

Today, marriage is a voluntary step that people choose with the goal of achieving a happier life shared with a loving companion. Sometimes this goal is achieved for a time, but changes take place in the relationship and the partners. Divorce frees people from marriages which have become destructive or unsatisfactory. The aftermath allows for growth, learning, development, and the passage into a new life that can lead to restructuring, resulting in greater happiness for everyone involved.

Those looking back after healing from divorce advise others to acknowledge the past, but then move ahead. "There will always be scar tissue, but it's important to take the time for catharsis and then get on with it," says Becky Ralston, now divorced for three years. "I still resent some things my ex did, but life goes on. People should try to enjoy just being human for awhile. I didn't do everything perfectly after my divorce, but it pains me to see some people swinging to such extremes. Some people swear they never want another relationship and go for years without even considering a date, then get into relationships that aren't the greatest because they're so lonely. I watch others bedding down everything in sight, trying desperately to hold onto a new partner. You have to realize that you're not going to get married again within a week!"

Frances Webb expresses similar sentiments. "The conflict eventually ended, even though we had experienced a high-conflict divorce. I was ready to move on! I have a friend who can't stop talking about her ex—she just hangs on. I want to tell her, 'Put it away!' When I moved from the East Coast to the Southwest last year, this friend told me she couldn't imagine picking up and moving across the country. I think she feels that way because she can't let go over her marriage. People have to put the past in the past."

Another key factor to successful divorce recovery, say those who have achieved it, is to look back on the marriage as another phase of life, not a failure. "It would help every divorced person to realize that because a marriage doesn't last a lifetime doesn't mean it was a failure," says Webb. "How could one conceive of a twenty-year marriage that produced two beautiful, happy children that are doing just great, as a failure? Every couple should be able to look at what they achieved and say to each other, we did okay, didn't we?"

Webb believes that we are conditioned by society to burden the institution of marriage with too many expectations. "It is our culture that has determined that any marriage that ends amounts to failure, and that's not accurate," she says.

"We need to realize that very few couples have a perfect marriage. Yet we enter marriage with such great expectations. Right away, couples start planning for their retirement, college for the children—almost all of the expectations we have for life are tied to this unit. We expect that Christmas and vacations and family visits will take place within this relationship. For a man or woman to suddenly face life without this unit which they've been a part of for so long—that's the greatest disappointment."

Counselors urge people recovering from divorce not to put off doing the things they enjoy until some event transpires, such as completing a course of therapy, moving to a new town, or finding a new mate. Many who have survived the aftermath of divorce also emphasize the importance of not neglecting your need for recreation and social contacts. "Take a class," advises Becky Ralston. "Not a career-related class, but something fun. My husband and I had gone dancing together when we were married, and I was just starting to learn more and enjoy it when we divorced," she explains. "So I enrolled in a West Coast Swing class. It was something fun to look forward to at least once a week, and gave me an opportunity to socialize, to meet new people with a common interest."

Those who have successfully healed after a divorce find themselves better prepared to face subsequent challenges, including another divorce. "I was divorced from my first husband when I was very young and had a young child," explains Kathleen Robertson, a family law attorney reflecting on being divorced for the second time. "The fear factor was much higher then. With hindsight, I can see it was a very positive step in my life. I experienced a lot of personal growth afterward. I learned who I was and who I wasn't, I went to college and graduate school. I had a career in genetic engineering, then went on to law school. I found that I could get emotional support from my own resources, and that I could live frugally.

Years later, when I realized that my second marriage was ending, I had a much different perspective, both as an attorney and from my own life experience. It was also a very weighty decision that took a long time to make. We tried counseling, made a real effort to work it out. Yet once I saw we were going nowhere and I made the decision to leave the marriage, I was anxious to get it done. I didn't want it to be a battle or emotionally devastating for either of us."

In *The Best is Yet to Come,* Ivana Trump says that she was inspired to write the book after her breakup with tycoon Donald Trump by letters she received during that very public divorce. Trump found the message that she was not alone extremely comforting. She writes that while every divorce is a tragedy representing the end of a dream, it can also be a new beginning. She urges women coping with divorce to take control and plan well. Her number one rule is never to look back, only forward, although she admits that she felt hopeless at times.

Trump counsels others reeling in the aftermath of divorce to always believe and remember that the best truly is yet to come. Attitude is everything, says Trump, and those who view this new phase of life as another adventure, an opportunity to cultivate new interests, learn new skills, make mistakes and learn from them, and find new ways to be of service, will blossom. She advises others facing the inevitable challenges that come after divorce to think creatively, and work at finding a solution to every problem, because there is one out there.

Trump warns that it is easy to be swamped by emotion that can obscure clear thinking, but a step-by-step approach to any problem can yield a solution. Her experience shows that even the rich and privileged suffer from a feeling of failure after a divorce. All the surface trappings and money cannot shield one from the emotional pain, fear, humiliation, and sense of failure that are universal. While financial survival was never a worry for Trump, she faced the same fear of the unknown and worries about how the split would affect her three children that all divorcing mothers encounter. She also knew that her career would change drastically, since she would not want to continue to work for her ex-husband. Trump also had to endure problems unique to her situation, such as the media circus that surrounded her every move after news of the split became public. Trump never lost confidence, however, and reminded herself that she would always have her children, which she considered her real treasure, as well as her skills and ambition. She reports that she blossomed after the divorce, when none of her dreaded middle-of-the-night fears came true, but her wildest dreams did.

Like many others, Trump experienced that being on her own allowed her to move in new directions and discover new resources. After the worst happened, she not only survived but flourished to become stronger and more confident. Trump states that if the marriage hadn't ended, she wouldn't have explored the new avenues that led her to fresh opportunities and different career options. Trump was presented in the newspapers as "a woman scorned." Yet she speaks of her divorce as a rebirth. She advises others to decide to do things they have always wanted to do, to figure out what they desire, to be determined to get it, and to work like the devil to do so—and they will.

KEEPING IT IN PERSPECTIVE: DIVORCE AND DEMOGRAPHICS

Gaining perspective can be one of the most effective balms for the sense of failure that often follows divorce, and one which usually begins to take shape in the final stage of healing. Remember, half of all marriages end in divorce—you are not alone, or odd, or unusual. Demographic studies of modern life indicate that people today change all aspects of their lives with far greater frequency than previous generations, in large part because change is an option that our predecessors often simply did not enjoy.

The high frequency of divorce today has much to do with sociological factors. In addition to longevity, baby boomers and subsequent generations have grown up in an era where there was much more freedom than in the past to experiment with different roles and identities and to end a marriage that wasn't working, as well as a great deal of societal pressure to live up to the impossible standard of "having it all." The drive toward affluence in the '80s left many people empty and exhausted, with little time and space for enjoying the pleasure of what they had accumulated, often including a marriage that was neglected.

Fortunately, the '90s have brought greater attention to the importance of a healthy inner life, with many hankering for simpler lifestyles and a return to greater involvement with spiritual values. Ironically, while a positive change, this too may have contributed to the end of many marriages, in which one partner experiences a profound shift in goals and values while the other partner does not.

Statistics reported in 1991 indicate that, on the average, Americans today change careers or occupations seven times throughout their lifetimes. The majority change residence or geographic location every five years. Thus, in other aspects of life, we have begun to accept that short-term relationships are not necessarily inferior to long-term ones. Quality, not quantity of time in a relationship, is what is important. People today have an average lifespan of seventy-five years. Yet we still base our expectations for marriage on ideals established when people lived to be only forty-five years old.

As those who study human behavior and development learn more about the human life cycle as it progresses through time, it is becoming clear that stable people with strong values simply change from stage to stage in life.

Sociological changes have also affected the restructuring of life cycles, especially in the twentieth century. Women today are becoming more confident, strong, and autonomous. This has had a profound effect on couples who married at a time when more traditional roles prevailed. In her book *New Passages*, sociologist and author Gail Sheehy reports that divorce rates for those who came of age during the Vietnam era, born between 1945 and 1950, soared as these couples began to reach their early forties. Sheehy reports that in earlier generations, the most common age for divorce was when the woman was around twenty-eight years old and the man around thirty. Women tended to remain in traditional roles, while men were more likely to grow faster and progress more rapidly through life changes. Now, Sheehy has found, the process has reversed. She states that divorce often dovetails with the midlife time of taking stock that brings about reevaluation of all facets of life, including career, education, and other endeavors.

Women today are achieving a new sense of balance between the traditional and nontraditional worlds. Some, including Sheehy, predict that the divorce rate will decline, due in part to the fact that people today tend to be older when they marry for the first time. Also, more young people are choosing not to marry at all. While the current rate of divorce remains at about 50 percent of all marriages, some, including researchers at the U.S. Census Bureau, predict a decline that will take the statistic closer to 40 percent.

LIFE AFTER DIVORCE

Those who indulge in favorite pleasures, enjoy the social support of old friends and new, enjoy their children, focus on their accomplishments and goals, and put their energy into working toward building satisfying new lives demonstrate to themselves, their ex-spouses, and others who may have doubted them that there is indeed life, and a very good life, after divorce. Psychologist Mel Krantzler urges that divorce can be an adventure instead of a disaster. He advises that the valuable components of a defunct marriage can become part of the bank of experience that enables an individual to become a more mature, capable, and wise human being.

Even those who have been through a horrific divorce and seemingly endless period of trying to get back on their feet usually manage to find their way to new lives, and new love. In the third year after a devastating divorce, in which his wife walked out with no warning on their first wedding anniversary, Tim met Suzannah, to whom he is now engaged. "I met her when I was back in my hometown visiting my family. Right away, I knew she was the woman for me, but I couldn't fall in love with her or really open up to her for a long time. I moved back to be close to her, but it took me a couple more years before I could tell her I loved her, or even admit it to myself. Even now, over eight years since the divorce, I still feel the aftershocks, I have to cope with it. Suzannah is incredibly patient to put up with me."

"He still has baggage from the divorce," Suzannah agrees. "He can be very difficult to live with. But he's a good man, a special person, so it's worth it. But sometimes I have to remind myself that his behaviors and reactions aren't about me, they're something he carries from the past. We're doing just fine."

For many, once the initial bridges of pain and grief have been crossed, divorce can be liberating. It is a license to explore avenues of change that you may have considered previously, but didn't feel were feasible or appropriate. Divorce presents an opportunity to rid yourself of old and unworkable objects and ideas, and to learn new and more effective ways to manage all facets of your life, including the emotional ones.

The stresses and demands of coping with a troubled marriage, as well as the put-downs and hostility that so often accompany the demise of an intimate relationship, are no longer an issue. These are the positive sides of the coin that come with the pain. An old Spanish proverb, translated by artist and businessperson Gerald Murphy, says it best: "Living well is the best revenge."

GOOD NEWS: CHANGING CULTURAL ATTITUDES ABOUT DIVORCE

Constance Ahrons, Ph.D., is a professor of sociology and associate director of the marriage and family therapy program at the University of Southern California. In her book *The Good Divorce*, Ahrons sets forth the principle that while no divorce is actually "good," we must accept that divorce is a fact of our society that acts as a safety valve for bad marriages. Most people today, particularly those who have been through an unpleasant marriage, agree that the temporary pain of a divorce is far more bearable than the endless suffering of a negative home life. Ahrons defines a "good divorce" as one in which the couple is able to part without destroying their lives, or the lives of those they love, especially their children. She considers a continued close relationship of both parents to the children to be the key factor.

Ahrons was the first social scientist to study normal divorced families—not those who have suffered interminable conflict and trauma, but rather those who have remained a family that spans two or more households, what she calls a binuclear family. Ahrons emphasizes that in a good divorce, former spouses have been able to develop a parenting partnership that is cooperative enough to permit the bonds of kinship to continue with and through the children. She states that with so many today involved in divorces and remarriages, society must begin to incorporate this reality into people's concepts of good and normal lives.

In her studies of divorced couples, Ahrons has found that most are able to forge a new relationship, similar to a business relationship, which she terms "cooperative colleagues." These parents, while usually not close friends, are able to cooperate reasonably well on issues concerning their children. Ahrons also found that the relationship between divorced parents often improves over the years, especially if both people are committed to the loving support of their children. Fortunately, among all those she studied, this group was the largest.

Other good news can be found in the way the media and entertainment industry have portrayed divorced parents in recent years. For most of this century, our culture expected divorced couples to either ignore one another or to be openly hostile. In recent years, however, movies such as *Mrs. Doubtfire*, media accounts of cooperative parenting between divorced celebrities, and stories written by those who have found solutions to their own parenting problems have given parents better role models.

Obviously, when a marriage has deteriorated beyond repair to the point that everyone in the home is miserable, divorce is the best and healthiest solution. Many inaccurate myths and unsupported fears stand in the way of society's acceptance of this basic truth. It is important to realize that much of what is reported in the media or hyped by those seeking to make divorce more difficult is only part of the story. For example, while it is true that many women experience a short-term drop in household income after a divorce, many ultimately find greater financial satisfaction due to their increased control and access over the money they earn. While children suffer when parents divorce, they suffer more from exposure to prolonged conflict in the home, and many are healthier and enjoy more one-on-one contact with each parent after the parents split and put an end to their hostility.

While the majority of people in our culture still seem to expect that those who divorce will be hostile or avoid each other, more and more couples are providing living proof that such animosity is no longer the norm. One couple, divorced for seven years, reports that they just smile when they get "weird looks" as they sit next to each other at their daughter's softball games, plays, and church music recitals. Another found amusement in friends' confusion when his ex-wife, a realtor, joined her former husband and his new wife for a dinner out to celebrate her sale of a new home to them.

For couples with children, the benefit of remaining friendly is obvious. But childless couples also speak of the value of respecting what they once felt for one another, and of appreciating the things in common that brought them together in the first place. For others, it simply makes sense to remain friends. "My first wife is great friends with the whole family," says my neighbor Dave. "We were just too young to know what we were doing when we got married—both of us were only twenty. Our decision to end the marriage was mutual, we did our own paperwork together. There was no hostility; we just realized that we would get along better as friends than as partners in a marriage. Over the years, that's proven true."

A recent article in the *Albuquerque Journal* described such couples as part of a "quiet movement" that doesn't draw the attention given to those who fight dramatic battles. But there is every indication that these peacemongers are becoming a silent majority. In 1997, Nailah Skami of Redmond, Washington, launched the first "National Get Along with Your Ex Month." The event had its second anniversary in July 1998.

Suggested Readings

Ahrons, Constance R. *The Good Divorce: Keeping Your Family Together When Your Marriage Comes Apart.* New York: HarperCollins, 1994.

Ban Brethnach, Sarah. *Simple Abundance: A Daybook of Comfort and Joy.* New York: Warner Books, 1995.

Bauer, Jill. *From "I Do" to "I'll Sue": An Irreverent Compendium for Survivors of Divorce.* New York: Plume/Meridian, 1993.

Belli, Melvin, and Mel Krantzler. *Divorcing.* New York: St. Martin's Press, 1988.

————. *The Complete Guide for Men and Women Divorcing.* New York: St. Martin's Press, 1990.

Berger, Stuart, M.D. *Divorce Without Victims.* Boston: Houghton Mifflin, 1983.

Berry, Dawn Bradley. "Let Freedom Ring!" *Healing Your Life After Divorce: A Divorce Recovery Newsletter.* June, 1991, p. 1.

————. *The Divorce Sourcebook,* 2d ed. Los Angeles: Lowell House, 1998.

————. *The Domestic Violence Sourcebook,* 2d ed. Los Angeles: Lowell House, 1998.

Bluestein, Jane, Judy Lawrence, and SJ Sanchez. *Daily Riches: A Journal of Gratitude and Awareness.* Deerfield Beach, Fla.: Health Communications, Inc., 1998.

Bolick, Nancy O'Keefe. *How to Survive Your Parents' Divorce.* New York: The Changing Family, 1994.

Bradshaw, John. *John Bradshaw on Surviving Divorce.* Santa Fe: Sagebrush Productions (Videotape), 1989.

Bridges, William. *Transitions.* New York: Perseus Press, 1980.

Buckman, Sid. "Ghosts From Your Past." *Healing Your Life After Divorce: A Divorce Recovery Newsletter.* June, 1991, p. 3.

"Child Support Payments Increase by 27 percent." *Albuquerque Tribune,* Jan. 9, 1998, p. A7.

Clapp, Genevieve. *Divorce and New Beginnings.* New York: John Wiley & Sons, 1992.

Clare, Bernard, and Anthony Daniele. *The Ex Factor: The Complete Do-It-Yourself Postdivorce Handbook.* New York: Donald I. Fine, Inc., 1986.

Curtis, M. Carol. "Rites of Passage—Rituals of Release." *Healing Your Life After Divorce: A Divorce Recovery Newsletter.* June, 1991, p. 2.

Engel, Marjorie. *Divorce Help Sourcebook.* Detroit: Gale Research/Visible Ink Press, 1994.

Fassel, Diane. *Growing Up Divorced: A Road to Healing for Adult Children of Divorce.* New York: Pocket Books, 1991.

Favaro, Peter J., Ph.D., and Charles Ferzola, Esq. *Divorced Parents' Guide to Managing Custody and Visitation.* San Jose, Calif.: R & E Publishers, 1995.

Fisher, Bruce. *Rebuilding When Your Relationship Ends,* 2nd ed. San Luis Obispo, Calif.: Impact Publishers, 1992.

Gold, Lois. *Between Love and Hate: A Guide to Civilized Divorce.* New York: Plenum Publishing, 1992.

Gray, John, Ph.D. *Mars and Venus Starting Over.* New York: HarperCollins, 1998.

Herman, Stephen P., M.D. *Parent v. Parent: How You and Your Child Can Survive the Custody Battle.* New York: Pantheon Books, 1990.

Hillman, Terry, and Pamela Weintraub. *The Complete Idiot's Guide to Surviving Divorce.* New York: Alpha Books, 1996.

Jong, Erica. *Fear of Fifty: A Midlife Memoir.* New York: HarperCollins, 1994.

Kass, Anne. "Don't Give Children a Sophie's Choice." *Albuquerque Tribune,* Oct. 8, 1989.

Lawrence, Judy. *The Budget Kit,* 2nd ed. Chicago: Dearborn Financial Publishing, 1997

———. *The Money Tracker.* Chicago: Dearborn Financial Publishing, 1996.

———. "Children, Divorce, and Budgets." *The New Mexico Verdict* 1, No. 4, August–September, 1994.

Levoy, Gregg. *Callings: Finding and Following an Authentic Life.* New York: Crown Publishers/Harmony Books, 1997.

Luhrs, Janet. *The Simple Living Guide.* New York: Broadway Books, 1997.

Minton, Lynn. "Fresh Voices: Getting Along with Stepparents: Teenagers Talk Frankly." *Parade,* Feb. 26, 1995, pp. 24–25.

Murphy, Patricia A. *Making the Connections: Women, Work, and Abuse.* Winter Park, Fla.: GR Press, 1993.

Murphy, Patricia A. *The Making the Connections Workbook: A Career and Life Planning Guide for Women Abuse Survivors.* Winter Park, Fla.: GR Press, 1995.

Pitzele, Sefta K. *Surviving Divorce: Daily Affirmations.* Deerfield Beach, Fla.: Health Communications, 1991.

Rosenberg, Stephen M., and Ann Z. Peterson. *Every Woman's Guide to Financial Security.* Capital Publishing, 1994.

Sheehy, Gail. *New Passages: Mapping Your Life Over Time.* New York: Random House, 1995.

Thompson, Dino. "Working Off the Big Mad." *Healing Your Life After Divorce: A Divorce Recovery Newsletter.* June, 1991, p. 2.

Trafford, Abigail. *Crazy Time: Surviving Divorce and Building a New Life.* New York: Harper Perennial/HarperCollins, 1992.

Trump, Ivana. *The Best is Yet to Come: Coping with Divorce and Enjoying Life Again.* New York: Simon and Schuster/Pocket Books, 1995.

Wallman, Lester, and Sharon McDonnel. *Cupid, Couples, and Contracts: A Guide to Living Together, Prenuptial Agreements, and Divorce.* New York: Master Media Ltd., 1994.

Walther, Anne N. *Divorce Hangover: A Step-by-Step Prescription for Creating a Bright Future After Your Marriage Ends.* New York: Simon and Schuster/Pocket Books, 1991.

Ward, Barbara. "Reconcilable Differences: Many Divorced Couples Put a Value on Staying Friendly." *Albuquerque Journal*, Aug. 23, 1998, p. C12.

Woodhouse, Violet, and Victoria Felton-Collins. *Divorce and Money*, 2d ed. Berkeley, Calif.: Nolo Press, 1993.

Resources

AGENCIES AND ORGANIZATIONS

Many of these organizations also maintain Internet Web sites. A search using the name of the organization will take you to the current site.

American Bar Association Section of Dispute Resolution
740 15th Street NW
Washington, DC 20005-1009
(202) 662-1680
E-mail: dispute@abanet.org
This section of the American Bar Association serves as an information clearinghouse on dispute resolution, conducts workshops, and provides technical services.

Academy of Family Mediators
5 Militia Drive
Lexington, MA 02173
(781) 674-2663
E-mail: afmoffice@mediators.org
This organization promotes mediation as an alternative to the adversarial system and publishes various periodicals, audiotapes, and videotapes.

Ackerman Institute for Family Therapy
149 E. 78th Street
New York, NY 10021
(212) 879-4900
Clinic, training, and research institute devoted to the study of family relationships, family change, and family healing. Sponsor lecturers and training films.

American Academy of Psychiatry and the Law
819 Park Avenue
Baltimore, MD 21201
(301) 539-0379
This group enables psychiatrists to exchange ideas and experience in areas where psychiatry and law overlap; develop standards of practice, encourage research, and produce information for the public.

American Association for Mediated Divorce
5435 Balboa Boulevard
Encino, CA 91316
(818) 986-9793

American Academy of Matrimonial Lawyers
150 N. Michigan Avenue, Ste. 2040
Chicago, IL 60601
(312) 263-6477
Attorneys who specialize in family law. The Academy publishes a list of members and other materials.

American Association for Marriage and Family Therapy
  Research and Education
1133 15th Street NW, Room 300
Washington, DC 20005-2710
1-800-347-AMFT
(202) 452-0109

Provides local referrals to family therapists and publishes a consumer's guide to marriage and family therapy.

American Association of Retired Persons (AARP)
601 E Street NW
Washington, DC 20049-0001
(202) 434-2277

Publishes information on grandparents' visitation rights, *Divorce After Fifty: Challenges and Choices*, and other information on related issues.

American Bar Association
Section on Family Law
750 North Lakeshore Drive
Chicago, IL 60611
1-800-621-6159
(312) 988-5000

National association of attorneys practicing in the family law field. Numerous publications, referrals to local members.

American Psychiatric Association
1400 K Street NW
Washington, DC 20005
(202) 682-6000

This group, composed of psychiatrists, has an extensive library and produces various publications.

American Academy of Child and Adolescent Psychiatry
3615 Wisconsin Avenue NW
Washington, DC 20016
1-800-333-7636
(202) 966-2891

Professional society of child and adolescent psychiatrists; produces journal and newsletters.

American Divorce Association of Men (ADAM)
1519 S. Arlington Heights Road
Arlington Heights, IL 60005
(708) 364-1555
Promotes reform in divorce laws and encourages counseling, mediation, education, and related services. Maintains a lawyer referral list.

American Family Therapy Academy
2020 Pennsylvania Avenue NW, Ste. 273
Washington, DC 20006
(202) 994-2776
Family therapists, researchers, and teachers working to advance the theory and type of therapy that regards the family as a unit, focused on improving knowledge of how to treat families.

American Psychological Association
1200 17th Street NW
Washington, DC 20036
(202) 955-7600
1-800-374-2721
Scientific and professional society of psychologists with numerous divisions, including a division of family psychology, and publications; provides various services.

American Self-Help Clearinghouse
St. Clares-Riverside Medical Center
Denville, NJ 07834
(973) 625-7101
Lists helplines and toll-free numbers for self-help groups nationwide.

Association for Children for Enforcement of Support
2260 Upton Avenue

Toledo, OH 43606
(419) 472-0047
1-800-537-7072

This organization has 350 chapters across the United States to advise custodial parents on how to collect child support.

Association of Family and Conciliation Courts
329 W. Wilson
Madison, WI 53703-3612
(608) 251-0604

Judges, attorneys, mediators, counselors, teachers, and others concerned with the resolution of family disputes and the effect on children. Numerous publications.

Big Brothers/Big Sisters of America
230 N. 13th Street
Philadelphia, PA 19107
(215) 567-7000

National program with many local chapters; provides children from one-parent homes with adult volunteers to act as friends, mentors, and role models.

Center for Dispute Settlement
1666 Connecticut Avenue NW, Ste. 501
Washington, DC 20009
(202) 265-9572

Promotes and evaluates mediation and similar programs, offers consulting and training, and manages a complaint center.

Center for Law and Social Policy
1616 P Street NW, Ste. 150
Washington, DC 20036-1413
(202) 328-5140

This public interest law firm works toward improvements in family law policy. Publishes materials on various issues, including opportunities for AFDC recipients, team parents, and child support enforcement.

Child Abuse Listening Mediation (CALM)
P.O. Box 90754
Santa Barbara, CA 93190-0754
(805) 965-2376
(805) 569-2255 (twenty-four-hour bilingual listening service)
This program is designed to prevent and treat all forms of child abuse. It offers intervention, referrals, and emergency assistance.

Child Find of America
P.O. Box 277
New Paltz, NY 12561-0277
(914) 255-1848
1-800-I-AM-LOST (for children who have been abducted and those who can identify missing children)
1-800-A-WAY-OUT (for mediation information)
This organization works to prevent child abduction and to locate missing children. It conducts mediation and counseling programs for parents involved in or concerned about child abduction. It produces various videos, publications, children's games, and other information and educational tools.

Children's Divorce Center
88 Bradley Road
Woodbridge, CT 06525
(203) 387-8887
Services, information, and publications for individuals and professionals to help children and parents deal with divorce and remarriage.

Children's Foundation
725 15th Street NW, Ste. 505
Washington, DC 20005-2109
(202) 547-6227
1-800-787-KIDS
Assistance, information, and publications for child care providers.

Children's Rights Council
220 I Street NE, Ste. 200
Washington, DC 20002
(202) 547-6227
This organization assists children of separated and divorced parents through advocacy and parenting education.

Children's Rights of America
8735 Dunwoody Place, No. 6
Atlanta, GA 30350
(770) 998-6698
Information, services, and publications for families of missing and exploited children; assistance and education for lawyers working on parental abduction cases; outreach programs and speaker's bureau.

Committee for Mother & Child Rights, Inc.
210 Ole Orchard Drive
Clear Brook, VA 22624-1647
(540) 722-3652
Offers emotional support and guidance for mothers with child custody problems, including referrals to attorneys and other experts in child custody issues.

Dads Against Discrimination
P.O. Box 8525

Portland, OR 97207
(503) 222-1111
Information, publications, referrals, and services for divorced fathers.

Divorce Support
5020 W. School Street
Chicago, IL 60641
(773) 286-4541
Support and assistance for members, information network.

Divorced Parents X-Change
P.O. Box 1127
Athens, OH 45701-1127
(614) 664-3030
This group of divorced parents, stepparents, and their children assist others with parenting after divorce, promotes healthy families, and advocates equality in parental custody. Provides information, children's services, speakers, and other resources.

Elisabeth Kübler-Ross Center
South Route 616
Headwaters, VA 24442
(703) 396-3441
A network of individuals serving families and individuals in personal crises. Programs, lectures, newsletter.

Family Law Council
P.O. Box 217
Fair Lawn, NJ 07410
Seeks reform in current divorce system; supports arbitration and mediation in settling family disputes.

Family Research Council
801 G Street NW
Washington, DC 20001
(202) 393-2100
    Information on parenting and family issues.

Family Resource Coalition of America
200 S. Michigan Avenue, Ste. 1600
Chicago, IL 60604
(312) 341-0900
E-mail: hn1738@handsnet.org
    Network of nationwide family support organizations; various publications and services.

Family Resources Database
National Council on Family Relations
3986 Central Avenue NE, Ste. 550
Minneapolis, MN 55421
(612) 781-9331
    References and information on programs and services offered by other organizations.

Families and Work Institute
330 7th Avenue, 14th Floor
New York, NY 10001
(212) 465-2044
(212) 268-4846 (The Fatherhood Project)
    Research, education, publications, and seminars on balancing work and family responsibilities.

Fathers for Equal Rights
P.O. Box 010847, Flagler Station
Miami, FL 33101
(305) 895-6351

Assists parents and grandparents involved in custody disputes. Various publications and self-help packages.

Fathers' Rights and Equality Exchange (FREE)
3140 De La Cruz Boulevard, Ste. 200
Santa Clara, CA 95054-2444
(650) 853-6877
Advocates for noncustodial fathers, produces educational materials.

Find the Children
11811 W. Olympic Boulevard
Los Angeles, CA 90064-1113
(310) 477-6721
Services and assistance for families and law enforcement personnel working to locate missing children. Provides referrals and a directory of missing children with pictures.

Foundation for Grandparenting
P.O. Box 326
Cohasset, MA 02025
Information, publication, and speakers' bureau dedicated to increasing public awareness of the importance of grandparents in children's lives.

Freedom Rings—Jewelry for the Divorced
P.O. Box 90502
Albuquerque, NM 87199-0502
1-800-600-RING
Provides divorce ceremony and custom design for new jewelry from wedding rings.

Grandparents Anonymous
1924 Beverly

Sylvan Lake, MI 48320
(810) 682-8384
Assists grandparents who have been denied visitation with grandchildren.

Grandparents' Rights Organization
555 S. Old Woodward Avenue, Ste. 600
Birmingham, MI 48009
(248) 646-7191 or 646-7177
Assists grandparents who have been denied visitation with grandchildren.

Institute for the Study of Matrimonial Laws
c/o Sidney Siller
11 Park Place, Ste. 1116
New York, NY 10007
(212) 766-4030
Promotes improvement in family law, encourages research, aids communities in programs to help single parents and children. Extensive library.

International Association for Financial Planning
5775 Glenridge Drive NE, Ste. B-300
Atlanta, GA 30328-5364
(404) 845-0011
Provides names of financial planners and analysts who have met rigorous requirements for membership.

International Association for Marriage and Family Counselors
5999 Stevenson Avenue
Alexandria, VA 22304
(703) 347-6647
1-800-545-AACD

This group of counselors works in the fields of marriage, divorce, and family counseling and therapy, as well as mediation. Provides referrals.

Joint Custody Association
1606 Wilkins Avenue
Los Angeles, CA 90024
(310) 475-5352
Information on joint custody and the law surrounding it.

Kevin Collins Foundation for Missing Children
P.O. Box 590473
San Francisco, CA 94159
(415) 771-8477
1-800-272-0012
Prevention of and education on child abduction. Publishes guide on prevention and maintains abduction response team.

Kids' Express
P.O. Box 782
Littleton, CO 80160-0782
Publishes a monthly newsletter for children of divorced parents.

LadyBug Press
P.O. Box 7249
Albuquerque, NM 87194-7249
1-800-244-1761
Fax 1-888-660-7108
www.mytwohomes.com
This company produces special products for children of divorced families and their parents, all developed by a team of divorce mediators, divorce attorneys, and designers. Featured

products include "My Two Homes," a divorce calendar for kids with stickers that give children and parents a colorful, fun way to keep track of their time-sharing schedules, holidays, activities, and changes; a "Mom & Dad Pad" with form notes that parents can use to quickly communicate information about children in a positive tone; a T-shirt, photo album, and handbook to help kids cope. Call, fax, or e-mail for a free brochure.

Lavender Families Resource Network (LFRN)
P.O. Box 21567
Seattle, WA 98111
(206) 325-2643
  Legal, financial, and emotional support for gay and lesbian parents dealing with child custody issues.

Men/Fathers' Hotline
807 Brazos, Ste. 315
Austin, TX 78701
(512) 472-3237
  Crisis line for men and fathers; provides referrals to other organizations.

Missing Children Help Center
410 Sware Boulevard, Ste. 400
Tampa, FL 33619
(813) 623-5437
1-800-USA-KIDS
  A division of the National Child Safety Council, this organization promotes programs and provides information and referrals to those concerned with missing children. Maintains a free hotline for reporting a missing child or a child's location.

Mothers Without Custody
P.O. Box 36
Woodstock, IL 60098
1-800-457-MWOC
Network for mothers without primary custody.

Ms. Foundation for Women
120 Wall Street, 33rd Floor
New York, NY 10005
(212) 742-2300
Funds and assists women's self-help organizing efforts; pursues changes in social policy and laws to end discrimination.

National Association of Child Advocates
1522 K Street NW, Ste. 600
Washington, DC 20005
(202) 289-0777
Although the NCAA and its forty-four member organizations do not provide individual services, they can provide information on the most current legislation and policy in the areas of health care, welfare reform, assistance programs for children, child care, and support enforcement. Affiliate groups include local organizations devoted to child support enforcement, single parents, noncustodial parents, father's rights, and stepfamilies.

National Association for Family Day Care
1361 E. Guadalupe, Ste. 201
Tempe, AZ 85283-3916
Promotes day-care services in private homes and operates an accreditation program for day-care providers.

National Association of Child Care Referral and Resource
Agencies
1319 F Street NW, Ste. 606

Washington, DC 20004
(202) 393-5501
Information and assistance on locating qualified child care.

National Association of Family and Consumer Services
3900 E. Camelback Road, Ste. 200
Phoenix, AZ 85018
(602) 912-5386
Conferences, volunteer training, and information for families coping with issues such as child care, nutrition, and budgeting.

National Association of Professional Organizers
1033 La Posada Drive, Ste. 220
Austin, TX 78752-3880
(512) 454-8626
Provides home organization services.

National Center for Missing and Exploited Children
2101 Wilson Boulevard, Ste. 550
Arlington, VA 22201
(703) 235-3900
Provides assistance and a clearinghouse of information for parents and law enforcement agencies. Merged with the Adam Walsh Child Resource Center. Publications and toll-free hotline to exchange information on sightings of missing children at 1-800-843-5678 or for the hearing impaired at 1-800-826-7653.

National Child Support Advocacy Coalition
P.O. Box 420
Hendersonville, TN 37077
(615) 264-0151
This group of individuals and organizations advocates improved child support enforcement, changes in related laws,

and public awareness of the effects of unpaid child support. Publications and referral service.

National Child Support Enforcement Association
Hall of States
444 N. Capital NW, Ste. 444
Washington, DC 20001
(202) 624-8180

National Clearinghouse on Child Abuse and Neglect and
   Family Violence Information
P.O. Box 1182
Washington, DC 20013-1182
(703) 385-7565
1-800-394-3366
   Provides information to professionals on family violence prevention.

National Coalition Against Domestic Violence
P.O. Box 18749
Denver, CO 80218-0749
(303) 839-1852
   Various publications and information services.

National Coalition of Free Men
P.O. Box 129
Manhasset, NY 11030
(516) 482-6378
   Advocates for men's legal rights in custody and other issues. Publications and speakers' bureau.

National Congress for Fathers and Children
9454 Wilshire Boulevard, Ste. 207

Beverly Hills, CA 90212
1-800-SEE-DADS
Promotes rights of fathers and divorce reform; electronic bulletin board, various publications.

National Council for Children's Rights
(Children's Rights Council)
220 Eye Street NE Ste. 140
Washington, DC 20002-4362
(202) 547-6227
Advocates for child support, joint custody, visitation, and custody reform.

National Court-Appointed Special Advocates Association
100 W. Harrison Street, No. 500
Seattle, WA 98119
(206) 270-0072
This organization, composed of juvenile court judges and attorneys, advocates support programs that provide court-appointed special advocates for abused or neglected children. Produces various publications.

National Domestic Violence Hotline
1-800-799-SAFE (7233)
1-800-787-3224 (TDD)
This hotline is staffed twenty-four hours a day by trained volunteers who can provide crisis assistance and referrals to local shelters and other sources of help.

National Foundation for Consumer Credit
8611 Second Avenue, Ste. 100
Silver Spring, MD 20910
(301) 589-5600
1-800-388-2227 for a directory of offices

Coalition of businesses and service agencies that sponsor consumer credit counseling services and distribute publications.

National Organization to Insure Survival Economics (NOISE)
c/o Diana D. DuBroff
12 W. 72nd Street
New York, NY 10023
(212) 787-1070
Seeks new ways to deal with support programs for families facing divorce, including changes in the insurance industry.

National Organization for Men
11 Park Place
New York, NY 10007
(212) 686-6253
(212) 766-4030
Both men and women working to promote equal rights for men in areas of alimony, child custody, domestic abuse, and divorce.

National Organization of Single Mothers
P.O. Box 68
Midland, NC 28107-0068
(704) 888-5437
Membership, publications, newsletter.

National Organization for Women (NOW)
1000 Sixteenth Street NW, Ste. 700
Washington, DC 20036
(202) 331-0066
Advocates for women's equal rights.

New Beginnings
13129 Clifton Road

Silver Spring, MD 20904
(301) 384-0111
Membership group for divorced and separated individuals, with workshops and activities.

NOW Legal Defense and Education Fund
99 Hudson Street, 12th Floor
New York, NY 10013
(212) 925-6635
Produces affordable resource kits on divorce and separation, child support, and child custody.

North American Conference of Separated and Divorced
Catholics
P.O. Box 1301
La Grande, OR 97850
(541) 963-8089
Helps develop regional groups of divorced Catholics; organizes workshops, retreats, and training programs and distributes resource materials.

Older Women's League (OWL)
666 11th Street NW, Ste. 700
Washington, DC 20001
(202) 783-6686
Provides information to older women facing divorce and related issues, such as health insurance rights.

Organization for the Enforcement of Child Support
1712 Deer Park Road
Finksburg, MD 21048
(410) 876-1826
Works with various branches of government to improve the child support enforcement system. Various publications, including a self-help guide.

Parents Anonymous
675 W. Foothill Boulevard, Ste. 220
Claremont, CA 91711-3416
(909) 621-6184

Works for prevention and treatment of child abuse; sponsors support groups for parents who have abused or fear they could abuse their children; local chapters throughout the nation.

Parents Sharing Custody Network International
420 S. Beverly Drive, Ste. 100
Beverly Hills, CA 90212
(310) 286-9171

A national network for divorced families involved in the cooperative raising of their children. Publications, training, and seminars; other resources and information.

Parents Without Partners
401 N. Michigan Avenue, Ste. 220
Chicago, IL 60611-4267
(312) 644-6610
1-800-637-7974

Support groups for single parents, with local chapters.

Rainbows
1111 Tower Road
Schaumberg, IL 60173-4305
(847) 310-1880

This international organization provides training and curricula for peer support groups aimed at those who have suffered a loss due to divorce or other reasons. Publications.

Single Parent Resource Center
31 E. 28th Street, 2nd Floor

New York, NY 10016-7923
(212) 947-0221
National group working to establish a network of regional single-parent organizations.

Stepfamily Association of America
650 J Street, Ste. 205
Lincoln, NE 68508
(402) 477-STEP
1-800-735-0329
Local chapters, numerous publications, educational resources.

Stepfamily Foundation
333 West End Avenue
New York, NY 10023
(212) 877-3244
1-800-SKY-STEP
Information and counseling for stepfamilies; training for professionals who work with them. Telephone counseling service, many publications.

United Fathers of America
595 The City Drive, Ste. 202
Orange, CA 92668
(714) 385-1002
This organization seeks equal rights for fathers in child custody; provides counseling, assistance, and referrals.

U.S. Department of Health and Human Services
Administration for Children and Families
Office of Child Support Enforcement
370 L'Enfant Promenade SW, 4th Floor
Washington, DC 20447
(202) 401-9373

This federal agency helps states develop, operate, and improve child support enforcement programs according to federal regulations. Its services include the Federal Parent Locator Service, which helps find parents who are not paying child support or those who have kidnapped children.

Vocal National Network
825 Circle Drive N, Ste. O
Colorado Springs, CO 80909
1-800-848-8778
Education, support, and advocacy for those unfairly accused of child abuse or neglect.

VOCAL (Victims of Child Abuse Laws)
7485 E. Kenyon Avenue
Denver, CO 80237
1-800-745-8778
This group seeks to provide protection for civil rights of people falsely accused of child abuse or neglect, and to protect children from real abusers.

Women in Transition
Women's Resource Center
Santa Fe Community College
P.O. Box 4187
Santa Fe, NM 87502
(505) 438-1274
Provides workshops for divorced and widowed women and for single mothers to help build self-esteem and prepare them to reenter the workforce.

Women's Legal Defense Fund
1875 Connecticut Avenue NW, Ste. 710
Washington, DC 20009
(202) 986-2600

This group of attorneys and other individuals seeks to secure equal rights for women through litigation, advocacy, legal counseling, and education.

Women on Their Own
P.O. Box 1026
Willingboro, NJ 08046
(609) 871-1499
Network of single women raising children alone. Offers referrals, support, workshops, advocacy, and other forms of assistance. Publications.

WomenWork! The National Network for Women's
    Employment
1625 K Street NW, Ste. 300
Washington, DC 20006
(202) 467-6346
Programs and services for displaced homemakers. Publishes a directory of programs and provides information and fliers.

INTERNET WEB SITES

As of 1998, excellent Web sites are found at the following locations:

Divorce Care
http://www.divorcecare.com

Divorce Support
http://www.divorcesupport.com/index.htm

Divorce Magazine
http://www.divorcemag.com/home.html

Divorce Wizards
http://www.divorcewizards.com/html

Divorce Online
http://www.divorce-online.com/

Divorcenet
http://www.divorcenet.com/

Office of Child Support Enforcement
http://www.acf.dhhs.gov/programs

Index

DATE DUE

DEC 16 2000			
APR -1 2001			
NOV 29 2002			
JAN -3 2003			
MAR 22 2003			
NOV 21			
JAN 11 2004			
DEC 16 2004			
MAR 22 2005			
SEP -4 2008			
SEP -4 2008 JAN 02 2012			
			Printed in USA

HIGHSMITH #45230